THE MOUNTAIN BIKER'S GUIDE

TO NEW MEXICO

Dennis Coello's America by Mountain Bike Series

THE MOUNTAIN BIKER'S GUIDE TO NEW MEXICO

Dennis Coello's America by Mountain Bike Series

Sarah L. Bennett

Foreword, Introduction, and Afterword
by Dennis Coello, Series Editor

MENASHA
RIDGE
PRESS

796.6
Bennett

T 61726

Library of Congress Cataloging-in-Publication Data
Bennett, Sarah L.
    The mountain biker's guide to New Mexico / Sarah L.
Bennett ; foreword, introduction, and afterword by
Dennis Coello.
        p.   cm.
        — (Dennis Coello's America by mountain bike series)
        ISBN 1-56044-219-0
        1. All terrain cycling—New Mexico—Guidebooks.
2. New Mexico—Guidebooks.   I. Title.   II. Series:
America by mountain bike series.
GV1045.5.N6B46   1993
796.6'4'09789—dc20   93-46387
                                                        CIP

Maps by Tim Krasnansky
Cover photo by Dennis Coello

Menasha Ridge Press
3169 Cahaba Heights Road
Birmingham, Alabama 35243

Falcon Press
P. O. Box 1718
Helena, Montana 59624

 Printed on Recycled Paper

Table of Contents

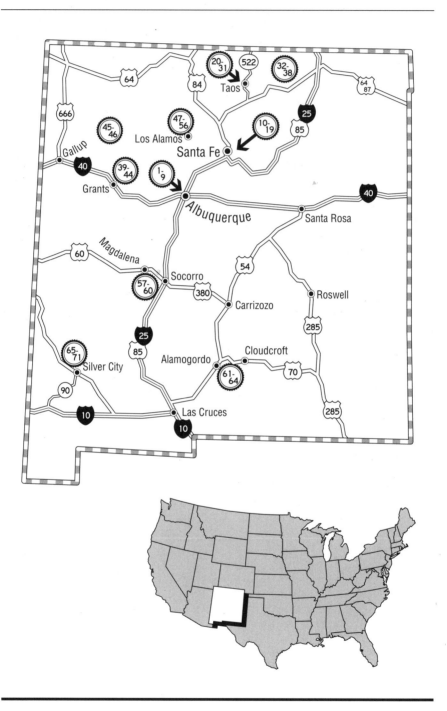

List of Maps

AMERICA BY MOUNTAIN BIKE   *MAP LEGEND*

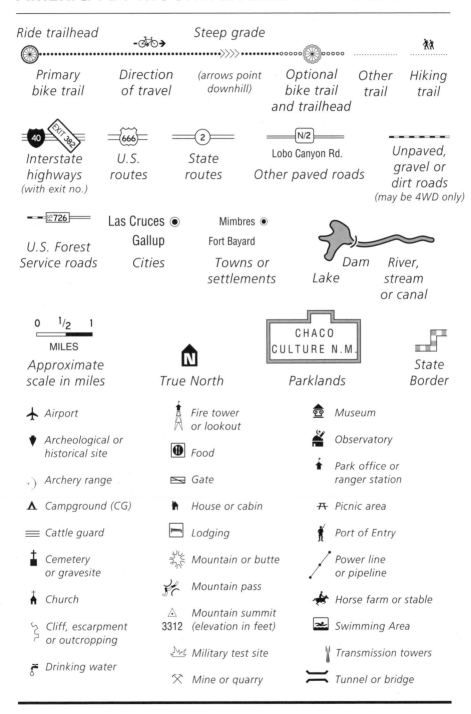

Ride trailhead

Steep grade

Primary bike trail

Direction of travel

(arrows point downhill)

Optional bike trail and trailhead

Other trail

Hiking trail

Interstate highways (with exit no.)

U.S. routes

State routes

Lobo Canyon Rd.
Other paved roads

Unpaved, gravel or dirt roads (may be 4WD only)

U.S. Forest Service roads

Las Cruces ◉
Gallup
Cities

Mimbres ◉
Fort Bayard
Towns or settlements

Lake

Dam

River, stream or canal

0   1/2   1
MILES
Approximate scale in miles

True North

CHACO CULTURE N.M.
Parklands

State Border

✈ Airport

♥ Archeological or historical site

·) Archery range

▲ Campground (CG)

≡ Cattle guard

† Cemetery or gravesite

♠ Church

⌇ Cliff, escarpment or outcropping

⚕ Drinking water

Fire tower or lookout

⊞ Food

⊠ Gate

♠ House or cabin

⊟ Lodging

Mountain or butte

Mountain pass

△ Mountain summit
3312 (elevation in feet)

Military test site

✕ Mine or quarry

♨ Museum

⚗ Observatory

♦ Park office or ranger station

Ħ Picnic area

Port of Entry

/ Power line or pipeline

Horse farm or stable

Swimming Area

∥ Transmission towers

Tunnel or bridge

Acknowledgments

Many, many thanks are due to the people who assisted me in the weeks and months I spent on the road gathering information for this project. The interest and enthusiasm I received from friends and strangers alike was overwhelming. Whether it was a shower and a bed, a meal, directions, or simply a smile and a slap on the back, these people gave me what it took to keep pushing on down the road. Without their help I doubt this book would have been possible.

My gratitude and respect also go out to the men and women who work for our National Forest Service and who have the difficult task of managing a wide range of public interests and demands upon our wildlands. We have these people to thank for building and maintaining most of the roads and trails in this book. They deserve special acknowledgment for the work they are doing now to accommodate the growing number of mountain bikers that will visit our national forests in the future. These folks need our input and deserve our cooperation.

The riders with whom I shared the trails, and who appear in the pages of this book, are deeply appreciated for their love of fat tires and the outdoors, and their spirit of adventure. I am convinced that their concern for all these things will keep the sport growing in the right direction.

And, last but not least, I would like to thank my editor and friend, Dennis Coello, for offering me this project and the chance to get out there into the beautiful country of the American Southwest.

Foreword

Welcome to *America by Mountain Bike,* a 20-book series designed to provide all-terrain bikers with the information they need to find and ride the very best trails everywhere in the mainland United States. Whether you're new to the sport and don't know where to pedal, or an experienced mountain biker who wants to learn the classic trails in another region, this series is for you. Drop a few bucks for the book, spend an hour with the detailed maps and route descriptions, and you're prepared for the finest in off-road cycling.

My role as editor of this series was simple: First, find a mountain biker who knows the area and loves to ride. Second, ask that person to spend a year researching the most popular and very best rides around. And third, have that rider describe each trail in terms of difficulty, scenery, condition, elevation change, and all other categories of information that are important to trail riders. "Pretend you've just completed a ride and met up with fellow mountain bikers at the trailhead," I told each author. "Imagine their questions, be clear in your answers."

As I said, the *editorial* process—that of sending out riders and reading the submitted chapters—is a snap. But the work involved in finding, riding, and writing about each trail is enormous. In some instances our authors' tasks are made easier by the information contributed by local bike shops or cycling clubs, or even by the writers of local "where-to" guides. Our sincere thanks go to all who have helped.

But the overwhelming majority of trails are discovered and pedaled by our authors themselves, then compared with dozens of other routes to determine if they qualify as "classic"—that area's best in scenery and cycling fun. If you've ever had the experience of pioneering a route from outdated topographic maps, or entering a bike shop to request information from local riders who would much prefer to keep their favorite trails secret, or know how it is to double- and triple-check data to be positive your trail info is correct, then you have an idea of how each of our authors has labored to bring about these books. You and I, and all the mountain bikers of America, are the richer for their efforts.

You'll get more out of this book if you take a moment to read the Introduction explaining how to read the trail listings. The "Topographic Maps" section will help you understand how useful topos will be on a ride, and will also tell you where to get them. And though this is a "where-to," not a "how-to" guide, those of you who have not traveled the backcountry might find the planning and equipment tips in "Hitting the Trail" of particular value.

In addition to the material above, newcomers to mountain biking might want to spend a minute with the Glossary, page 241, so that terms like *hardpack, single-track,* and *water bars* won't throw you when you come across them in the text.

Finally, the tips in the Afterword on mountain bike etiquette and the land-use controversy might help us all enjoy the trails a little more.

All the best.

Dennis Coello
Salt Lake City

Preface

Before I set out on the road to begin my field work for this series I had spent very little time in the Southwest. Except for what I had seen in glossy magazines and in nature journals I was completely unfamiliar with the country that is New Mexico. The peaks of the Sangre de Cristo Mountains lit up by stands of fiery aspens looked fabulous in travel brochures. What I had learned about the Spanish colonial history of the state, reaching back beyond the time the Pilgrims first landed at Plymouth Rock, fascinated me. I could only imagine the cool shadows and imposing walls of 500-year-old adobe pueblos built by the ancestors of the Pueblo Indians who live in those structures today. The intricate passageways and the stillness at the ruins of Chaco Canyon—an Anasazi masterpiece—filled me with a sense of mystery and magic.

When the chance came to explore and ride in New Mexico I was thrilled— I jumped on it. All that country, and barely a million people! Never in all my imaginings and daydreaming while packing in the weeks before I left did I dream how truly spectacular New Mexico would be. I never imagined how these places would leap to life, vibrate with color and mystery, until I was standing there, breathing them in.

I knew I would find mountains, and deserts, and cities full of people in New Mexico, but I had no idea how dramatic and diverse they would be. Landscape, history, and cultures have come together in New Mexico to create an atmosphere that is completely unique. New Mexico is a place well suited to the adventurous. With a mountain bike and a little curiousity, you'll be equipped to explore one of the most beautiful and intriguing regions of the American West.

THE WEATHER

When people start planning a trip to the desert Southwest, the first thing they worry about is the weather. The climate can be extreme in this part of the country and does play a very important part in the safety and enjoyment of exploring by mountain bike. The wide variations in elevation and terrain throughout New Mexico, however, can provide comfortable temperatures for biking during every month of the year, if you know where to go. There are few places in this country that offer so much rideable terrain year-round. While concerns about heat will shape most vacation plans in the Southwest, other weather factors can pose a serious threat as well. Here is a brief introduction to the seasonal weather patterns and dangers of different areas of the state.

Below 5,000 Feet

Riding anywhere below 5,000 feet in the summer months in New Mexico is difficult because there tends to be little cooling at night. In the spring and fall months in the lower deserts the days still get good and hot but the nights cool off sufficiently to make early morning and evening riding very pleasant. The temperatures for riding in these lower elevations are just about perfect during the winter months when higher elevations are impassable due to snow.

Desert Conditions

If you are coming from another part of the country and are unaccustomed to the strength of the desert sun and the aridity, you will need several days to acclimate yourself to these conditions. The dry air, heat, and elevation will at first take a substantial toll on your strength and endurance, so start out slow. A bad sunburn, high exertion, and low liquid intake can combine to create a number of very dangerous situations. You should know the warning signs and dangers of these heat-related conditions. (See "Desert Health and Safety" on page xxiii).

The Rainy Season

New Mexico, while generally considered to be a desert state, has a bona fide monsoon season. During late summer and fall, weather patterns begin to change in the Southwestern deserts. Moisture begins pumping into the upper and middle levels of the atmosphere from the Gulf of Mexico, sending humidity levels soaring. This moist warm air rises as it travels over the hot desert, creating beautiful towers of billowing cumulonimbus storm clouds that can lash out violently with lightning, hail, and torrential rains.

Within an eight- to twelve-week window beginning sometime in mid-July and running through September, cycles of cloud building and storms can become a daily routine, especially at higher elevations. These storms generate a tremendous amount of electricity, so by mid- to late afternoon it is a good idea to be off high or exposed places and close to shelter. Avoid driving through, or camping in, aryoyos or drainages this time of year. These can become raging torrents in a matter of seconds, without warning. Sometimes flash flooding occurs far downstream from where the rain has fallen. While those kind of storms tend to be isolated, they can wreak havoc on your outing, so get an early start if afternoon thunderstorms are predicted.

Besides receiving the lion's share of summer thunderstorms, higher elevations are prone to rapid temperature changes. After a storm moves in, temperatures can plummet. It's a good idea to carry a weatherproof shell along on your ride, especially if you are riding in the mountains. Snow is not uncommon in the late spring or early fall in some of the higher ranges. Here again, it is prudent to be aware of the signs of hypothermia. You will find these outlined in "Desert Health and Safety," page xxiii.

THE LAND

The land that lies within the borders of New Mexico can be thought of as a giant wedge that starts high in the north and runs out to lower elevations in the south. Elevations range from 13,161 feet atop Wheeler Peak in the Sangre de Cristo Mountains near Taos, to below 2,500 feet in the extreme southeastern corner of the state—a topographical relief of over 10,000 feet. The landscape of New Mexico, the fifth largest state in the union, is incredibly diverse; it includes portions of the Colorado Plateau, the Rocky Mountains, the Great Plains, and the Sonoran and Chihuahuan deserts.

Of all the landscapes and formations you'll find in New Mexico probably none is so massive and so distinct as the Rio Grande Rift Valley. Beginning in Colorado, cutting across the entire length of New Mexico and extending well into the Mexican state of Chihuahua, the Rio Grande Rift is a major break in the earth's crust and one of the largest geological formations in the world.

A rift valley is formed when a narrow block of the earth's crust that lies between two parallel fault zones drops. Faults associated with a rift are often extremely deep, reaching all the way to the earth's core. As a result volcanic activity is often found along rift faults. The Jemez Mountains and the numerous cinder cones and lava formations near Albuquerque are evidence of this type of vulcanism. Once the rift is formed it is usually found by coursing water; the river then carves a valley in the rift floor, adding layers of sediment in which vegetation can take hold. The Rio Grande River, running almost the entire length of the rift, has served as the life blood of this region, allowing people to survive in a country that would otherwise be an inhospitable desert.

The Colorado Plateau is an enormous uplifted landmass that ranges between 5,000 and 8,000 feet above sea level. The plateau extends across much of northern New Mexico and Arizona and into the southern reaches of Utah and Colorado as well. In places the plateau's crust has given way to powerful volcanic events, leaving numerous shield volcanoes and cinder cones across the northeastern section of the state. Mount Taylor, just north of Grants, is the largest of these shield volcanoes; it rises to 11,301 feet and is one of the four sacred mountains of the Navajo. In northwestern New Mexico the plateau forms the long mesas and canyons which were home to various Indian cultures over the centuries, the most prominent of these being the Anasazi. The Anasazi left the Colorado Plateau dotted with endless stone ruins, from tiny grain storage bins and primitive one-room shelters to the enormous, intricately designed and built pueblos at Chaco Canyon.

The Sangre de Cristo Mountains of northern New Mexico, accompanied by the smaller but adjoining Culebra, Cimarron, and Santa Fe subranges, form the most southern extension of the Rocky Mountains. The Jemez Mountains, just north of Albuquerque, are the remains of a massive collapsed volcano, or caldera.

Many of the state's smaller mountain ranges to the south, such as the Sandia, the Sacramento, the San Andreas, the Magdalena, the San Mateo, and the Organ, are fault blocks forced skyward by the rifting Rio Grande Valley. These ranges may not be as high as the Rockies to the north, but they are often more dramatic, with steep slopes and spiny ridges. Other mountain ranges in southern New Mexico—the Black, Mimbres, Mogollon, Pinos Altos, and Animas—belong to a system of fault blocks known as the Basin and Range.

Most of New Mexico's smaller mountain ranges have complex systems of volcanic intrusions that helped to create some fairly substantial deposits of gold, silver, lead, zinc, and copper ores. These mineral deposits have been mined as far back as the 1600s by the Spanish, and they brought thousands of American fortune hunters to this country in the mid-1800s. Small towns such as Magdalena, Pinos Altos, Silver City, and Soccoro were once wild frontier towns where gold seekers lived hard and died young. Today Soccoro is home to the New Mexico Institute of Mining and Technology, which has an excellent mineral museum on its campus. While most of the old mines are silent now, due to rising costs and depleted ore bodies, there is still a good amount of mining activity in the state. Coal is mined in the northwest part of the state; enormous molybdenum (used as an alloy for steel) mines are in operation near Questa, in the Sangre de Cristo Mountains; and copper, silver, and gold ores are still brought out of mines near Silver City.

THE PEOPLE

The country that we know as New Mexico has supported a colorful variety of peoples over the centuries, both native and European, endowing the state with a rich cultural heritage. The land has been inhabited for 20,000 years, beginning with a nomadic band of Paleo-Indians who left behind only a few spear points to tell of their travels. Scientists now believe that these were some of the first ancestors of native North Americans, who crossed over from Asia during the last ice age when North American and Asian continents were joined by a bridge of snow and ice. Small bands continued to migrate through New Mexico until they learned the agricultural skills that allowed them to erect more permanent settlements. Success at farming meant a rise in population; small villages became bustling societies.

Evidence of New Mexico's earliest known inhabitants was discovered in a cave in the Sandia Mountains just north of Albuquerque in 1936. Bits of bone and fur found at this site, and at several sites nearby, reveal that the first inhabitants of the Southwest successfully hunted such animals as the woolly mammoth and giant ground sloth, animals that have been extinct for some 10,000 years. Some scientists theorize that a change in the climate turned the grasslands and forests that supported the big animals into desert, forcing them into extinction.

Until about 500 B.C., small bands survived by hunting rabbits, grouse, and other small game, and gathering what seeds, berries, and roots they could find. At this time squash and beans were introduced into the local diet, probably by Indians traveling north from Mexico or Central America, and agriculture became the main source of subsistence. These first farming cultures lived in pit houses and manufactured crude pottery for storing and cooking beans and grains.

With more time and resources on their hands, people practiced complex religious rituals, became highly crafted, constructed beautiful stone cities, and developed extensive trade networks reaching deep into Mexico and South America. Gradually, distinct cultural groups emerged: the Anasazi of the Colorado Plateau, the Mogollon and Mimbres of the central highlands, and the Hohokam of Arizona's southern deserts. These cultures flourished roughly from A.D. 500 to A.D. 1100, at which time they mysteriously began to disappear. Drought, disease, and pressure from tribes moving into the area are all possible reasons for their demise. Behind them they left hundreds of beautifully constructed stone houses as well as complex irrigation and road systems. Large Anasazi ruins can be found at Bandelier National Monument just south of Los Alamos, or near Aztec, northwest of Farmington. Thousands of smaller ruins populate the Four Corners area. The most fantastic of all these ruins are those at Chaco Canyon. Anyone traveling in the Southwest would miss a unique experience should they fail to visit a few of the many ruins scattered throughout New Mexico and the Four Corners region.

Today Native Americans in New Mexico belong to one of three main tribes: the Apache, the Navajo, or the Pueblo. The Pueblo are generally considered to be the descendants of the Anasazi and have been in the area the longest. The Pueblo people continue to live in stone pueblos today, some of which are over 500 years old. They are open to the public for viewing and tours but a fee is charged and taking pictures is usually forbidden. There are five distinct languages spoken among the Pueblo people. A deeply religious people, they revere ancient customs and crafts, and celebrate their heritage in a number of ceremonies and festivals held throughout the year. The Pueblo are masters of exquisitely crafted pottery whose designs vary greatly from tribe to tribe.

The Navajo most likely arrived in the Southwest sometime around A.D. 1300, about the time the Anasazi and other ancient cultures of this region disappeared. Although the Navajos were a fairly peaceful people, moving their herds of sheep from range to range throughout the Four Corners area, once European settlers arrived there was conflict. In 1868 they were alotted their 25,000-acre reservation, the largest in the lower 48 states. The Navajo are superb silversmiths, known for their work with silver and turquoise around the world. Their weaving is also greatly admired; an authentic Navajo rug, with its bright colors and geometric patterns identifying the clan from which it came, can fetch a high price. Old, authentic rugs and those woven by certain individuals are highly sought after by collectors.

The Apache people were the most nomadic of the three tribes. Farming seasonally, hunting and gathering, they ranged widely across what is now New Mexico. They fought fiercely against Spanish, Mexican, and American encroachment and gained the reputation as a violent and warring people, when in fact they sought only to hold on to their homeland. At one point more than a third of the nation's cavalry was engaged in their pursuit, and ruthless gangs of scalpers were paid by the U.S. and Mexican governments to track and kill them. The eradication program virtually wiped out Apache culture, social customs, and traditional crafts, along with most of their population. Today Apache crafts and customs are being revived on two reservations, the Jicarilla Apache Indian Reservation, between Chama and Farmington, and the Mescalero Apache Indian Reservation, in the Sacramento Mountains south of Ruidoso.

Anglo peoples have a long and colorful past in the region as well. More than a hundred years before the Pilgrims set foot on the Atlantic coast and settled in New England, the Spanish had penetrated deep into the New World to what is now the American Southwest, bringing armies, missionaries, and priests to Christianize its native inhabitants. According to legend, the very first Europeans entered the Southwest in 1527: a small group of Spaniards who survived the sinking of their ship somewhere in the Gulf of Mexico. They spent the next ten years traveling west and then south to a Spanish settlement in Mexico, where they told stories of having seen seven huge cities built out of gold and turquoise. The viceroy of New Spain (what is now Mexico) promptly organized an exploration party guided by the missionary Fray Marcos de Niza. Instead of the golden cities he expected, Niza found the stone city of the Zuni Pueblo. Just south of where Gallup, New Mexico, is today, Niza sunk a cross in the ground and claimed the country for Spain.

Niza returned to Mexico City with news of his discovery. The tales of his journey inspired Francisco Vasquez de Coronado to organize his own exploration party. Coronado was convinced the Indians were hiding a vast wealth of gold, and he laid plans to conquer them. In the winter of 1540 the Spanish, led by Coronado, attacked the Zuni Pueblo. The Indians offered no resistance. With more than three hundred soldiers and over one thousand Mexican Indians, Coronado explored the Southwest for nearly two years, subjugating defenseless Indians at pueblos all across what is now New Mexico. Coronado and his army ranged from the Grand Canyon in the west to as far east as Kansas but nowhere did he find a city of gold.

In 1598 Don Juan de Onate made the first real effort to colonize the American Southwest. He was cruel to the native Indians and his settlers found the climate too dry. The expedition failed. The next attempt at colonization and rule was made by Don Pedro de Peralta, who set up operations in what is now modern-day Santa Fe. He appointed himself, with the blessing of the King of Spain, as the governor of New Mexico. At this point the effort to Christianize the Indians of New Mexico began in earnest. The Spanish used extremely harsh methods to convert the Indians: those who refused were often tortured or killed. The Indians became increasingly angry at their treatment and began to rebel. There were a number of very bloody revolts by the region's Pueblo Indians, the most successful being the Pueblo Revolt of 1680. For almost ten years the Pueblo again ruled themselves. Eventually the Spanish regained control, after a long and violent campaign from 1692 to 1696.

For the next hundred years the Spanish ruled this region, but began to lose their grip of power and dominance around the world. In 1821 Mexico won its independence from Spain. Anglos began filtering into what is now Arizona and New Mexico, trapping, prospecting, and trading. After the discovery of precious minerals in the mountains and hills of New Mexico the tide of settlers became enormous, and temporary settlements sprang up, along with some permanent towns.

The United States won the region that is now Arizona and New Mexico in the Mexican-American War of 1846–48. This was a war aimed primarily at winning Texas and California; the desert country that lay between them was not considered truly valuable. The Gadsden Purchase of 1853 added the southernmost chunk of Arizona and New Mexico to the territory, and statehood was declared for both in 1912.

Today New Mexico's human landscape is a virtual kaleidoscope of cultures. Indian, Spanish, Mexican, and Anglo cultures are woven together into a richly textured fabric of past and present, making New Mexico seem exotic and almost otherworldly to travelers from other parts of the country.

There are families in New Mexico today who can trace their heritage directly to their Spanish ancestors, many of whom were ceded enormous tracts of land by the King of Spain. Some of these tracts have remained intact, shown on maps as "land grants." In the mountains of northern New Mexico, some "land grant" families have remained isolated, their customs and their language unchanged for hundreds of years. The Mexican-American community in New Mexico is quite distinct from that of Spanish heritage and is estimated to make up more than 20% of the state's population.

People from all over the world come to New Mexico for its art. A tradition that began with Anasazi and Mimbres pottery is carried on today by a large community of contemporary artists and writers living and working in towns such as Taos and Santa Fe. Hundreds of art galleries, Spanish and Indian art markets, and art fairs held in almost every town in the state allow visitors to sample the fruits of New Mexico's creative communities.

THE FLORA AND FAUNA

The plant and animal life of New Mexico is as rich and varied as that of any region of North America. Over the 10,000 feet of elevation change in New Mexico you will find six of the world's seven life zones (based on the Merriam system that combines elevation and rainfall). In the Chihuahuan Desert, classified as

Lower Sonoran, you'll find everything from cactus and mesquite to scorpions, diamondback rattlers, and javelina (a type of wild boar). In the higher Transition and Canadian zones of the Sangre de Cristo Mountains, aspen and spruce forests are home to black bear, cougar, and elk.

The enormous expanse of dry flatlands known as the Chihuahuan Desert extends across the southern quarter of New Mexico, punctuated only by the small but dramatic mountains of the Basin and Range, and is classified as Lower Sonoran (below 4,500 feet). In the Lower Sonoran life zone you will find honey mesquite, creosote, salt bush, soaptree yucca, tar bush, and desert holly as well as prickly pear, ocotillo, cholla, agave, and Turk's head cactus. After the winter rains of February and March this desert comes alive with the blossoms of little golden zinnia, desert marigold, buffalo gourd, and the towering flower stalks of several varieties of yucca, whose blossoms are usually a creamy white. Cactus and their blossoms in the Chihuahuan Desert come in a rainbow of colors, shapes, and sizes, and within the short span of a few weeks in April and May they cover the desert floor like shy, delicate dancers.

For the most part, the remaining three-quarters of the state of New Mexico falls within the Upper Sonoran life zone (4,500–6,500 feet), characterized by the elegant shapes of fragrant pinyon and juniper trees. In many places you will find several varieties of oaks intermixed. In the higher reaches of the Upper Sonoran life zone, pinyon and juniper give way to ponderosa pine.

Because ponderosa tend to grow straight, tall, and close together, they are very appealing to the lumber industry and have been logged extensively throughout northern and central New Mexico. Environmentalists contend that certain areas such as the Jemez Mountains have been suffering from overlogging. Some of the only old-growth ponderosa surviving in the Southwest is found on the Kaibab Plateau, protected inside Grand Canyon National Park. The Upper Sonoran life zone in New Mexico is also heavily grazed by herds of cattle and sheep. In the last few years ranchers have met with some stiff opposition from New Mexicans who feel that their public land has been overgrazed. Timber, mining, and ranching industries have left widespread road systems on which mountain bikers can travel quickly and easily into remote country.

Mountain bikers should educate themselves on these issues. Don't hesitate to ask the forest ranger about logging or grazing practices where you may be riding. These forests belong to all of us and it is important for mountain bikers to speak up and express our viewpoints to those who are making decisions concerning our public lands.

The mixed spruce, fir, and aspen forests that are found throughout the Canadian and Hudsonian life zones above 8,000 feet make for classic alpine riding conditions in the mountains of New Mexico. These higher climes receive most of the moisture that the Southwest gets during the year in the form of winter snows and summer thunderstorms. Up here it stays nice and cool during the heat of the summer months. Elk, mountain goats, and bighorn sheep retreat to these higher elevations during the summer months. You'll certainly see marmots, pikas, and some of the other native rodents busily scurrying around when the ground is free of snow. This high country is steep and sensitive to trail traffic, and it's where you'll find the bulk of land designated as Wilderness Areas. Wilderness Areas are off-limits to all mechanized vehicles, and that includes mountain bikes. It is important that we acknowledge this restriction; there are some places mountain bikes just don't belong. The Alpine zone occurs above 12,000 feet and can be found only in a few spots in New Mexico. Here you'll find only stunted plants and shrubs and the occasional bristlecone pine.

DESERT HEALTH AND SAFETY

Water, Water, Water

The single most important thing riders can take with them into the desert is water. Riders exerting themselves in an arid climate in high temperatures need tremendous amounts of water to stay healthy and to keep functioning properly. Not only does this precious fluid constitute the bulk of our body mass, it is critical to our survival. Good hydration can increase physical performance and is vital to aiding the body's functions and maintaining mental acuity.

It is easy to underestimate the amount of fluids your body uses when exercising in the desert. Don't let thirst regulate your water intake; by the time you begin to feel thirsty you are already experiencing a fluid deficit. For long rides in hot weather you will want to carry some kind of fluid or drink mix that is high in salt, potassium, and glucose, such as Gatorade or Exceed. These will help to replace the electrolytes you need to metabolize fuel into energy.

Heat-related Stress and Illness

In hot weather, your body's system for regulating its internal temperature, at rest and when at work, remains quite effective, but it can only work up to its maximum potential with your knowledge and cooperation. The volume of water that must be maintained in the body has very narrow parameters. Severe problems can result if critical levels of water, salts, potassium, glucose, and electrolytes are not maintained in the body when it is subjected to high temperatures as well as exertion. Here is a list of heat-related problems, from the mildest to the most severe.

Heat cramps: These are muscle spasms that occur during periods of exposure to heat and dehydration. They are caused by the constriction of blood vessels to the muscles in response to heat, and by the loss of bodily salts that comes from sweating. If heat cramps are ignored a more serious situation will result. You can relieve these symptoms by drinking plenty of water and replenishing salt and electrolytes to your system. If you make a point of drinking extra fluids containing salt and electrolytes before a ride, you can prevent this condition from developing.

Heat exhaustion: This is a condition caused by stress to your circulatory system combined with a reduction of blood volume in your body due to extensive fluid loss. Symptoms of heat exhaustion include dizziness, nausea, headaches, and a general feeling of weakness. Your pulse rate becomes weak and rapid and you lose the ability to sweat. If you experience these symptoms you should stop exercising immediately, find a cool spot in which to rest, and consume large amounts of fluids. Some of these symptoms may appear hours after you get out of the sun and finish your ride, as your body struggles to recuperate.

Heat stroke: This is the most dangerous of all heat-related conditions and requires immediate action. Heat stroke is what happens when the internal body temperature has risen so high that the body loses the ability to control sweating, heart rate, and the reactions that protect internal organs. Symptoms of heat stroke include the inability to sweat, hot and dry skin, and a dangerously high internal body temperature. Victims of heat stroke can suffer disorientation, hallucinations, and seizures. Heat stroke causes excessive strain on the circulatory system, which can result in permanent liver, heart, or kidney damage. It may also damage the central nervous system and result in permanent disabilities. If left untreated, this condition will lead to complete circulatory collapse and death—it *is* a serious medical emergency. Action you can take while waiting for medical help includes finding a cool place for the victim, immersing the person's body in a cold stream if possible, or rubbing water over the skin. Riders on the trail need to listen to their bodies and monitor each other for signs of heat cramps and heat exhaustion. These can lead to heat stroke if untreated.

Keeping the desert sun off your skin can help prevent these heat-related conditions. A loose, white, or light-colored long sleeve shirt, a hat or visor to keep the sun off your face, and lots of sunscreen will help prevent a damaging sunburn and will aid your body in its fight to stay cool.

Timing your rides so you are not out in the hottest part of the day or during the hottest season of the year will also help prevent heat stress. Early morning and evening are excellent times for riding. You may even want to do half your ride in the morning and half in the evening, with a siesta in a cool spot planned for the afternoon. Spring and fall are the best times for enjoying the desert, but even then temperatures in the middle of the day can climb to 90 degrees and above. Stopping frequently to drink and snack in the shade is the best strategy for avoiding stress to your system from the desert heat.

Hypothermia

At the other end of the spectrum is a condition that develops from exposure to cold. It is called hypothermia, and it can strike even in the middle of summer in the desert. Getting caught out after dark or in a rainstorm at high elevations without proper clothing to protect you from the elements, can result in this life-threatening condition.

Hypothermia is caused by an alarming drop in the body's core temperature. Symptoms include slurred speech, poor coordination, mental dullness and confusion, sleepiness, and a loss of color in the face and extremities. Immediate action is required to reduce further heat loss. Remove wet clothing and pile on dry clothes, sleeping bags, quilts, tarps, or anything that will hold in heat. Drink hot fluids, warm the body next to a fire or next to the body of another person. Prevent hypothermia by bringing a thin layer for warmth and a weatherproof shell with a hood when riding at high elevations or on a day when foul weather is predicted.

Food

A long day's ride requires the proper fuel. Eating enough of the right kinds of foods to maintain energy levels throughout the day is not difficult, but there are a few important things to remember.

During an exciting ride on a long, hot day, your body may be exhausted and your appetite suppressed. Eating throughout the day, however, is very important and should not be left until hunger strikes. As with thirst, once you sense you are hungry, you are already experiencing a depletion in your fuel stores. Once glycogen levels, or energy stores, in your muscles have been depleted it takes several days to replace them. If you have several days of riding planned, you'll want to avoid this scenario.

Before a big ride, or any ride for that matter, you should eat several well-balanced meals. The morning of the ride it is a good idea to eat carbohydrates—bread, cereals, rice, and pasta—that can be easily metabolized into polysacchaarides, or sugars. There is no need for "carbo-loading." Filling up on huge plates of pasta the night before a ride is simply overeating and only stresses your digestive system.

During a ride you will want to consume both simple and complex sugars in liquids and foods. Sugars provide fuel that the body can quickly and easily convert into energy. Simple sugars are the easiest to digest, making them a good ingredient in snacks when exercising. Fruit, juice, and honey are good sources.

After your ride you will want once again to eat a well-balanced meal. This is the time of day when it is okay to eat foods high in protein and foods which contain some fat. Both fat and protein take much longer to digest, about four to five hours, making them ideal to eat the night before a ride. Fatty acids can be burned up during sustained exercise, after sugars are used up. Fats, despite their bad reputation, contribute to the body's store of slow-release energy and can benefit athletes when consumed in small quantities. Fats are found in foods such as meat, cheese, butter, nuts, and avocados.

The best plan is to snack all day. Take time off the trail to snack for a few minutes every couple of hours, taking care to drink enough water to aid digestion.

Avoid hunger. Once you are hungry you have already depleted your energy stores which may haunt you into the next day. Eat smart, well-balanced meals at night without overeating and you will be rebuilding those precious energy stores for future rides.

I have included this information not to scare you, but to make you aware of New Mexico's special conditions so you can enjoy your ride in safety. Once you are prepared to take the proper precautions, you can ride with confidence into the spectacular New Mexico backcountry, with nothing but adventure ahead.

Sarah L. Bennett

Introduction

TRAIL DESCRIPTION OUTLINE

Information on each trail in this book begins with a general description that includes length, configuration, scenery, highlights, trail conditions, and difficulty. Additional description is contained in eleven individual categories. The following will help you understand all of the information provided.

Trail name: Trail names are as designated on United States Geological Survey (USGS) or Forest Service or other maps, and/or by local custom.

Length: The overall length of a trail is described in miles, unless stated otherwise.

Configuration: This is a description of the shape of each trail—whether the trail is a loop, out-and-back (that is, along the same route), figure eight, trapezoid, isosceles triangle, or if it connects with another trail described in the book.

Difficulty: This provides at a glance a description of the degree of physical exertion required to complete the ride, and the technical skill required to pedal it. Authors were asked to keep in mind the fact that all riders are not equal, and thus to gauge the trail in terms of how the middle-of-the-road rider—someone between the newcomer and Ned Overend—could handle the route. Comments about the trail's length, condition, and elevation change will also assist you in determining the difficulty of any trail relative to your own abilities.

Condition: Trails are described in terms of being paved, unpaved, sandy, hard-packed, washboarded, two- or four-wheel-drive, single-track or double-track. All terms that might be unfamiliar to the first-time mountain biker are defined in the Glossary.

Scenery: Here you will find a general description of the natural surroundings during the seasons most riders pedal the trail, and a suggestion of what is to be found at special times (like great fall foliage or cacti in bloom).

Highlights: Towns, major water crossings, historical sites, etc., are listed.

General location: This category describes where the trail is located in reference to a nearby town or other landmark.

Elevation change: Unless stated otherwise, the figure provided is the total gain and loss of elevation along the trail. In regions where the elevation variation is not extreme, the route is simply described as flat, rolling, or possessing short steep climbs or descents.

Season: This is the best time of year to pedal the route, taking into account trail condition (for example, when it will not be muddy), riding comfort (when the weather is too hot, cold, or wet), and local hunting seasons.

Note: Because the exact opening and closing dates of deer, elk, moose, and antelope seasons often change from year to year, riders should check with the local Fish and Game department, or call a sporting goods store (or any place that sells hunting licenses) in a nearby town before heading out. Wear bright clothes in fall, and don't wear suede jackets while in the saddle. Hunter's-orange tape on the helmet is also a good idea.

Services: This category is of primary importance in guides for paved-road tourers, but is far less crucial to most mountain bike trail descriptions because there are usually no services whatsoever to be found. Authors have noted when water is available on desert or long mountain routes, and have listed the availability of food, lodging, campgrounds, and bike shops. If all these services are present, you will find only the words "All services available in . . ."

Hazards: Special hazards like steep cliffs, great amounts of deadfall, or barbed-wire fences very close to the trail are noted here.

Rescue Index: Determining how far one is from help on any particular trail can be difficult due to the backcountry nature of most mountain bike rides. Authors therefore state the proximity of homes or Forest Service outposts, nearby roads where one might hitch a ride, or the likelihood of other bikers being encountered on the trail. Phone numbers of local sheriff departments or hospitals have not been provided because phones are almost never available. If you are able to reach a phone, the local operator will connect you with emergency services.

Land Status: This category provides information regarding whether the trail crosses land operated by the Forest Service, Bureau of Land Management, a city, state, or national park, whether it crosses private land whose owner (at the time the author did the research) has allowed mountain bikers right of passage, and so on.

Note: Authors have been extremely careful to offer only those routes that are open to bikers and are legal to ride. However, because land ownership changes over time, and because the land-use controversy created by mountain bikes still has not completely subsided, it is the duty of each cyclist to look for and to heed signs warning against trail use. Don't expect this book to get you off the hook when you're facing some small-town judge for pedaling past a "Biking Prohibited" sign erected the day before. Look for these signs, read them, and heed the advice. And remember there's always another trail.

Maps: The maps in this book have been produced with great care, and, in conjunction with the trail-following suggestions, will help you stay on course. But as every experienced mountain biker knows, things can get tricky in the backcountry. It is therefore strongly suggested that you avail yourself of the detailed information found in the 7.5 minute series USGS (United States Geological Survey) topographic maps. In some cases, authors have found that specific Forest Service or other maps may be more useful than the USGS quads, and tell how to obtain them.

Finding the trail: Detailed information on how to reach the trailhead, and where to park your car is provided here.

Sources of additional information: Here you will find the address and/or phone number of a bike shop, governmental agency, or other source from which trail information can be obtained.

Notes on the trail: This is where you are guided carefully through any portions of the trail that are particularly difficult to follow. The author also may add information about the route that does not fit easily into the other categories.

ABBREVIATIONS

The following road-designation abbreviations are used in the *America by Mountain Bike* series:

CR	County Road
FR	Farm Route
FS	Forest Service road
I-	Interstate
IR	Indian Route
US	United States highway

State highways are designated with the appropriate two-letter state abbreviation, followed by the road number. *Example:* UT 6 = Utah State Highway 6.

Postal Service two-letter state codes:

AL	Alabama	LA	Louisiana
AK	Alaska	ME	Maine
AZ	Arizona	MD	Maryland
AR	Arkansas	MA	Massachusetts
CA	California	MI	Michigan
CO	Colorado	MN	Minnesota
CT	Connecticut	MS	Mississippi
DE	Delaware	MO	Missouri
DC	District of Columbia	MT	Montana
FL	Florida	NE	Nebraska
GA	Georgia	NV	Nevada
HI	Hawaii	NH	New Hampshire
ID	Idaho	NJ	New Jersey
IL	Illinois	NM	New Mexico
IN	Indiana	NY	New York
IA	Iowa	NC	North Carolina
KS	Kansas	ND	North Dakota
KY	Kentucky	OH	Ohio

OK	Oklahoma	UT	Utah
OR	Oregon	VT	Vermont
PA	Pennsylvania	VA	Virginia
RI	Rhode Island	WA	Washington
SC	South Carolina	WV	West Virginia
SD	South Dakota	WI	Wisconsin
TN	Tennessee	WY	Wyoming
TX	Texas		

TOPOGRAPHIC MAPS

The maps in this book, when used in conjunction with the route directions present in each chapter, will in most instances be sufficient to get you to the trail and keep you on it. However, these maps cannot begin to provide the detailed information found in the 7.5 minute series USGS (United States Geological Survey) topographic maps. Recognizing how indispensable these are to bikers and hikers alike, many bike shops and sporting goods stores now carry topos of the local area.

But if you're brand new to mountain biking you might be wondering "What's a topographic map?" In short, these differ from standard "flat" maps in that they indicate not only linear distance, but elevation as well. One glance at a "topo" will show you the difference, for "contour lines" are spread across the map like dozens of intricate spider webs. Each contour line represents a particular elevation, and at the base of each topo a particular "contour interval" designation is given. Yes, it sounds confusing if you're new to the lingo, but it truly is a simple and wonderfully helpful system. Keep reading.

Let's assume that the 7.5 minute series topo before us says "Contour Interval 40 feet," that the short trail we'll be pedaling is two inches in length on the map, and that it crosses five contour lines from its beginning to end. What do we know? Well, because the linear scale of this series is 2,000 feet to the inch (roughly 2¾ inches representing 1 mile), we know our trail is approximately ⅘ of a mile long (2 inches × 2000 feet). But we also know we'll be climbing or descending 200 vertical feet (5 contour lines × 40 feet each) over that distance. And the elevation designations written on occasional contour lines will tell us if we're heading up or down.

The authors of this series warn their readers of upcoming terrain, but only a detailed topo gives you the information you need to pinpoint your position exactly on a map, steer you toward optional trails and roads nearby, plus let you know at a glance if you'll be pedaling hard to take them. It's a lot of information for a very low cost. In fact, the only drawback with topos is their size—several feet square. I've tried rolling them into tubes, folding them carefully, even cutting them into blocks and photocopying the pieces. Any of these systems is a pain, but no matter how you pack the maps you'll be happy they're along. And you'll be even happier if you pack a compass as well.

Major universities and some public libraries also carry topos; you might try photocopying the ones you need to avoid the cost of buying them. But if you want your own and can't find them locally, write to:

USGS Map Sales
Box 25286
Denver, CO 80225

Ask for an index while you're at it, plus a price list and a copy of the booklet *Topographic Maps*. In minutes you'll be reading them like a pro.

A second excellent series of maps available to mountain bikers is that put out by the United States Forest Service. If your trail runs through an area designated as a national forest, look in the phone book (white pages) under the United States Government listings, find the Department of Agriculture heading, and then run your finger down that section until you find the Forest Service. Give them a call and they'll provide the address of the regional Forest Service office, from which you can obtain the appropriate map.

TRAIL ETIQUETTE

Pick up almost any mountain bike magazine these days and you'll find articles and letters to the editor about trail conflict. For example, you'll find hikers' tales of being blindsided by speeding mountain bikers, complaints from bikers about being blamed for trail damage that was really caused by horse or cattle traffic, and cries from bikers about those "kamikaze" riders who through their antics threaten to close even more trails to all of us.

The authors of this series have been very careful to guide you to only those trails that are open to mountain biking (or at least were open at the time of their research), and without exception have warned of the damage done to our sport through injudicious riding. My personal views on this matter appear in the Afterword, but all of us can benefit from glancing over the following International Mountain Bicycling Association (IMBA) Rules of the Trail before saddling up:

1. *Ride on open trails only.* Respect trail and road closures (ask if not sure), avoid possible trespass on private land, obtain permits and authorization as may be required. Federal and State wilderness areas are closed to cycling.

2. *Leave no trace.* Be sensitive to the dirt beneath you. Even on open trails, you should not ride under conditions where you will leave evidence of your passing, such as on certain soils shortly after a rain. Observe the different types of soils and trail construction; practice low-

impact cycling. This also means staying on the trail and not creating any new ones. Be sure to pack out at least as much as you pack in.

3. *Control your bicycle!* Inattention for even a second can cause disaster. Excessive speed can maim and threaten people; there is no excuse for it!

4. *Always yield the trail.* Make known your approach well in advance. A friendly greeting (or a bell) is considerate and works well; startling someone may cause loss of trail access. Show your respect when passing others by slowing to a walk or even stopping. Anticipate that other trail users may be around corners or in blind spots.

5. *Never spook animals.* All animals are startled by an unannounced approach, a sudden movement, or a loud noise. This can be dangerous for you, for others, and for the animals. Give animals extra room and time to adjust to you. In passing, use special care and follow the directions of horseback riders (ask if uncertain). Running cattle and disturbing wild animals is a serious offense. Leave gates as you found them, or as marked.

6. *Plan ahead.* Know your equipment, your ability, and the area in which you are riding—and prepare accordingly. Be self-sufficient at all times. Wear a helmet, keep your machine in good condition, and carry necessary supplies for changes in weather or other conditions. A well-executed trip is a satisfaction to you and not a burden or offense to others.

For more information, contact IMBA, P.O. Box 412043, Los Angeles, CA 90041, (818) 792-8830.

HITTING THE TRAIL

Once again, because this is a "where-to," not a "how-to" guide, the following will be brief. If you're a veteran trail rider these suggestions might serve to remind you of something you've forgotten to pack. If you're a newcomer, they might convince you to think twice before hitting the backcountry unprepared.

Water: I've heard the questions dozens of times. "How much is enough? One bottle? Two? Three?! But think of all that extra weight!" Well, one simple physiological fact should convince you to err on the side of excess when it comes to deciding how much water to pack: a human working hard in 90-degree temperature needs approximately ten quarts of fluids every day. Ten quarts. That's two and a half gallons—*12* large water bottles, or *16* small ones. And, with water weighing in at approximately 8 pounds per gallon, a one-day supply comes to a whopping 20 pounds.

In other words, pack along two or three bottles even for short rides. And make sure you can purify the water found along the trail on longer routes. When writing of those routes where this could be of critical importance, each author has provided information on where water can be found near the trail—if it can be found at all. But drink it untreated and you run the risk of disease. (See *Giardia* in the Glossary.)

One sure way to kill both the bacteria and viruses in water is to boil it for ten minutes, plus one minute more for each 1,000 feet of elevation above sea level. Right. That's just how you want to spend your time on a bike ride. Besides, who wants to carry a stove, or denude the countryside stoking bonfires to boil water?

Luckily, there is a better way. Many riders pack along the effective, inexpensive, and only slightly distasteful tetraglycine hydroperiodide tablets (sold under the names Potable Aqua, Globaline, and Coughlan's, among others). Some invest in portable, lightweight purifiers that filter out the crud. Yes, purifying water with tablets or filters is a bother. But catch a case of Giardia sometime and you'll understand why it's worth the trouble.

Tools: Ever since my first cross-country tour in 1965 I've been kidded about the number of tools I pack on the trail. And so I will exit entirely from this discussion by providing a list compiled by two mechanic (and mountain biker) friends of mine. After all, since they make their livings fixing bikes, and get their kicks by riding them, who could be a better source?

These two suggest the following as an absolute minimum:

> tire levers
> spare tube and patch kit
> air pump
> allen wrenches (3,4,5, and 6 mm)
> six-inch crescent (adjustable-end) wrench
> small flat-blade screwdriver
> chain rivet tool
> spoke wrench

But, while they're on the trail, their personal tool pouches contain these additional items:

> channel locks (small)
> air gauge
> tire valve cap (the metal kind, with a valve-stem remover)
> baling wire (ten or so inches, for temporary repairs)
> duct tape (small roll for temporary repairs or tire boot)
> boot material (small piece of old tire or a large tube patch)
> spare chain link
> rear derailleur pulley
> spare nuts and bolts
> paper towel and tube of waterless hand cleaner

First-aid kit: My personal kit contains the following, sealed inside double Ziploc bags:

sunscreen
aspirin
butterfly-closure bandages
Band-Aids
gauze compress pads (a half-dozen 4″ × 4″)
gauze (one roll)
Ace bandages or Spenco joint wraps
Benadryl (an antihistamine, in case of allergic reactions)
water purification tablets
Moleskin/Spenco "Second Skin"
hydrogen peroxide, iodine, or Mercurochrome (some kind of antiseptic)
snakebite kit

Final considerations: The authors of this series have done a good job in suggesting that specific items be packed for certain trails—raingear in particular seasons, a hat and gloves for mountain passes, or shades for desert jaunts. Heed their warnings, and think ahead. Good luck.

Dennis Coello
Salt Lake City

Albuquerque Area Rides

The mile-high city of Albuquerque is situated just north of dead center of the state of New Mexico. Albuquerque sprawls along the banks of the Rio Grande River with the Sandia Mountains towering to the east, and volcanic terraces and mesas stretching away to the west. Although Albuquerque is not the capital city of New Mexico, a distinction that belongs to Santa Fe, it is the state's financial hub and home to more than a third of its entire population—slightly over a half million people.

Albuquerque and the surrounding area have a fascinating history, both keyed to the river that neatly cuts the state in half. With a constant supply of water, fertile soils, and relatively mild summer and winter temperatures, it's no wonder this desert valley became a popular place to settle. From the Paleo-Indians who hunted here 10,000 years ago, to the Indians who farmed the sandy soils of the riverbanks, to the Spanish and eventually American settlers who made their homes here, the Rio Grande, or "Great River," has nurtured its people through the ages.

Evidence of the area's earliest known inhabitants—a few spear points and a sloth's claw—was found in a cave at the base of the Sandia Mountains in the 1930s and is thought to be at least 12,000 years old. The banks of the Rio Grande were farmed for corn, beans, and squash by the Indians who learned their agricultural skills from their cousins in South and Central America as many as 2,000 years ago. Some historians believe these Indians were so successful that they eventually became overcrowded. By A.D. 800, after a dramatic decrease in numbers, individuals banded together and left their primitive pit houses to begin building stone houses and practicing religion in more organized communities. These people probably came under the influence of the Anasazi to the north, who had begun to leave their original homes and filter south about this time.

Today there are nineteen different Pueblo tribes within the Pueblo Nation who live in separate stone pueblos scattered between Albuquerque and Santa Fe. The Pueblo Indians are most likely the descendants of the Anasazi. Some of the pueblos built by the ancestors of today's Pueblo Indians have been lived in since ancient times. The Acoma Pueblo, perched high on a mesa top near Grants, New Mexico, has been occupied since the twelfth century, making it one of the oldest cities in America. Although these people are referred to collectively as "the Pueblo Indians," there are great differences among them. The Pueblo speak five different languages and each are further distinguished by special designs, styles, and emphasis in the production of their crafts. The majority of their pueblo dwellings are open to the public at specified times. Visitors are required to pay a fee and are assigned an Indian guide. Taking pictures of the pueblos or their inhabitants is usually forbidden, but you can buy crafts from the gift shops for mementos instead.

It was the Pueblo people who Francisco Vasquez de Coronado and his expedition discovered in 1540, living and farming along the banks of the Rio Grande. He found them living humbly in stone houses as they had for 1,500 years, not in cities of gold as had been rumored throughout Mexico and Spain. The Indians received abominable treatment from the Spanish who sought to dominate and Christianize them under the name of their god and king. The Indians' anger continued to mount under Spanish domination resulting in a series of bloody revolts culminating with the Pueblo Revolt of 1680. The Indians briefly regained their freedom only to be brutally subjugated by the Spanish in 1696. The Pueblo Revolt of 1680 was the longest and most successful uprising of native North Americans against European colonists.

The site of Albuquerque's old town square was originally an Indian pueblo probably occupied since the early 1300s. A spanish settler supposedly befriended the Indians and settle near the pueblo in 1632. There he built several structures, all of which were destroyed in the Pueblo Revolt of 1680. Albuquerque was founded in 1706 when a group of Spanish families was granted the land by the King Felipe V. The town was named for don Francisco Fernandez de la Cueva Enrique, the Duke of Albuquerque and viceroy of New Spain. In 1779 Spanish authorities ordered settlers to band together for protection from increasingly hostile Indian tribes; it is at this time that the plaza that exists today began to take shape.

Albuquerque grew as an important trade route and stopover along the Chihuahua Trail from Mexico to Santa Fe. Activity increased in later years with the establishment of the Santa Fe Trail. The center of town moved and began to grow up around the railroad that reached Albuquerque in 1880. Albuquerque also became an important military outpost and commerce center. Raw materials such as mineral ore, lumber, and livestock were shipped to both the East and West coasts from here. Agriculture has long been an important part of Rio Grande River Valley's economy, and many crops are still grown here today. The city's biggest employer, Sandia Laboratories, researches and develops nuclear weapons capabilities for the federal government. A number of high-tech industries now make the Albuquerque area home.

The Rio Grande River never had to cut rock like the Colorado River did to find its way to the ocean; its work was done for it by a rift valley. The rift valley was formed 30 million years ago when a narrow block of the earth's crust dropped between two parallel faults that reached all the way down to the earth's mantle. The rifting fault movement of the Rio Grande Valley continues to this day. Erosion and the river have been able to fill the trough left by this dropping sliver of the earth's crust with soft, poorly consolidated volcanic ash, gravel, and sand sediments referred to as the Santa Fe Group. Were it not for the constant deposition of these sediments, the trench that would be left would most probably be a sea. Where the rift valley begins in Colorado it is only a few feet wide. By the time it reaches the Albuquerque area it is about 30 feet wide, and to the south it broadens into the heavily faulted country of the Basin and Range.

To the west of Albuquerque you can see the remnants of the kind of volcanic action that is common along the edges of deep, rifting faults. Here, five main volcanos and numerous cinder cones have produced a thick layer of exposed basalt. This basalt provided the ancient inhabitants of this area with a canvas on which they inscribed many fascinating petroglyphs, now protected in Petroglyph National Monument. This new monument also incorporates the volcanos on the mesa to the west that used to exist separately inside Volcano State Park. The extremely rugged western face of Sandia Peak to the east of Albuquerque is the eastern fault block of the rift fault system. Almost five miles below the earth's surface, buried by millions of years of river deposition, lies the rock that matched up with Sandia Peaks before the rift was formed.

The low-lying area surrounding Albuquerque, like much of the state, is classified as an Upper Sonoran life zone (4,500–6,500 feet above sea level). Here you will find desert grasses, including blue gramma—a favorite for cattle ranchers; cholla and prickly pear cactuses; yucca; and pinyon, juniper, and oak trees. On the higher slopes within the Upper Sonoran life zone, ponderosa pine will begin to appear. In the Sandia Mountains and foothills, Transition, Canadian, and Hudsonian life zones are found as well.

Ponderosa pine completely dominate the Transition zone, but will allow spruce and fir in amongst their ranks at elevations close to 8,000 feet. As the climate grows cooler and wetter these other conifers begin to outnumber their warm weather friends. At the top of the Sandia Crest you will find bristlecone pine, subalpine fir, blue spruce, and only the hardiest of plants and animals—those designed to survive at the high altitudes of the Alpine life zone.

The Albuquerque area features yet another kind of ecological zone—a "bosque" (pronounced *bos-kay*). A bosque is a rare type of mature riparian woodland found in desert regions, naturally occurring along the banks of the Rio Grande River. Dominated by the large Rio Grande cottonwood, this rare woodland also includes several types of willows, Russian olive, New Mexico olive, false indigo, and the beautiful silverleaf buffalo berry. This river habitat used to extend all the way into Mexico, providing shelter for wildlife and wood for settlers to build and furnish their homes. Today, after centuries of farming and tree harvesting on the flood plain, only very small portions remain. What remains is protected in several nature and wildlife preserves.

In the higher reaches of the mountains surrounding Albuquerque you can expect to see mule deer, white-tailed deer, and maybe a porcupine or two. Reintroduction and rehabilitation programs for bighorn and desert sheep, as well as for mountain goats, has brought these natives back to several ranges in New Mexico, but you would be extremely lucky to spot one. If you are spending any amount of time out and about in the wilds of New Mexico you will more than likely see a large, rather odd-looking bird zipping across the desert on foot. This is none other than the state bird, the roadrunner, also called a medicine bird, a lizard bird, and a chaparral cock.

While you are in the Albuquerque area there are several stops worth making.

Coronado State Park and Museum gives insight into Indian life-styles before Spanish contact, the nature of Coronado's expedition, and the aftermath of the fateful meeting of these two cultures. The New Mexico Museum of Natural History features displays on the history of the earth and its life forms, including a great dinosaur exhibit (the kids will love this stop). The Pueblo Indian Cultural Center gives a good introduction to the Pueblo people who are such an integral part of this state's history and culture. The Atomic Energy Museum may be a blast for some. Petroglyph National Monument and the Rio Grande Nature Center were two of my favorite stops and are featured in rides 1 and 2 in this section. If you happen to be in town for the Albuquerque Balloon Festival, which usually lasts at least a week in October, you don't want to miss it. Hop on your bike and head to the fairgrounds. This is the largest gathering of balloonists in the world, bringing in over 700 entries in the last few years. Here are a few places to contact for more information about the Albuquerque area:

Albuquerque Convention and Visitors Bureau
P.O. Box 26866
625 Silver Avenue S.W.
Suite 210
Albuquerque, New Mexico 87125
(505) 243-3696
(800) 284-2282

Albuquerque Chamber of Commerce
P.O. Box 25100
Albuquerque, New Mexico 87125
(505) 764-3700

City of Albuquerque
Open Space Division
P.O. Box 1293
Albuquerque, New Mexico 87103
(505) 873-6620

Cibola National Forest
Sandia Ranger District
Star Route Box 174
Tijeras, New Mexico 87059
(505) 281-3304

Bike Coop
3407 Central N.E.
Albuquerque, New Mexico 87106
(505) 265-5170

Two Wheel Drive
1706 Central S.E.
Albuquerque, New Mexico 87106
(505) 243-8448

Harvard Bike House
123 Harvard S.E.
Albuquerque, New Mexico 87106
(505) 255-8808

RIDE 1   *VOLCANO AND PETROGLYPH TOUR*

This is an easy ride that traverses hard-packed dirt roads, with only a few rocky spots, out around the volcanoes and along the volcanic escarpment where the petroglyphs are found. There are miles of fun, level, and rolling roads out here, giving riders many different options. There are some short, steep technical climbs around the most southern and most northern of volcanos for those looking for a challenge. Sections of the trail near the mesa escarpment are covered with polished round stones crafted by the river when the ground here lay at the level of the floodplain. Any way you choose to go, out-and-back or around in a big loop, this is a good place to get out, have a look around, and get some exercise. Views of the city of Albuquerque, the Sandias, Mount Taylor, the Jemez Mountains, and up toward Santa Fe are expansive from up here. Proximity to town makes this ride convenient for a shorter outing.

What was once called Volcano Park has recently been incorporated into Petroglyph National Monument. The five main volcano cones that distinguish Albuquerque's western horizon are included within Petroglyph Monument. These volcanos were created as basalt lava forced its way to the surface from hundreds of miles beneath the earth's crust along fissures created by the rifting Rio Grand Valley. The two northern cones are Bond and Butte Volcano. On the northeast side of Bond Volcano is Boca Negra Cave, which is a lateral vent or "blowhole." Excavation of this cave produced evidence of some 10,000 years of human use. There are indications that in more recent historic times Boca Negra Cave was used by the Pueblo Indians for religious purposes. Desert grasslands surround the cones with fourwing saltbush, squawbush, Apache plume, sagebrush, yucca, prickly pear, and hedgehog cactus. A few gnarled junipers cling to life in the rocky outcrops near the cones.

Parallel to the dirt road that brings you up onto the mesa to the volcanos you will find an escarpment of volcanic rock dropping off just a few hundred yards to the east. On this escarpment of black rock the ancients of this area doodled over

RIDE 1 *VOLCANO AND PETROGLYPH TOUR*

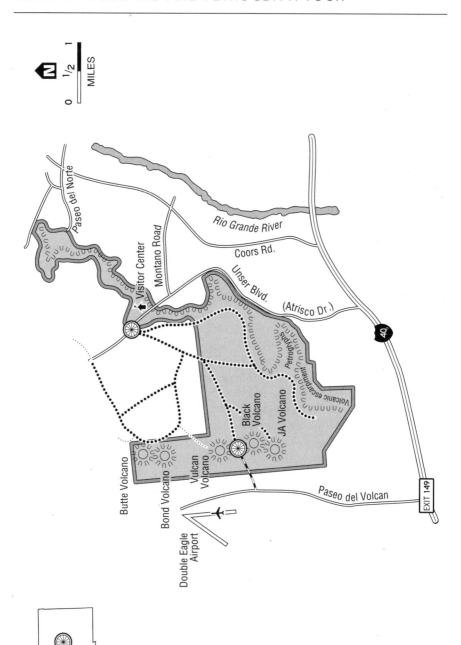

10,000 interesting designs and figures, called petroglyphs, dating from 1000 B.C. The petroglyphs were made by pecking at and abrading the thin layer of varnish that coats these basalt boulders. Several roads lead out to the escarpment; you can leave your bike, climb down, and hunt through the boulders on foot to find this ancient artwork. Do not ride across untracked ground but leave your bike at the end of the road or trail and walk across to the escarpment. You may choose to begin your ride at the monument's Visitor Center, where you can see some petroglyphs first and learn about the symbols and their possible interpretations.

General location: Petroglyphs National Monument is located just outside the western perimeter of Albuquerque.

Elevation change: On the mesa, around the volcanos, and near the escarpment the elevation is between 5,300′ and 5,800′.

Season: This is a great place to ride year-round. Though the city and surrounding areas can receive a dusting of snow now and then, it is not likely to stick around too long. Violent summer thunderstorms produce a lot of electricity as they move through this region, and you are very exposed up here, so take action if you see dark clouds building and lightning in the distance. Seek shelter or head back to your car if bad weather is heading your way.

Services: All services are available in Albuquerque. There are several great bike shops in town.

Hazards: When I was here the petroglyphs at Boca Negra Canyon were in one state park and the volcanos were in another, with most of the escarpment being open to public use. At this time you could ride anywhere along the escarpment and around the volcanos. At the time this book was written mountain bikes were allowed on all the existing roads now within the monument. Since its publication, however, some areas may have been restricted to mountain bikes. Please check in at the Visitor Center for current status on road access within the monument.

Weather is really your biggest concern out here, but you've got a good view in all directions so you'll have plenty of time to seek shelter if a storm starts coming your way.

Rescue index: You are never far away from help out here. There is a ranger on duty during daylight hours at the Petroglyph National Monument Visitor Center. Otherwise, help can be found in surrounding suburbs.

Land status: Petroglyph National Monument, National Park Service, U.S. Department of the Interior.

Maps: Use the USGS 7.5-minute quad for Los Griegos.

Finding the trail: From Albuquerque go west on I-40 to Exit 149. This is the road to the city shooting range and the Double Eagle Airport and model airplane park. Go north on this nameless road for approximately 4.5 miles, past the shooting range. Just before the steel gates to the airport there will be a sign for Petroglyph National Monument. Turn right onto a dirt road. It is another

One of the thousands of intriguing figures and designs found in Petroglyph National Monument just outside of Albuquerque.

1.5 miles to parking inside the monument. (There is also parking at the model airplane park, but it can get pretty busy on the weekends.)

You may also reach the trail by parking at the Visitor Center in Petroglyph National Monument. Take the exit for Unser Boulevard and head north until it enters the national monument. (There is also parking at the top of the hill just past the entrance to Petroglyph National Monument.) You can see the petroglyphs at the Visitor Center and then ride out to the volcanos via Artisco Drive. Artisco Drive will take you up onto the mesa. From there you will see a number of dirt roads heading out across the mesa's terrace.

Sources of additional information: City of Albuquerque, Open Space Division, P.O. Box 1293, Albuquerque, New Mexico, 87103, phone (505) 873-6620.

Notes on the trail: There are many possibilities for creating your own routes out here. The open nature of this country and the good views to various landmarks make it hard to get lost. While supplementary topographical maps are interesting they are not really necessary here.

RIDE 2 *CORRALES BOSQUE PRESERVE*

This is not so much a specific route as it is a good place to get out and explore. Trails run for almost eight miles along the length of the Rio Grande river through the Corrales Bosque Preserve, protected and maintained by the Nature Conservancy as an example of a mature riparian woodland. The single-track trails in the preserve are easy to ride and are made of hard-packed sandy soils, as is the maintenance road on top of the dike that parallels these trails. You will find sections of loose sand that are hard to pedal through on both the trails and the road that run along the banks of the river. Head down on a trail and come back on the road or vice versa. The dikes that border both sides of the Rio Grande are also dirt roads that are great for mountain biking. Access to these dikes is found at various points throughout the city.

Corrales Bosque is a cool, peaceful, and really beautiful deciduous forest along the banks of the "big river." The preserve gives an intimate look at an unusual riparian habitat that used to range all along the Rio Grande. The dominant tree of this river woodland is the Rio Grande cottonwood, which depends upon intermittent flooding to germinate and disperse its seeds. At one time the bosque almost entirely disappeared due to wood harvesting and farming. A devastating flood in 1904 wiped out the remaining bosque as well as an enormous amount of farmland. Silt and sand raised the level of the floodplain and made conditions ripe for the bosque to make a comeback. Once again the bosque became a healthy habitat for a variety of waterfowl, over 260 species of birds, raccoons, gray foxes, muskrats, beavers, and bobcats. To learn more about the riparian woodlands of the Rio Grande visit the Rio Grande Nature Center located on the east side of the river just north of Interstate 40 off Rio Grande Boulevard and Candelaria Street.

General location: The Corrales Bosque Preserve is located just outside the northern limit of the city of Albuquerque near the village of Corrales. The preserve is bordered on the west by the village and on the east by the Rio Grande.
Elevation change: The river bottom is at an elevation of approximately 5,000'. No elevation is gained or lost in the distance you will travel along the floodplain.

RIDE 2 *CORRALES BOSQUE PRESERVE*

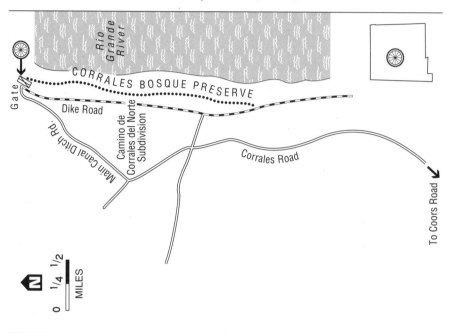

Season: Riding is excellent in the preserve and on the river's dikes year-round. In wet weather some of the trails become muddy while the sandy sections become firmer. This is an especially beautiful ride in the fall when the cottonwoods provide a golden canopy overhead. The brilliant yellow leaves of these giants create a light of their own and are a wonderful contrast against a deep blue desert sky.

Services: All services are available in Albuquerque.

Hazards: Few hazards exist out here. Sandy spots can frustrate your progress from time to time.

Rescue index: Many people use the trails of the preserve and the dikes along the river for walking, jogging, and horseback riding. Help is never far away. The dikes are also lined by homes.

Land status: The Corrales Bosque Preserve is the property of the Nature Conservancy.

Maps: Use USGS 7.5-minute quads for Los Griegos, Alameda, and Bernalillo.

Finding the trail: To reach the Corrales Bosque Preserve find Corrales Road. On I-40 go west to the Coors Road Exit. Coors Road will turn into Corrales Road once you cross over Alameda Boulevard. Or from I-25 head north until you reach the Alameda Boulevard exit. Alameda will intersect Corrales Road immediately after you cross over the Rio Grande River. Turn right and head north through

The "bosque," or riparian woodland of the Rio Grande River, protected within the Nature Conservancy's Corrales Bosque Preserve.

the village of Corrales until you see the road head up the side of a sandy mesa. Just before the road climbs you will see a sign for Corrales del Norte subdivision. Turn right (east) immediately onto a dirt road, the Main Canal Ditch Road. Proceed along this road until it ends at a fenced area marked with a sign: Corrales Bosque Nature Preserve. Park here and enter through the opening in the fence.

Sources of additional information: The Nature Conservancy, Santa Fe Office, (505) 988-3867. The Rio Grande Nature Center (2901 Candelaria N.W., Albuquerque, New Mexico 87107, (505) 344-7240) has some good exhibits on the wildlife and woodlands of the bosque as well as a selection of informative books and field guides.

Notes on the trail: Create your own route using the trails of the preserve and the dike road. Bring a picnic and relax in the shade under the arms of hundred-year-old cottonwoods. Enjoy!

RIDE 3   *OTERO CANYON*

This is a moderately difficult out-and-back that will take intermediate and advanced riders about one to two hours to complete. You will bike up and down Otero Canyon on a hard-packed dirt single-track trail that becomes rocky as it crosses over the drainage bottom. This trail follows Otero Canyon for approximately 2.5 miles before climbing up to a ridge. At the top of the ridge the land becomes the property of the U.S. Department of Defense, which has made it off-limits to the public. The trail does continue however, dropping down into Madera Canyon. Ride back the way you came. Total distance of this ride is just under six miles.

This is really pretty pinyon-juniper country with stands of oak intermixed. Clump grasses and woody shrubs make up the ground cover here. This is a great short, single-track ride that is perfect for someone wanting to challenge themselves on a single-track trail for the first time. Trail surface is excellent for the most part, with only a few rocky sections.

General location: Cibola National Forest, Sandia Ranger District, just east of Albuquerque.
Elevation change: At the trailhead marker at the beginning of Otero Canyon the elevation will be 6,800' above sea level. From there you will climb up this drainage to the ridge to reach a high elevation of 7,500'. Total elevation gain is 700'.
Season: This is a great trail to ride almost any time of year except for when the trail is snow-covered or wet.
Services: All services are available in Albuquerque.

RIDE 3 *OTERO CANYON*

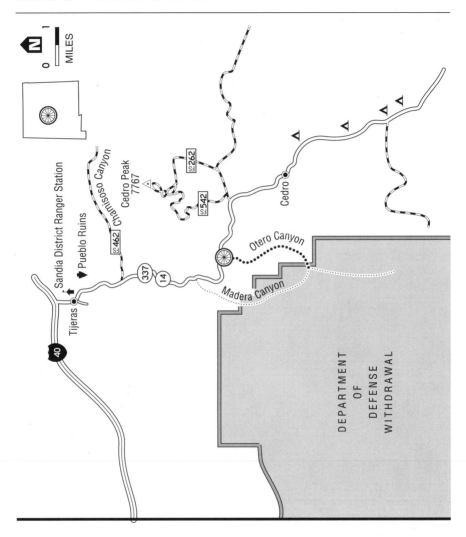

Hazards: Only 2.5 miles of this trail heading up Otero Canyon is in the public domain; beyond this point, which is not marked, the trail becomes the property of the Department of Defense and is off-limits to the public. The trail does continue down Madera Canyon, the next drainage to the west. Eventually this trail hits NM 337.

The trail does become rocky as it drops into the creek bottom of Otero Canyon, so use caution. This is a fast downhill, so check your speed and be courteous to those riding uphill.

The single-track trail up Otero Canyon is a trail that riders of all abilities should try.

Rescue index: NM 337 is a fairly well traveled road where help could be flagged down. Your next best option is to head to the town of Tijeras 5 miles back the way you came. The Sandia District Ranger is located in Tijeras.

Land status: Cibola National Forest, Sandia Ranger District.

Maps: The 7.5-minute USGS topo for Tijeras covers this area but does not show the trail. The Cibola National Forest map does not show this trail.

Finding the trail: From Albuquerque take Interstate 40 heading east to the town of Tijeras in Tijeras Canyon. Exit at Tijeras and head south on NM 337 for approximately 4 miles. Look for a pulloff to the right just past a rock outcrop. Park here and pick up the trail at the sign marker: Otero Canyon.

Sources of additional information: Cibola National Forest, Sandia Ranger District; address and phone are listed in the introduction to this section.

Notes on the trail: Trails leave from both sides of the parking area but join in a few hundred yards. You will ride on a fast, hard-packed single-track trail for the first 2 miles before dropping into the rocky drainage bottom. Turn around once you reach the ridge and head back down. This is a straightforward, out-and-back affair so it's pretty hard to get lost. Ride up and come back the way you came. Don't forget your brain bucket and have a blast!

RIDE 4 *CEDRO PEAK*

The ride up and around Cedro Peak is an easy to moderately difficult seven-mile loop that will take riders of beginning to intermediate riding ability about two hours to complete. This trail follows maintained gravel and hard-pack dirt roads that take you up to the top of Cedro Peak and to a fire lookout.

This country falls within the Upper Sonoran and Transition zones where you'll find mature stands of pinyon and juniper, with good views up to the Sandias and surrounding foothills. This is a pretty area and a fun, short ride that will give you a good feel for New Mexico's rolling uplands. There are many trails in the Cedro Peak area, making it a popular spot for local mountain bikers.

General location: Cedro Peak is located in the Cibola National Forest, east of Albuquerque.

Elevation change: At the point where FS 242 begins, the elevation will be 6,995' above sea level. From here you will climb gradually to an elevation of 7,767' high atop Cedro Peak. Elevation gain is 772'.

Season: Most of this ride is at 7,000' and above so you will probably run into snow in the midwinter months. April through mid-November should be great for riding except for when the trail surface is wet.

RIDE 4 *CEDRO PEAK*

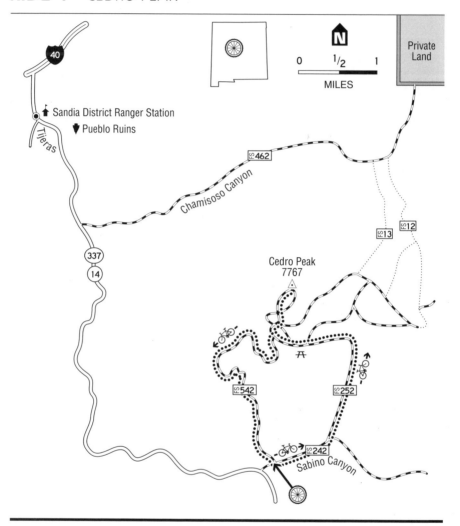

Services: All services are available in Albuquerque.

Hazards: Wet weather makes the going messy out here. Don't get stuck atop the fire lookout in a storm. Check in at the Sandia Ranger Station in Tijeras for local hunting season schedules and weather forecasts. They have lots of other interesting information about the flora, fauna, and history of the area.

Rescue index: In case of an emergency you could flag help down on the well-

The Cedro Peak area includes a whole system of trails perfectly suited to mountain biking.

traveled NM 337. Your next best option is to head to the town of Tijeras five miles back the way you came. The Sandia District Ranger is located in Tijeras.

Land status: Cibola National Forest, Sandia Ranger District.

Maps: Cibola National Forest, Sandia Ranger District Map. USGS 7.5-minute quad for Sedillo.

Finding the trail: From Albuquerque take Interstate 40 heading east to the town of Tijeras in Tijeras Canyon. Exit at Tijeras, stop by the Sandia District Ranger Station, say hi, and see what valuable information they might have to offer. You'll probably want to go for a short walk behind the station to see what remains of the Tijeras Pueblo ruins while you are here. Then drive south on NM 337 for approximately five miles, turning left when you reach Forest Service Road 242. Park here.

Sources of additional information: Cibola National Forest, Sandia Ranger District; address and phone are listed in the introduction to this section.

Notes on the trail: From where you parked you will ride almost a mile to where FS 242 will branch right; stay left here, on what is now FS 252. You will take this road all the way to the top of Cedro Peak. As you come back down the spur road that took you to the top, you will bear right and take FS 542 back to where you left your car.

There are lots of roads and several really fun single-track trails running off every direction in the Cedro Peak area, all of which make for excellent mountain biking. Supplementary topographical maps are really worthwhile here.

RIDE 5   *CHAMISOSO CANYON*

This ride is a six-mile tour up Chamisoso Canyon that most riders will find moderately difficult. Riders of beginning to intermediate riding ability in good physical condition will take two to three hours to complete this ride. The trail follows hard-packed dirt jeep roads and a double-track with a grassy median.

This ride traverses the rolling foothills south of the Sandia Mountains. Here you will find lots of pinyon and juniper trees mixed in with clumps of oak. This is great terrain for mountain biking and there are lots of really fun trails that run throughout this area. You can pick up a map of all the mountain biking trails in this area at the Sandia District Ranger Station in Tijeras.

General location: Chamisoso Canyon is located in the Cibola National Forest, east of Albuquerque.

Elevation change: At the point where FS 462 begins, the elevation is 6,424' above sea level. From here you will climb to a height of 7,100' at the point where FS 462 reaches the ridge between Chamisoso and Tablazon canyons. Total elevation gain is almost 680'.

Season: Early spring through late fall is the best time to do this ride, provided the ground is not saturated.

Services: All services available in Albuquerque.

Hazards: This jeep road receives moderate use and can become rutted in spots. Be aware of other riders in this area.

Rescue index: NM 337 is a fairly well traveled road, and the town of Tijeras and the Sandia District Ranger Station are less than a mile from where this trail leaves the road. Help is not far away.

Land status: Cibola National Forest, Sandia Ranger District.

Maps: Use the Cibola National Forest, Sandia Ranger District map. You can also get the USGS 7.5-minute quad for Sedillo. Cibola National Forest also puts out a Cedro Peak Multiple-Use Trails map that is excellent for getting around in this area.

Finding the trail: From Albuquerque take Interstate 40 heading east to the town of Tijeras in Tijeras Canyon. Exit at Tijeras and drive south for about .7 miles to the Sandia Ranger Station. Stop in for a chat with the local ranger and see what

RIDE 5 *CHAMISOSO CANYON*

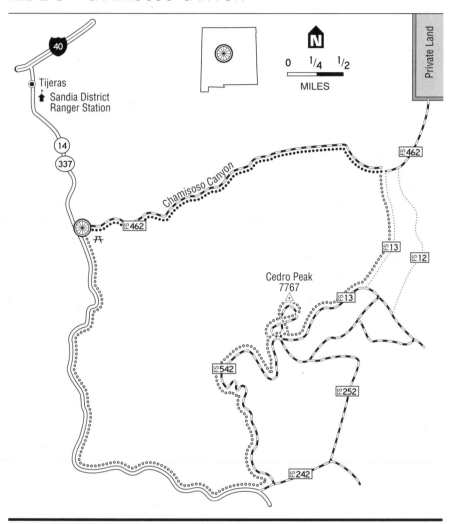

interesting information they might have. Then drive approximately 1 mile past the ranger station heading south on NM 14 to where Forest Service Road 462 branches off on the left. Park here.

Sources of additional information: Cibola National Forest, Sandia Ranger District; address and phone are listed in the introduction to this section.

Notes on the trail: You will follow FS 462 up Chamisoso Canyon for approximately 2.8 miles to a ridge top where the trail forks. The fork to the right is FS

The trail up Chamisoso Canyon belongs to the system of trails in the Cedro Peak area.

Trail 13, which will take you around the eastern flank of Cedro Peak. The trail to the left is the continuation of FS 462, which follows Tablazon Canyon down to where it joins a frontage road paralleling the freeway. FS 462 is interrupted by about a half a mile of private land in Tablazon Canyon. Turn around and ride back down the way you came.

There are quite a few roads and trails back in these hills, so you have lots of options for creating your own routes and doing some exploring. One of the best options is to continue around the eastern flank of Cedro Peak on FS Trail 13. From the top of Cedro Peak you can then head down FS 542 to where it joins FS 242. FS 242 comes out on NM 14; go right and ride back down Cedro Canyon to FS 462 where you left your car.

Supplementary topographical maps are going to be a must for wandering around back here as the Forest Service maps do not show much detail.

RIDE 6   *LOS HUERTES or WATERMELON TRAIL*

This ride is a 14-mile up-and-back affair that traverses pavement, graded gravel, hard-packed dirt, and somewhat rougher jeep roads. Riders in good physical condition and of intermediate riding ability will take about four hours to complete this ride. While the trail itself is not extremely technical, the substantial gain in elevation makes this a moderately difficult to difficult or strenuous ride.

This beautiful ride begins in the northern foothills of the Sandia Mountains and follows Las Huertes Creek up, up, up to its source at Capulin Spring Campground. The Sandia Man Cave or cliff dwellings make for an interesting stop at about mile 4.5 on the way up. Sit in the cool shade of alpine spruce and aspens at the campground and enjoy your snack before the ride down.

General location: The Los Huertes Trail is located northeast of Albuquerque, on the north slope of Sandia Mountain, in the Cibola National Forest.

Elevation change: From where this ride begins in the town of Placitas, your elevation is approximately 6,075′ above sea level. From there you will climb, gently at first and then more steeply, to an elevation of 8,800′ at Capulin Spring Campground. The elevation gain is 2,725′.

Season: Because of its high elevation, this trail will be rideable from April through sometime in late October or November.

Services: All services are available in Albuquerque. Water and convenience groceries are available in Placitas.

Hazards: You will want to be wary of car traffic on this road (Forest Service Road 16)—it can be heavy at times. This can be a very fast descent in places, so use caution and always wear your helmet.

Rescue index: This road receives moderately heavy traffic during the summer months. Other help can be found in the town of Placitas, at the picnic grounds on the way up, or when you reach the Sandia Crest road or NM 536.

Land status: Cibola National Forest, Sandia Ranger District.

Maps: Use the Cibola National Forest map for the Sandia Mountain Wilderness or USGS 7.5-minute quads for Sandia Crest and Placitas.

Finding the trail: From Albuquerque head north on Interstate 25 for 16 miles until you reach the exit for Placitas. Exit here and head east another 6 miles on NM 165 to the town of Placitas. Park anywhere in town.

Sources of additional information: Cibola National Forest, Sandia Ranger District; address and phone are listed in the introduction to this section.

Notes on the trail: Once on your bike, begin by heading east out of Placitas on NM 536 for about 1 mile until it turns to dirt and becomes FS 16. You will then

RIDE 6   *LOS HUERTES OR WATERMELON TRAIL*

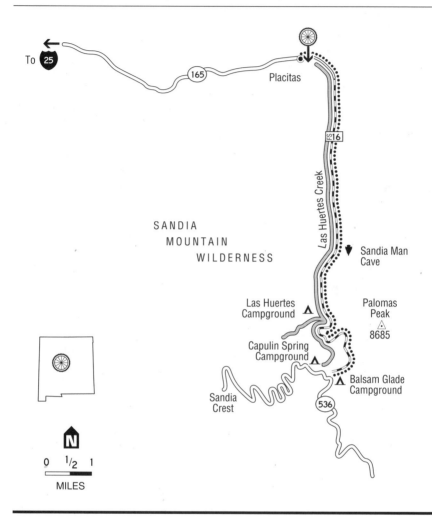

ride FS 16 as it follows Las Huertes Creek for the next 6 miles. This is a straight up-and-back ride with little or no possibility of getting lost.

You can adjust the length of this ride by driving through the town of Placitas on NM 536 and parking farther along on that road. Where the road turns to dirt is a good alternate starting point.

RIDE 7   *10K to TREE SPRING TRAIL*

This ride is a moderate to strenuous loop connecting two trails and traversing nine miles of the back side of Sandia Mountain. Riders in good to excellent physical condition with good riding skills will take about three hours to complete this loop. Trail surfaces on this ride include pavement, hard-packed dirt road, and single-track. Though a lot of this single-track is smooth, you will encounter water bars as well as some rocky sections.

This is classic alpine riding: you will be winding your way through deep, cool stands of mixed conifer and aspens at elevations above 8,000 feet. The single-track of the 10K and Tree Spring trails is great riding that everyone from intermediate to advanced riders will enjoy.

General location: The two trails are located on the east side of Sandia Mountain within the Cibola National Forest, just east of Albuquerque.

Elevation change: From where you begin this ride at the Tree Spring trailhead parking lot the elevation is approximately 8,400′ above sea level. From there you will climb to an elevation of 9,900′ near where you pick up the 10K trail heading downhill. Total elevation gain is 1,500′.

Season: Because you are at a high elevation your season for riding is short. Late April through mid-November will be the best time to ride this trail.

Services: All services are available in Albuquerque.

Hazards: These trails get a lot of pressure from all different kinds of trail users. If you can plan your ride to avoid peak traffic times, mainly weekends, all the better. Remember uphill riders and all other trail users have the right of way. Pull over, stop, say hi, and smile as they pass you by.

Temperatures can drop quickly at this elevation at sundown or during storms. A lightweight layer of Capilene (a type of polyester used in the manufacture of long underwear) is easy to carry and great to have along when the day cools off.

Rescue index: This trail receives a lot of use from hikers and bikers—you are not in the outback here. Also, help may be found on NM 536, the busy road that leads to Sandia Crest.

Land status: Cibola National Forest, Sandia Ranger District.

Maps: Sandia Mountain Wilderness Map issued by Cibola National Forest shows the 10K and Faulty trails but does not show the Oso Corridor Trail. Use USGS 7.5-minute quads for Tijeras and Sandia Crest.

Finding the trail: From Albuquerque take Interstate 40 heading east, take the next exit for the town of Tijeras and head north on NM 14. Continue heading north on NM 14 5.5 miles before turning left onto the Crest Highway—also NM 44 and 536. You will then drive approximately 5 miles to the Tree Spring Campground and the Tree Spring trailhead. Park here.

RIDE 7 *10K TO TREE SPRING TRAIL*

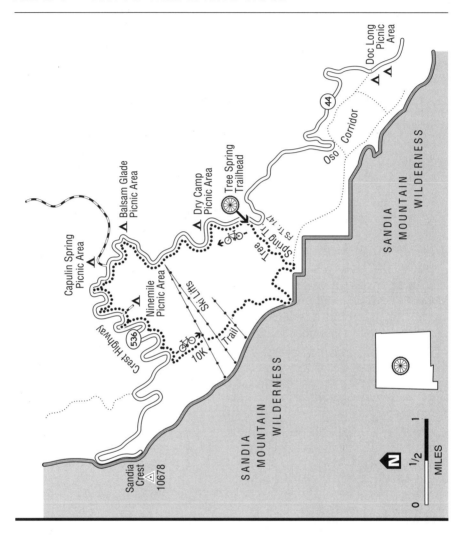

Sources of additional information: Cibola National Forest, Sandia Ranger District; address and phone are listed in the introduction to this section.

Notes on the trail: Begin this ride by heading back out to the Crest Highway. Go left, riding uphill just over 4.5 miles to where you will go left again onto the 10K Trail. As you climb up this paved portion of the Sandia Crest Highway you will pass Dry Camp, Balsam Glade, Capulin Spring, and Ninemile picnic areas. Immediately after you pass the Ninemile Picnic Area you will start climbing up switchbacks that get longer as you go. The 10K Trail leaves from the uphill side of the seventh switchback, a right-turn switchback. If you cannot find the trail at this point of this switchback, ride up the road another 200 to 300 yards to where the 10K Trail crosses the road and pick it up here. You will then ride the 10K Trail heading in a south-southeasterly direction for 1.7 miles, at which point it intersects the Tree Spring Trail (Forest Service Trail 147). Go left onto the Tree Spring Trail down to your car.

There is a great alternate route here called the Oso Corridor Trail. It branches off of the Tree Spring Trail only a few hundred yards from the trailhead and heads southwest downhill, paralleling the Crest Road for about 2 miles to where it comes out at the Doc Long Picnic Area. A short trail branches from the trail you rode in on just above this picnic area and takes off heading west, leading to the Cienega Canyon Picnic Area, where you can pick up the Faulty Trail, the next trail that is outlined in this section.

Do not be tempted to ride other trails leading into the Sandia Mountain Wilderness Area; they are off-limits to mountain bikes.

RIDE 8   *FAULTY TRAIL LOOP*

This ride follows an 11-mile loop on graded dirt roads and a great buffed-out (smooth) single-track trail. This loop will take about three hours to complete for riders of intermediate to advanced riding ability in good physical condition.

Once again you will be riding through gorgeous alpine forests of pine, spruce, and aspen. This is another great moderate trail with some really nice single-track riding, perfect for someone wanting to get comfortable riding off-road.

General location: The Faulty Trail is located on the east side of Sandia Mountain within the Cibola National Forest, just east of Albuquerque.

Elevation change: Where you begin this ride at the Cole Springs Campground and Picnic Area the elevation is 7,500' above sea level. From there you will ride back down to NM 14 at 6,850', up to the Sulphur Canyon Picnic Area at 7,400', and then along the Faulty Trail, which contours the hillside at elevations between 7,600' and 7,800'. Highest elevation reached is 7,800'. Total elevation gain is approximately 1,500'.

Season: This route should be clear of snow by sometime in the beginning of April and will be rideable until the snows come again in November.

Services: All services are available in Albuquerque.

Hazards: These trails get a lot of pressure from all different kinds of trail users. If you can plan your ride to avoid peak traffic times, weekends mainly, all the better. Remember, uphill riders and all other trail users have the right of way. Pull over, stop, say hi, and smile as they pass you.

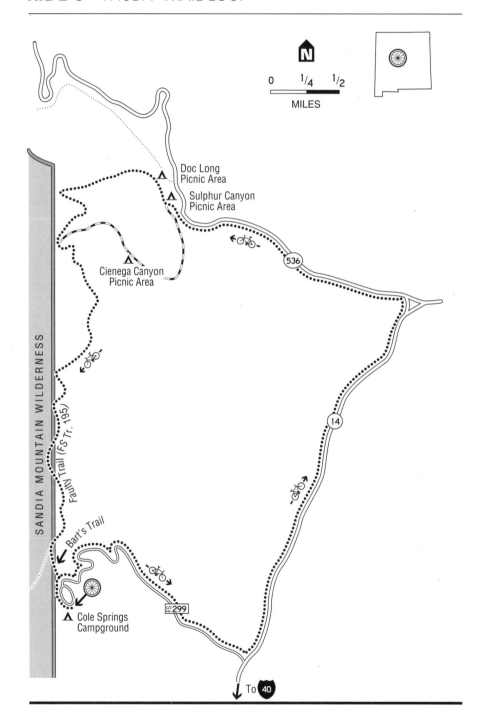

0   1/4   1/2
MILES

Doc Long
Picnic Area

Sulphur Canyon
Picnic Area

536

Cienega Canyon
Picnic Area

SANDIA MOUNTAIN WILDERNESS

Faulty Trail (FS Tr. 195)

14

Bart's Trail

Cole Springs
Campground

299

To 40

The single-track of the Faulty Trail and other trails outside the wilderness area on the back side of nearby Sandia Mountain are some of the best in the Albuquerque area.

Rescue index: This trail receives a lot of use from hikers and bikers—you are not in the outback here. Also, help may be found on NM 536, the busy road leading to Sandia Crest.
Land status: Cibola National Forest, Sandia Ranger District.
Maps: The Cibola National Forest map for the Sandia Mountain Wilderness is

good for finding these trails. You can also use the USGS 7.5-minute quads for Tijeras and Sandia Crest.

Finding the trail: From Albuquerque take Interstate 40 heading east; take the exit for the town of Tijeras, and head north on NM 14. Proceed for 3.5 miles to Forest Service Road 299, which takes off to the left at the settlement of Canoncito. Drive up FS 299 to the Cole Springs Campground. Park here.

Sources of additional information: Cibola National Forest, Sandia Ranger District; address and phone are listed in the introduction to this section.

Notes on the trail: From Cole Springs Campground, ride back out FS 299 to NM 14. Go left, and ride just over 2 miles on NM 14 to where the Sandia Crest Highway (NM 536) takes off to the left. Turn left onto this road and ride another 1.5 miles on the pavement to Sulphur Canyon Picnic Area. This picnic area is on the left-hand side of the Sandia Crest Road. A trail leaves from the end of the road that takes you to Sulphur Canyon Picnic Area and heads west for a couple hundred yards before intersecting the Faulty Trail, or FS Trail 195. Go left onto the Faulty Trail.

The Faulty Trail follows the contour of the hillside for about 3 miles before intersecting Barts Trail. Go left onto Barts Trail, which will take you down to FS 299, the road to the Cole Springs Campground where you left your car. It is about a third of a mile back to the campground from where the trail hits the road. You will know if you have missed the left-hand turn at Barts Trail when the trail starts heading uphill. At this point you will be entering the Sandia Mountain Wilderness Area, which is off limits to mountain bikes.

There aren't a whole lot of options here due to the wilderness area boundary. If you're feeling up to it, ride up the Oso Corridor Trail, Ride 7, just beyond the Doc Long Picnic Area, and try your skills going uphill on that single-track.

RIDE 9   *FOOTHILLS TRAIL*

This trail is accessible at several different points and runs for a distance of almost seven miles along the base of the Sandia Mountains. This out-and-back single-track trail is smooth for the most part but has some rocky, sometimes unrideable, sections where it dips down into arroyos or drainages that come out of these mountains.

This is a good area for riders of all ability levels to get out, do some exploring, and test their skills without having to drive out of town. You will be riding through brushy foothills country with great views looking west over the city of Albuquerque and the Rio Grande River Valley.

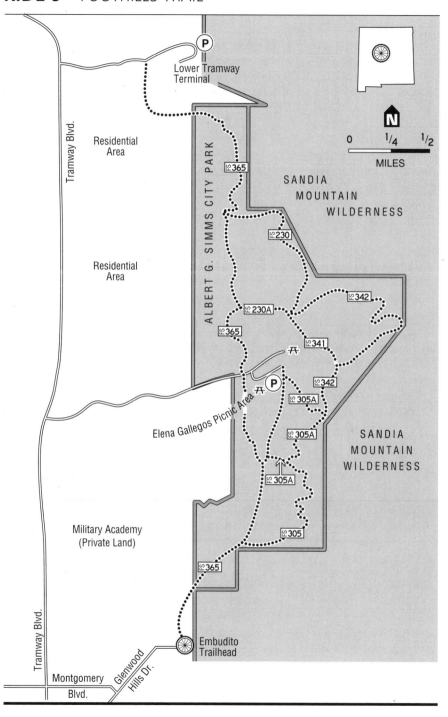

Tramway Blvd.

Residential Area

Residential Area

Military Academy (Private Land)

Lower Tramway Terminal

ALBERT G. SIMMS CITY PARK

FS 365

FS 230

FS 230A

FS 342

FS 365

FS 341

FS 342

FS 305A

FS 305A

FS 305A

FS 305

FS 365

Elena Gallegos Picnic Area

SANDIA MOUNTAIN WILDERNESS

SANDIA MOUNTAIN WILDERNESS

N

0   ¼   ½
MILES

Tramway Blvd.

Montgomery Blvd.

Glenwood Hills Dr.

Embudito Trailhead

General location: The Foothills Trail is located just east of Albuquerque, along the base of the Sandia Mountains.

Elevation change: This is rolling terrain with only moderate changes in elevation. Elevation at the Embudito trailhead is approximately 6,500' above sea level. High elevations along this route do not exceed 6,800'.

Season: This is a great place to get out and ride almost any time of year, provided the ground is not saturated.

Services: All services are available in Albuquerque.

Hazards: Keep an eye out for other trail users as you whiz along. Equestrians sometimes ride here, so give them the right of way, let them know well in advance if you are approaching from behind, smile, and say hello.

Rescue index: You are riding along the eastern margin of the city in an area that is well used by bikers, runners, and hikers. Help is not far away.

Land status: Cibola National Forest, Sandia Ranger District, and Open Space, City of Albuquerque.

Maps: Sandia Mountain Wilderness Map put out by the Cibola National Forest shows the area but not the trail. Use USGS 7.5-minute quads for Sandia Crest and Tijeras.

Finding the trail: From downtown Albuquerque head east on Montgomery Boulevard. Continue on Montgomery past the intersection with Tramway Boulevard into a residential area, where Montgomery intersects Glenwood Hills Drive. Go left onto Glenwood Hills Drive and head north for approximately half a mile before turning right onto a short road that dead ends at the Embudito trailhead access area. Park here.

You may also reach this trail from the Elena Gallegos Picnic Area in Albert G. Simms Park, farther north, off Tramway Boulevard.

Sources of additional information: Cibola National Forest, Sandia Ranger District; address and phone are listed in the introduction to this section.

Notes on the trail: From wherever you pick up the Foothills Trail it will roll along between the suburbs of Albuquerque and the boundary of the Sandia Wilderness Area. Double back on the trail to return to your starting point. Be ready for those dips into rocky arroyos and have fun!

Santa Fe Area Rides

In the winter of 1610, the city of Santa Fe was christened "Holy Faith" by its founder, Don Pedro de Peralta, making it the oldest capital city in the country. The Spanish colonial heritage of this town, the rich influences of the region's Native American tribes, the artistic community that lives and works here, and the fantastic natural beauty of the area all come together to create a fascinating picture that will intrigue anyone who passes through Santa Fe. Thousands of visitors are drawn by these things to Santa Fe each year. Situated at the southern tip of the Sangre de Cristo Range, Santa Fe is comfortably nestled up against the pinyon-dotted pink foothills surrounding this most southern extension of the Rocky Mountains. At an elevation of 7,000 feet above sea level, Santa Fe experiences four distinct seasons. While a severe winter storm might bring only a foot of snow to town, the Santa Fe Ski Area, only eighteen miles away, has chair lifts reaching to the summit of a 12,000-foot peak where there is enough snow to entertain skiers until early April. Santa Fe and the surrounding country are where desert and mountains meet, providing mountain bikers with many excellent and varied riding opportunities throughout the year.

The town of Santa Fe was constructed on the site of an abandoned Tano Indian village and was originally intended to be the capital of the "Kingdom of New Mexico." Santa Fe was founded as the Spanish colonial government's northernmost military outpost and mission. The Spanish were determined to settle this new land and convert the native Pueblo Indians to Catholicism. Political, religious, and military leaders ruled from the fortress at Santa Fe, which eventually earned the name "Palace of Governors." From here the Spanish led a well-documented campaign of terror against the Indians who refused to convert. The Pueblos' sacred kivas were destroyed, their people were tortured, enslaved, and often mutilated before they finally abandoned their sacred rituals and denounced their gods.

By 1680 the Pueblo people could no longer tolerate the abuse of the ruthless and domineering Spanish. Led by a San Juan Indian medicine man named Popé, the Pueblo people started a well-planned revolt that began in the outlying Pueblos to the north. The Indians set fire to homes, churches, and any structure that would burn along the way, killing settlers and priests as they tried to flee. The Indians spent weeks seeking out and destroying anything that represented the Spanish, including the Palace of Governors and all of the early historical documents of the settlement at Santa Fe. Popé himself took up residence in the palace and attempted to maintain his power and influence over the people he had helped to lead to victory. The Pueblo Revolt of 1680 is considered by historians to be the most organized and most successful Indian uprising in the New World. Still, conflict among various tribes and distrust of Popé eventually sent most

Indians back to their pueblos. By 1692, Vargas, the newly appointed governor of Santa Fe, had only unorganized resistance to contend with when he showed up. He was able to bring Santa Fe and all of New Mexico back under Spanish control.

For most of the next century the Spanish continued to rule the territory of Nueva Mexico from Santa Fe, where increasing numbers of white traders and settlers began to stop on their travels. In 1821 Mexico won its independence from Spain and, soon after, settlements all over the West began to grow with settlers and supplies that moved along the Santa Fe Trail. During this time America was undergoing a period of reckless expansion all across the continent, legitimized by the concept of "Manifest Destiny." This nineteenth-century doctrine gave the United States the self-designated "right and duty" to expand and civilize North America. In 1846 the United States declared war against Mexico—under the doctrine of Manifest Destiny—in order to secure the territories of Texas and California. By the end of the Mexican-American War, the United States had also won the vast tracts of land between. The bulk of what are modern-day New Mexico and Arizona was simply included in the spoils of victory. In 1846 General Stephen Kearney marched into Santa Fe and claimed the territory for the United States. No blood was ever shed in this takeover: Mexican government officials and troops fled Santa Fe before Kearney's men arrived.

In 1848 the Treaty of Guadalupe Hidalgo was signed by Mexican government officials, ceding a large portion of the Southwest to the United States. In 1853 the ten-million-dollar Gadsden Purchase added another chunk of land to America's southwestern territories; it would eventually become the southernmost part of Arizona and New Mexico. Finally, in 1912, one of the first areas of this country to be settled by Europeans was granted statehood and admitted to the Union.

Well before the turn of the century, artists and thinkers discovered the magnificent beauty, wonderful climate, and cultural heritage of Santa Fe. The Bohemian atmosphere of Santa Fe, as well as its beautiful surroundings, makes it one of the most popular tourist destinations in New Mexico. More recently, the Santa Fe area has become a popular center for the learning and practice of holistic medicine, as well as a kind of New Age spiritualism. Today the town of Santa Fe still strongly identifies with its Spanish and Indian heritage. Strict building codes require that all structures mimic the style of the original adobe pueblos that once stood here—just one of the ways Santa Fe guards its historical heritage. Santa Fe also celebrates a variety of cultural festivals and art fairs throughout the year. These events are always good opportunities to get out and experience the unique atmosphere and spirit of this city.

The pink hills and mesas that characterize the land surrounding Santa Fe have been created by horizontal layers of sedimentary rock. Hard sandstones and limestones form the mesa tops, cliffs, and ledges, while softer mudstones and siltstones erode into slopes. The layers of sedimentary rock in this area catalog the geological history of the Sangre de Cristo Mountains. Uplifting; erosion; the creation of beaches, shallow seas, and desert dunes; and river deposition are all recorded in the colored sands, soils, and rocks of this area. The reds, browns, pinks, and yellows that band the hills around Santa Fe have been created by tiny grains of iron oxides that exist in the rocks and eroded materials: hematite, biotite, and horneblende. The mountains behind Santa Fe are the Sangre de Cristos, which, like the rest of the Rocky Mountains, were created by faulting and uplifting. These mountains are primarily comprised of granite, with dikes and veins of very hard black and green gneiss running through their western flank.

The country surrounding Santa Fe is where the high desert and the Rocky Mountains meet and mingle. The hilly country that butts up against the mountains is speckled with the fragrant greens of pinyon and juniper and support a mixture of desert plants, including chamiso, sagebrush, agave, yucca, cholla, and prickly pear cactuses. Large, old cottonwoods and a variety of conifers grace the drainages and some of the streets in and around Santa Fe. Evergreen cone-bearing trees such as ponderosa pine, blue spruce, and Douglas fir identify the slopes and peaks around Santa Fe ranging from the Transition to the Canadian and Hudsonian life zones. The very highest points in the range, such as Truchas Peak (13,103 feet), are well within the Alpine life zone. In the fall, stately stands of quaking aspen turn a fiery gold in the canyons behind Santa Fe, making this a spectacular time of year for touring the mountains by mountain bike. In the summer the wildflowers bloom a spectrum of brilliant colors to rival those of any other slope in the Rockies.

The wildlife you are most likely to see in the high desert environment of Santa Fe and surrounding area include wild turkey, quail, coyote, cottontails, jackrabbits, and even bobcat. Mule deer and white-tailed deer will come down into the desert canyons in winter to browse on woody shrubs and dried grasses, but are mostly found higher up in the forests and meadows of the mountains. In the more remote reaches of the Sangre de Cristo and Santa Fe mountains you may be lucky enough to spot elk, mountain lion, black bear, or even a ring-tailed cat. In the sky over the foothills of Santa Fe a wide variety of raptors soar on thermals— air heated by the desert that rises as it runs against the flanks of the Sangre de Cristos.

Because Santa Fe is such a tourist mecca it is a good idea to reserve accommodations well in advance of your visit. While Santa Fe is great to visit anytime spring through fall, you may want to plan your visit to coincide with one of the many festivals, Santa Fe Opera performances, or Indian markets held throughout the year. You can find the usual chain hotels here, but also a good selection of charming bed-and-breakfast establishments. You'll see literally hundreds of boutiques, galleries, curio shops, and restaurants to spend your money in, but don't forget to visit some of the places that reflect Santa Fe's unique history. These include the Mission San Miguel, the oldest mission in the United States, dating from 1610; the Palace of Governors Museum; the Cathedral of St. Francis of Assisi; the Museum of Fine Arts; and the Wheelwright Museum of the American Indian. Here are a few places to contact when planning your biking trip to Santa Fe:

Santa Fe Convention and Visitors Bureau
201 West Marcy Street
Santa Fe, New Mexico 87501
(505) 984-6760

Santa Fe National Forest
Supervisors Office
P.O. Box 1689
Santa Fe, New Mexico 87504
(505) 988-6940

Santa Fe National Forest
Española Ranger District
P.O. Box R
Española, New Mexico 87532
(505) 753-7331

Santa Fe Schwinn
1611 St. Michaels Drive
Santa Fe, New Mexico 87501
(505) 983-4473

Coyote Bikes
1722 St. Michaels Drive
Santa Fe, New Mexico 87501
(505) 471-1682

RIDE 10 *CAJA DEL RIO PLATEAU*

This is an easy 18-mile loop that most riders will find takes them about three hours to complete. The route follows maintained dirt and gravel Forest Service roads, unmaintained dirt roads that have become a double-track for the most part, and some single-track. This is a good ride to do during the winter months when the higher elevations around Santa Fe are impassable due to snow.

The Caja del Rio Plateau is a wide open expanse punctuated by a few modest mountains sparsely covered by high desert chaparral, pinyon, and juniper. The plateau is a terrace of volcanic material left behind by the enormous volcano that was once the Jemez Mountains. There are excellent views in all directions out here as well as lots of options for exploring. Once you reach the edge of the gorge, you may even want to hike down to the Rio Grande for a refreshing swim.

General location: The Caja del Rio Plateau is located 9 miles north and west of Santa Fe, and is included within the Santa Fe National Forest.

RIDE 10 *CAJA DEL RIO PLATEAU*

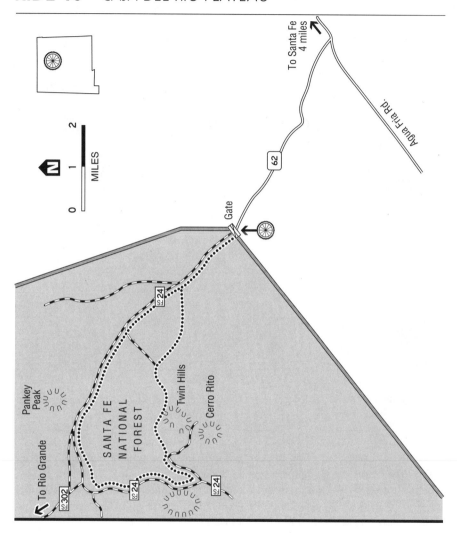

Elevation change: Where you begin this ride at the boundary of the Santa Fe National Forest, the elevation is approximately 6,400′ above sea level. You will gain a modest 300′ in this ride to reach an elevation of 6,700′.

Season: This is an excellent early spring, late fall, and winter ride. It is usually warm and dry out on this plateau when the trails are wet and muddy higher up. It can be scorching out here in the summer.

Services: All services are available in Santa Fe.

The Caja del Rio Plateau offers some great mountain biking when higher elevations are unrideable due to snow.

Hazards: It can be very hot and dry out here in the summer months, so if you come then be sure to bring lots of water and cover up.

Rescue index: While you are not far away from Santa Fe, this area does not get a lot of traffic. Your best place to seek help in case of an emergency is the settlement of Agua Fria, which you will pass on your way in.

Land status: Santa Fe National Forest, Española Ranger District.

Maps: The Santa Fe National Forest Map is adequate for finding this route and following it. You can also use the USGS 7.5-minute quad for Agua Fria.

Finding the trail: From downtown Santa Fe head southwest out of town on Agua Fria Road. Continue heading in this direction for about 4 miles until you reach NM 62. Go right onto NM 62 and continue for another 5 miles to the boundary of the national forest, marked by a fence and a gate, where it turns into Forest Service Road 24. Park here.

Sources of additional information: Santa Fe National Forest, Española Ranger District; address and phone are listed in the introduction to this section.

Notes on the trail: From the parking area at the national forest boundary you will continue on FS 24, heading northwest. Stay left at the first fork you encounter. At about mile 5 you will be even with Pankey Peak, to your right. Soon you will encounter a fork in the road; the right fork will take you to the intersection with FS 302. FS 302 is a right-hand turn that ends up at the Rio Grande River Gorge in about four miles.

If you take the left fork, FS 24, it will bend around and head south. You will pass another road to the west (right) shortly after this bend. Three miles after the bend there will be a road to your left; this is your turn. This road will double back and head northeast for 1 mile before making a sharp turn to the south toward the saddle of Twin Hills and Cerro Rito. As it turns south you will see a rough, abandoned road cutting straight ahead; follow the abandoned road for 3.5 miles to where it rejoins FS 24. Turn right to ride back to your car.

There are many options to create your own routes out here, but use supplementary maps and have a working knowledge of a compass if you do.

RIDE 11   *PACHECO CANYON*

This ride is an 18-mile up-and-back affair that will be moderate to difficult for most intermediate riders. The long climb and change in elevation add substantially to the difficulty of this trail, which follows a graded dirt road for the entire way. Sections of loose gravel, ruts, and washboard can crop up along this route. Allow three to four hours to complete this ride.

This beautiful canyon road begins in a drainage of leafy cottonwoods and then winds up through meadows and aspen glades into an alpine wonderland. This route serves as a good introduction to the mountains around Santa Fe. It is also a ride that will let you work on conditioning and acclimating to altitude without the stress of a super-technical ride.

General location: Pacheco Canyon is 8 miles north of Santa Fe in the Santa Fe National Forest.
Elevation change: At the point where NM 590 bears right off the Bishop's Lodge Road, just past the settlement of Tesuque, the elevation is 6,609' above sea level. Where you turn right onto the Pacheco Canyon Road the elevation is 7,204'. From there you will climb, climb, climb steadily, but not too steeply, to where the Pacheco Canyon Road, or Forest Service Road 102, intersects the paved Hyde Park or Ski Basin Road. At this point in the ride your elevation is 9,765'. Elevation gain is 2,560'.

RIDE 11 *PACHECO CANYON*

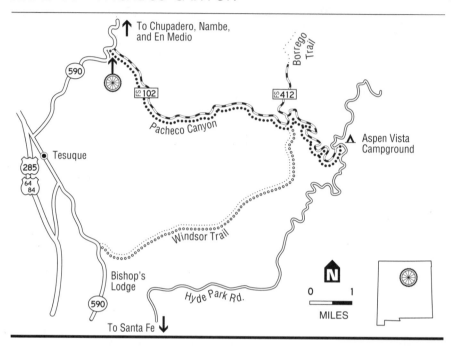

Season: Because of elevation, this ride is best taken late spring through fall. The road can get washed out and rutted in wet weather. The monsoon season, which begins in July and runs through September, can generate sudden, violent thunderstorms with heavy rains in the afternoon.

Services: All services are available in Santa Fe.

Hazards: Pacheco Canyon Road receives a fair amount of vehicle traffic. Be aware, ride to the right and in single file, allowing cars to pass. A bright piece of clothing or helmet cover will help alert motorists to your presence.

Rescue index: The Pacheco Canyon Road is a popular route for tourists driving down from the Santa Fe Ski Basin Road during the spring, summer, and fall, so you can expect to find help there. You will also find lots of traffic once you reach the paved Santa Fe Ski Basin or Hyde Park Road. Help may also be sought at any of the settlements off the Bishop's Lodge Road.

Land status: Santa Fe National Forest, Española Ranger District.

Maps: The Santa Fe National Forest Map is fine for finding this route and trails nearby. You can also get the USGS 7.5-minute quad for Aspen Basin and Tesuque.

Finding the trail: From Santa Fe drive north on NM 590 (Bishop's Lodge Road) for about 7 miles until just past the settlement of Tesuque where NM 590 branches

The Pacheco Canyon Road provides a tour of one of the Santa Fe area's prettiest canyons.

off to the right, heading toward the settlements of Chupadero and Nambe. Take this right and drive about 3.5 miles to where a dirt road enters on your right. This is FS 102. Here, you are about a mile short of Chupadero and Nambe. Park here.

Sources of additional information: Santa Fe National Forest, Española Ranger District; address and phone are listed in the introduction to this section.

Notes on the trail: Take FS 102 straight up Pacheco Canyon, all the way to the Hyde Park Road. It's hard to get lost on this ride unless you decide to take one of the many trails that branch off to the side.

There are several great route options once you reach the top of the canyon. This is one of the best: 6 miles from the start of this ride and 3 miles from where FS 102 intersects the Hyde Park Road, take a left on FS 412 and head north. FS 412 can be ridden to the end, where it turns into a single track known as the Borrego Trail (FS Trail 150). The Borrego Trail eventually drops down to join the Rio Capulin Trail (FS Trail 179). The Rio Capulin Trail then heads downward becoming a dirt road just above the settlement of Nambe. This dirt road turns into NM 590 3 miles above where you left your car at the beginning of FS 102. This is a rough single-track that can get very washed out and rocky in sections. It's not recommended for inexperienced riders, but the adventurous should give it a try.

Another great option is the Windsor Trail. This option requires a shuttle or drop-off, but allows riders to head straight back to Santa Fe about 4 miles on NM 590. From where you parked, take FS 102 past the point where FS 412 takes off on the left (6 miles) and continue another 1.6 miles to Windsor Trail, on the right. This trail is well marked but is most easily seen when coming down the road from the other direction.

Another option: get dropped off and ride FS 102 all the way to Hyde Park Road, then simply ride the paved Hyde Park Road all the way down to Santa Fe.

RIDE 12 *ASPEN VISTA ROAD*

Another up-and-back route that earns a moderate to difficult rating because of high altitudes and a sustained climb, this 12-mile ride follows a well-maintained dirt road and will take riders in good to excellent physical condition two to three hours to complete. There is a good loop option on this ride as well.

The Aspen Vista Road begins at 10,300 feet and traverses forests of mixed conifer and aspen to take you up to Tesuque Peak at 12,300 feet. As you climb higher you will emerge from these big trees to find altitude-stunted pines and the tundralike vegetation that characterizes Alpine life zones. Once you reach the radio towers you will have some spectacular views to take in. Lake Peak (12,400 feet) and Penitente Peak (12,250 feet) rise immediately to the north and east of you. Santa Fe Lake is just below you.

General location: The Aspen Vista Road takes off from the Santa Fe Ski Basin Road 15 miles north and east of Santa Fe in the Santa Fe National Forest.
Elevation change: Where this ride begins at the Aspen Vista Campground the elevation is approximately 10,000′ above sea level. From here you will climb to some radio towers that are at an elevation just over 12,000′ on top of Tesuque Peak. Total elevation gain is 2,000′.
Season: This is a summer and fall ride. The high altitude of this route means snow stays on the ground late into the spring. You are very exposed up here and should keep an eye out for afternoon thunderclouds. If they should start to rumble, take cover.
Services: All services are available in Santa Fe.
Hazards: The extremely high elevation of this ride will make it difficult if not uncomfortable for anyone who is not properly acclimated to high altitude or at least in good physical condition.

The threat of thunderstorms is a hazard to be taken very seriously when riding at high elevations where you are exposed and far from shelter. Check with the local weather service or the National Forest supervisor's office in Santa Fe for current weather forecasts. The monsoonal storms that belt this region daily for

RIDE 12 *ASPEN VISTA ROAD*

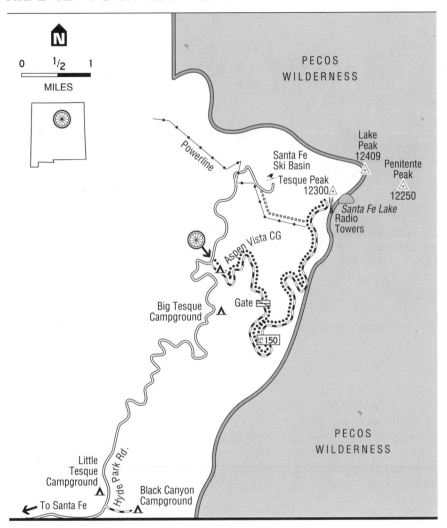

several weeks during the summer and early fall produce large amounts of rain, hail, and lightning and can deal a lethal blow to the foolhardy or unsuspecting. An early start is a good way to avoid these storms altogether.

Rescue index: This is a popular area for mountain bikers and hikers to get up and out in the cool air in the summer. Your best chance for finding help quickly in the case of an emergency is on the busy Hyde Park Road that you drive up on.

Land status: Santa Fe National Forest, Española Ranger District.

Healthy stands of quaking aspen set the Sangre de Cristo Mountains ablaze with color in fall.

Maps: The Santa Fe National Forest Map is adequate for seeing how to get to the trailhead and following this route. You can also use the USGS 7.5-minute quad for Aspen Basin.

Finding the trail: From Santa Fe head north out of town on Washington Road, taking a right on Artist Road. Artist Road turns into the Hyde Park Road. Continue heading up Hyde Park Road for approximately 13.5 miles until you reach Forest Service Road 150 and the Aspen Vista Campground. Park here.

Sources of additional information: Santa Fe National Forest, Española Ranger District; address and phone are listed in the introduction to this section.

Notes on the trail: From the Aspen Vista Campground ride FS 150 up, up, up, all the way to the radio towers. Two miles into this ride you will encounter a locked gate that prevents motorized vehicles from using this road; go around it and continue on your ride. Enjoy the views and don't forget to check the weather forecast before you go.

There's one alternate route you could try: from the radio towers, follow a rough road used for maintenance that runs along the power lines across and down to the Santa Fe Ski Basin and to the top of the paved Hyde Park Road.

From here you can ride down Hyde Park Road to where you left your car at the Aspen Vista Campground.

RIDE 13 *WINDSOR TRAIL AND WINDSOR TRAIL SYSTEM*

The Windsor Trail is a 17-mile single-track that belongs to a system of trails that give many options for creating your own routes, all of which fall into the moderate to difficult range. While the trail surface is excellent—smooth, hard-packed, alpine soil—there are numerous water bars and tree roots, and just a few rocks. These, combined with the sustained, and sometimes steep climbs, make this a favorite area for more advanced riders and a good challenge for the intermediate riders looking to improve their single-track riding skills.

Many different combinations of the trails in the Windsor Trail System are possible and will give varying distances, but any combination ridden out-and-back or in a loop will not exceed 20 miles and most usually fall into the 10- to 15-mile range. It's up to you: ride a whole loop or just a section out-and-back. You may want to ride up on the pavement and come down on the single-track, or, if you're super-aggressive, ride up *and* back down on the single-track. Allow three hours to complete the Windsor Trail.

The Windsor Trail System traverses the west-facing slopes of the southern extension of the Sangre de Cristo Mountains. This alpine setting features deep, shady stands of mixed conifers. Sprinkled across the slopes and canyons of these mountains you will find small, sunny meadows rimmed by glades of quaking aspen.

This is some five-star mountain biking! Scenery, location, trail grades, and surface condition all combine to make this system of trails some of the best you'll find in New Mexico. This area gets a good deal of attention from all types of trail users and so can become congested during certain times of year. Please be especially sensitive to other trail users here as conflicts in the past have threatened to close these trails to mountain bikers.

General location: The Windsor Trail System is located just north and east of Santa Fe in the Santa Fe National Forest.
Elevation change: The Windsor trailhead, where you begin this ride, is at an elevation of 7,200' above sea level. From there you will be climbing. Where the Chamiza Trail joins the Windsor Trail, your elevation will be just under 8,080'. Where the Borrego Trail meets the Windsor Trail, your elevation is 8,600'. The Windsor Trail crosses the Pacheco Canyon Road (Forest Service Road 102) at an elevation of 9,000', leaves this road at 9,300', and continues climbing to where it meets the Hyde Park or Ski Basin Road, at the Aspen Vista Campground, at an elevation of 10,307'. Elevation gain is approximately 3,100'.

RIDE 13 *WINDSOR TRAIL AND WINDSOR TRAIL SYSTEM*

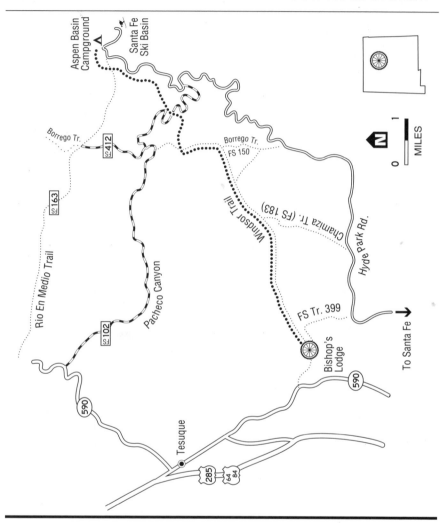

Season: This trail system is rideable midspring through fall provided ground is dry. If the ground is thoroughly wet and muddy, stay off the trails. Mountain bike tires can make a real bog in trail depressions; this makes the trail difficult for hikers and is considered environmentally incorrect as well.

Services: All services are available in Santa Fe.

Hazards: Because this system of trails is so close to the city of Santa Fe, it gets heavy use from other types of trail users and can become very busy on the weekends. There have been hard feelings between mountain bikers and other trail

The Windsor Trail and Windsor Trail System, just minutes outside downtown Santa Fe, offer mountain bikers some five-star riding.

users over this particular group of trails. It is therefore extremely important to be courteous to hikers and equestrians while you are riding. Remember, uphill traffic always has the right of way.

Rescue index: You are likely to see other folks on the trails here. Your best option for finding help in case of an emergency is to get out to the Hyde Park or Ski Basin Road where you will find plenty of car traffic year round.

Land status: Santa Fe National Forest, Española Ranger District.

Maps: The Santa Fe National Forest Map shows this and several other trails in the area but with little detail. Use the USGS 7.5-minute quad for Aspen Basin.

Finding the trail: To reach the Windsor trailhead drive north out of Santa Fe on Washington Street, which turns into Bishop's Lodge Road (also NM 590). Approximately 5 miles from town and 1 mile past Bishop's Lodge, there will be a dirt road on the right; turn here and drive through a housing settlement for about another mile before the road ends at the trailhead. Park here.

Sources of additional information: Santa Fe National Forest, Española Ranger District; address and phone are listed in the introduction to this section.

Notes on the trail: As you start riding keep an eye out for FS Trail 399, which takes off to the right several hundred yards from the trailhead. You can take this route out to the Hyde Park Road if you want to do the uphill section of this ride on the pavement. Otherwise, just continue on up. At miles 4 and 5 you will encounter two different branches of the Borrego Trail coming in from the right. In another 1.5 miles you will come across the Pacheco Canyon Road, or FS 102. Go left onto this road and ride for approximately a quarter of a mile around a right-hand elbow, looking all the time for where the trail takes off again on the right-hand side of the road. After you pick up the trail again, it is another 2.5 miles to the end of the trail at the Aspen Basin Campground.

There are many ways of combining the Windsor, Chamiza, and Borrego trails to create a multitude of great rides. If you take FS Trail 399, which leaves just beyond the Windsor trailhead sign to the right, it will take you over to the paved Hyde Park Road. You can then ride up Hyde Park Road until you reach the Chamiza trailhead in about 2 miles or the Borrego Trail head in another 4 miles. Both these trails also intersect the Windsor Trail. You can take the Windsor Trail back down to where you started, making a shorter loop. You may also want to take the paved Hyde Park Road all the way to the top.

One very popular option is beginning at the Chamiza trailhead, riding up the Chamiza Trail (FS Trail 183) to where it joins the Windsor Trail, and then continuing on the Windsor Trail to its end at the Aspen Vista Campground, a 6-mile trip, one way. The Chamiza Trailhead can be reached by taking the Hyde Park Road northeast out of Santa Fe for about 7 miles. Chamiza Trail is listed on Forest Service maps as FS Trail 183 and leaves on the left-hand side of the road. You can also start at the Borrego Trailhead, 4 miles past the Chamiza Trailhead on the left. The Borrego Trail (FS Trail 150) intersects the Windsor Trail 1.5 miles from where it begins. This is a 4-mile ride one way.

RIDE 14 *ATALAYA MOUNTAIN*

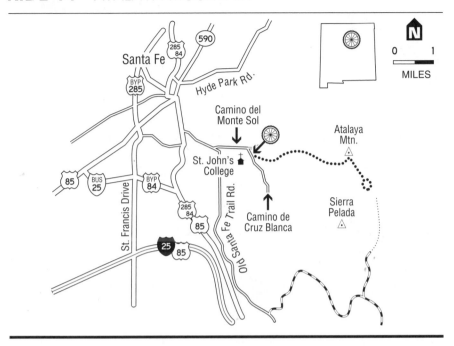

RIDE 14 *ATALAYA MOUNTAIN*

This ride is a strenuous, but short, seven-mile round-trip grunt up to the top of Atalaya Mountain. For intermediate or advanced riders in excellent physical condition, it will take about two hours to complete this ride. The route up is a mostly packed sand single-track trail that can get loose and gravelly in spots.

The sandy foothills that include Atalaya Mountain are lower than the mountains to the north of Santa Fe. They are characterized by pinyon, juniper, agave, clump grasses, and cactus—plants you'd expect to find in the high desert. Wonderful views of Santa Fe and west to the Jemez Mountains await you once you have made it to the summit.

General location: Atalaya Mountain is located just east of Santa Fe in the Santa Fe National Forest.
Elevation change: At the beginning of this ride the elevation is 7,400' above sea level. At the top of Atalaya Mountain you will have reached an elevation of 9,120'. Total elevation gain is 1,720'.

Strawberry hedgehog cactus grows throughout the foothills behind Santa Fe and is easy to spot in the spring with its display of showy pink blossoms.

Season: This trail should be rideable spring through fall provided the ground is dry.

Services: All services are available in Santa Fe.

Hazards: This is a short, but very steep, technical ride. You will encounter some rocks and roots, but it is the nature of the trail surface and not so much the obstacles that make this ride technical. Not recommended for beginners.

Rescue index: This trail is fairly well used by hikers, so you will probably see some on the trail. You are very close to town on this one and do not have far to go to find help in the event of an emergency.

Land status: Santa Fe National Forest, Española Ranger District.

Maps: The Santa Fe National Forest map is not of a scale that can show this short route with any detail, but it is good to have for finding most of the other routes in this section. Use the USGS 7.5-minute quad for Santa Fe.

Finding the trail: From Santa Fe drive out of town heading southeast on Old Santa Fe Trail Road. Take a left and head east on Camino del Monte Sol and then take your second right, on Camino de Cruz Blanca. Take this road to Wilderness Gate Road, and pass through a large adobe gate, which is the entrance to a subdivision. A hundred yards past this gate is a dirt road heading uphill on your left. (When I was here, this road and surrounding area looked like it was about to become another subdivision, so this road may no longer be dirt.) Turn left here and continue to the end, a small cul-de-sac. Some steps and a Forest Service sign mark the trailhead. Park here.

Sources of additional information: Santa Fe National Forest, Española Ranger District; address and phone are listed in the introduction to this section.

Notes on the trail: This is a straight up-and-back affair with little chance of getting seriously sidetracked.

RIDE 15 *GLORIETA GHOST TOWN*

This ride is an easy to moderate 6.5-mile out-and-back jaunt up Glorieta Canyon to the ruined remains of the town of Glorieta. The route follows a dirt road that becomes a more deteriorated jeep road and then turns into a wide single-track. There is one steep section on this ride and there are several loose spots. Riders in good physical condition can expect to take two hours to complete this ride.

This ride is in the rolling foothills at the southern tip of the Sangre de Cristo Mountains. Here you will find pinyon and juniper dominating, giving way to mixed conifers as you ride higher into the canyon. In an open meadow you will discover the remains of the old mining town of Glorieta, including a two-story hotel and several cabins that are now collapsed. A short hike across from the site of these ruins up to Rock Peak offers some great views of surrounding country.

General location: The remains of the town of Glorieta are located 20 miles southeast of Santa Fe in the Santa Fe National Forest.
Elevation change: Trailhead elevation is 7,520' above sea level. The high elevation reached at the ghost town is 8,400'. Total elevation gain is 880'.
Season: Midspring through fall is the best time to do this ride.
Services: All services are available in Santa Fe.
Hazards: You will encounter two gates on this ride; be sure to close them behind you after you pass through.

Do not climb in or around any of the old structures in Glorieta—they are very unstable and may collapse if disturbed.

If you think you may be riding close to hunting season, or if you don't know, be sure to contact the local Forest Service office for schedules and hunting areas. If you have to ride during hunting season, make sure you wear some piece of bright clothing.
Rescue index: This trail receives light use most of the year. Your best bet for finding help is in the (populated) settlement of Glorieta, just south of where you begin this ride.

RIDE 15 *GLORIETA GHOST TOWN*

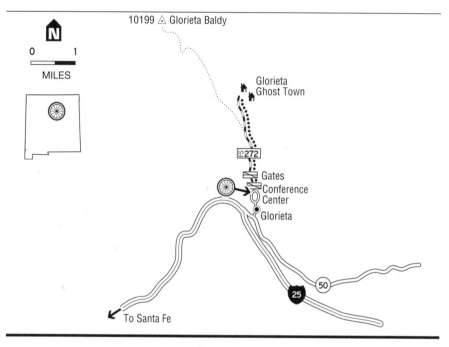

Land status: Santa Fe National Forest, Pecos Ranger District. Glorieta Baptist Conference Center's private property.

Maps: The Santa Fe National Forest map shows both the route up to the ruins at Glorieta and how to get there. You can also get the USGS 7.5-minute quad for Glorieta Baldy.

Finding the trail: From Santa Fe, get on Interstate 25 northbound (this section of I-25 actually heads in a southeast direction) until you reach the exit for Glorieta and Pecos. Exit here, cross over I-25, and then go left onto NM 50, which will take you right into Glorieta. Head north through town following signs to the Glorieta Baptist Conference Center. Park here. You will need to stop at the security gate here and register because you will be on their private property at the start of the ride. You can also pick up a map here.

Sources of additional information: Santa Fe National Forest, Española Ranger District; address and phone are listed in the introduction to this section. You may also want to contact the Glorieta Baptist Conference Center; phone: (505) 757-6161.

Notes on the trail: Once you are past the gate you will be on the Glorieta Canyon

The ruins of old stone cabins that were left behind by miners, herders, and homesteaders can be found throughout New Mexico.

Road and Trail (Forest Service Trail 272). This route is easy to follow and will take you straight up to the ghost town, with no chance to get lost.

RIDE 16 *GLORIETA BALDY*

The trail up to Glorieta Baldy is a rough, four-wheel-drive jeep road that is rocky, loose, and steep for long sections. This 20.5-mile loop is difficult and very strenuous. Even the most experienced riders in excellent physical condition will find this route a grueling test of strength and endurance. You will climb for approximately 12 miles and gain a substantial 3,000 feet in elevation. The radical single-track descent off the top of the peak, which eventually smooths out for a really fun ride down, will test the technical abilities of any riders who come this way. Allow at least five hours for the round-trip assault on this peak, with time to take in the view when you get to the top.

RIDE 16 *GLORIETA BALDY*

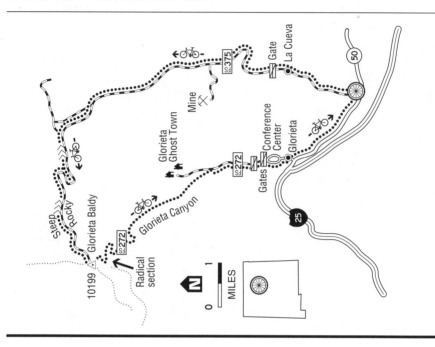

After sliding through pinyon and juniper in the lower elevations you will enter alpine forests of mixed conifers and aspen that break open onto grassy hillsides and meadows. The views on this ride are fantastic all along the way, but the cherry on the cake is the 360-degree view from atop the lookout at the peak.

General location: Glorieta Baldy trailhead is located east and south of Santa Fe, eight miles as the crow flies, and just over twenty miles driving.

Elevation change: Where this ride begins at the start of Forest Service Road 375 the elevation is approximately 7,200' above sea level. Elevation at the top of Glorieta Baldy is 10,199'. Elevation gain is 3,000'.

Season: Late spring through fall is the time to do this ride, provided roads and trails are dry.

Services: All services are available in Santa Fe.

Hazards: The very high altitudes reached on this ride may make exertion a painful experience for those who are unaccustomed to them or who are not in good physical condition.

When riding at this elevation, rapid temperature changes and dangerous lightning storms can be a problem. It would be a good idea to check the weather

Glorieta Baldy is at the southern end of the Rocky Mountains and rises to 10,199 feet.

forecast for afternoon thundershowers before heading out. If storms are predicted, get an early start so you can avoid them. This way you can keep from having to cut your ride short.

Rescue index: FS 375 receives light to moderate use in the dry seasons. In case of an emergency, help should be sought at the settlement of La Cueva or in Glorieta Pass, the small town at the beginning of FS Trail 272.

Land status: Santa Fe National Forest, Pecos Ranger District.

Maps: The Santa Fe National Forest map is good for finding how to get to the start of this trail. It also shows the trail itself but not with a lot of detail. For more detail, get the USGS 7.5-minute quads for Pecos, Glorieta, Rosilla Peak, and McClure Reservoir.

Finding the trail: From Santa Fe get on Interstate 25 northbound (this section of I-25 actually heads in a southeast direction for about 10 miles before swinging north) until you reach the exit for Glorieta and Pecos. Exit here and then turn left, crossing over I-25. Turn right onto NM 50 heading east towards Pecos. You will continue on NM 50 for about 2 miles until you reach FS 375. FS 375 is a dirt road leaving from the left-hand side of the road. Park here, at the intersection of NM 50 and FS 375.

Sources of additional information: Santa Fe National Forest, Pecos Ranger District, P. O. Drawer 429, Pecos, New Mexico 87552-0429; (505) 757-6121.

Notes on the trail: Begin your ride by heading up FS 375 for 2 miles to La Cueva, a small settlement of just a few homes. Past the houses you will go through a gate. You will then climb, climb, climb. About 5 miles past La Cueva you will encounter a fork in the road; bear left. In another mile you will encounter another fork; go left again. After this last fork you will be facing the final push up the last very steep, rocky section to the top. Keep going, go all the way to the lookout. Once atop Glorieta Baldy you will find FS Trail 272 heading down the south side of the mountain and dropping into Glorieta Canyon. The first half mile of this descent on this single-track trail is extremely rough and mostly unrideable, but after that the trail smooths out for an excellent ride down. You will pass through the remains of the old mining town of Glorieta at about mile 5 on this descent. Soon you will hit a dirt road with a gate marking the private property of the Glorieta Baptist Convention Center. (There is a second gate closer to the convention center on this same road.) It is legal to pass through these gates, but be sure to close them behind you. Ride out of the Baptist Center on the paved road and go left onto NM 50, which will take you back to your vehicle at the intersection of NM 50 and FS 375.

There are several trails off the west side of Glorieta Baldy, but as far as I know they have yet to be blazed by mountain bikers. If you are going to do any exploring in this area, supplementary maps and a call to the forest ranger are a necessity.

If you are not interested in the steep, rocky descent, you can just return the way you came.

RIDE 17 *ELK MOUNTAIN*

The ride up to Elk Mountain is a fairly strenuous assault on a peak that will take you to a high elevation of 11,659 feet just below the summit of Elk Mountain. This trail is approximately 25 miles round-trip and will take experienced riders in good to excellent physical condition at least five hours to complete. This route follows rough jeep roads, double-track, and abandoned roads that all have rough, rocky spots. An alternate starting point will shorten the distance of this ride to 17 miles round-trip.

This is an alpine environment, with mixed conifers and aspens giving way to more open, grassy slopes as you near the peak. Allow yourself some time to absorb the views from up here—they're fantastic. You can see the jagged Truchas Peaks, Penitente Peak, Santa Fe Baldy, Pecos Baldy, and a host of other peaks inside the Pecos Wilderness.

RIDE 17 *ELK MOUNTAIN*

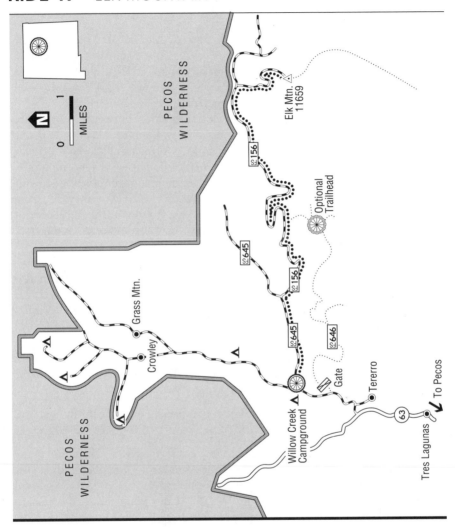

General location: Elk Mountain is located about 15 miles east of Santa Fe, as the crow flies, in the Santa Fe National Forest. It is about 35 miles to the trailhead (a 45-minute car ride).

Elevation change: At the point where this ride begins, at the Willow Creek Campground, the elevation is approximately 7,816' above sea level. You will reach a high elevation on this ride of 11,659'. Total elevation gain is 3,840'.

Season: Because of the high altitudes, this is a late spring through fall ride. Aspens are beautiful in fall.

Services: All services are available in Santa Fe. Gas, water, and convenience groceries are available in Pecos.

Hazards: This is a strenuous ride at high altitude. A good solid base of physical fitness will help make this ride more enjoyable, but even riders in excellent physical condition will suffer if they are not acclimated to these elevations. Save this ride to do after you have been riding in the area for 3 or 4 days; this will allow your body to perform up to its full potential.

You are very exposed for a good portion of this ride. Summertime and early fall monsoonal thunderstorms can come up in a few hours and lash these peaks and ridges with rain, hail, and lots of lightning. Storms usually aren't a threat until the afternoon, so if thunderstorms are predicted, make this a morning ride.

Rescue index: Although this area receives a good amount of recreational traffic in the summer months, it is still fairly remote country. You may find help at any of the summer cabins along the road on the way in, at the settlement of Tererro. Or, try the Panchuela Ranger Outpost or the summer community at Green Mountain, both at the end of Forest Service Road 223.

Land status: Santa Fe National Forest, Pecos Ranger Station.

Maps: The Santa Fe National Forest map is adequate for this ride. You can also get the USGS 7.5-minute quad for Elk Mountain.

Finding the trail: From Santa Fe go north on Interstate 25 for about 16.5 miles to the Glorieta/Pecos Exit. Exit here, go left, and cross over I-25 to NM 50. Turn right onto NM 50 and drive 6 miles to the town of Pecos. At the four-way stop in Pecos, go left onto NM 63 and drive for 12.5 miles to the town of Tererro. After you pass through town, NM 63 turns into gravel. Drive another mile on NM 63 to the Willow Creek Campground. Park here.

Sources of additional information: Santa Fe National Forest, Pecos Ranger Station, P. O. Drawer 429, Pecos, New Mexico 87552-0429; (505) 757-6121.

Notes on the trail: Begin this ride by heading across NM 63 and heading up the hill on FS 645. This road quickly deteriorates into a rough double-track. (This section of road can be a muddy bog when wet.) Two miles up FS 645 you will encounter a fork; bear right here onto FS 156. At this point the road begins to climb more steeply and becomes quite rocky. Ride FS 156 as it follows the ridge. Just over 7 miles from the start of this ride FS 156 forks right and goes downhill, then begins climbing again. Keep going; this is the last push to the top. Go back down the way you came up.

No real route options exist for this ride as you are bordered by the Pecos Wilderness to the north and by watershed land to the south. You can shorten this ride by driving to a different trailhead. From NM 63, go right onto FS 646 (approximately 1 mile before you reach FS 645 and the Willow Creek Campground). Drive for 3.5 miles on FS 646. At the first fork you come to, bear left and go downhill. Just over 5 miles from where you turned off NM 63 you will come to a three-way intersection. Park here. Take your bike down the left-hand road. It will deteriorate into a rough double-track, and then a single-track, before intersecting FS 156 just over 2 miles from where you left your car. When you reach FS 156 go right and continue on up to the top of Elk Mountain. Total distance from this starting point is 15 miles.

RIDE 18 *BARILLAS PEAK*

This is a great 20-mile out-and-back ride with a short loop for intermediate to advanced riders in good physical condition. The route up to Barillas Peak follows hard-packed dirt roads that deteriorate to rough, rocky jeep roads along certain sections. You should allow at least four hours to complete this ride, plus time spent gazing out from the lookout once you reach the peak.

You are in transition country here: after riding through the pinyon and juniper of the high desert, you will ascend into the pines and aspens of the Rocky Mountains. Open, sweeping views abound. This is a beautiful ride. Keep your eye out for raspberries along the trail; they grow thick up here. Enjoy!

General location: Barillas Peak is located east and slightly south of Santa Fe in the Santa Fe National Forest. Allow about an hour to get to the trailhead from Santa Fe.
Elevation change: At the intersection of Forest Service Road 83 and FS 203 where you begin this ride the elevation is approximately 8,000' above sea level. From here you will climb to a high elevation atop Barillas Peak of 9,371'. Total elevation gain is 1,371'.
Season: Midspring through late fall this route should be free of snow.
Services: All services are available in Santa Fe. Food, gas, and water are available in Pecos.
Hazards: You should be aware of schedules for hunting season when riding in this area, as it is very popular for deer hunting. Check with the forest service before you go if you will be in this area during the spring or fall. A bright piece of clothing will help to alert hunters and motorists to your presence.

When you are exposed on a mountain peak like this it is a good idea to keep an eye on the weather. During the summer monsoon season wild thunder and lightning storms can come up quickly. Lightning loves to strike high ridges and peaks—these are good places to avoid if you should see one of these monsters approaching.
Rescue index: While you are not miles and miles from civilization, you are in the wilderness here. This area sees light to moderate use during the summer months

RIDE 18 *BARILLAS PEAK*

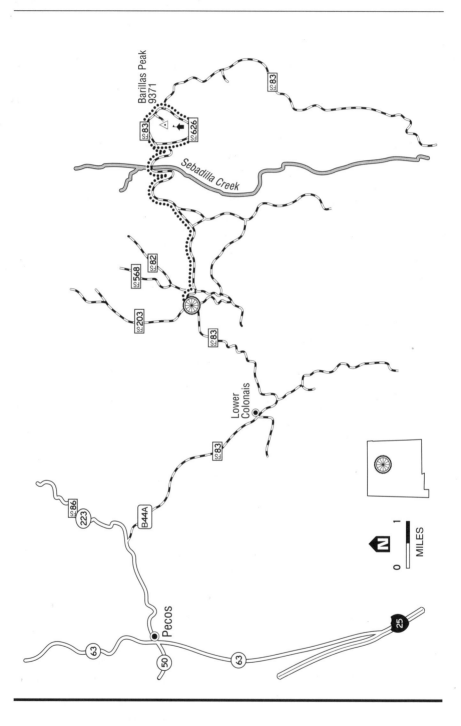

Barillas Peak
9371

FS 83

FS 626

FS 83

Sebadilla Creek

FS 82

FS 568

FS 203

FS 83

FS 83

Lower
Colonais

FS 83

FS 86

223

B44A

MILES

0   1

N

Pecos

25

63

50

63

The ride up to Barillas Peak traverses the beautiful mountainous wilds east of Santa Fe.

and somewhat heavier traffic during hunting season. Your best bet for finding help is in the town of Pecos or at the settlement of Lower Colonias, both of which you will pass on your way in.

Land status: Santa Fe National Forest, Pecos Ranger District.

Maps: The Santa Fe National Forest map is adequate for finding this ride. You can also use USGS 7.5-minute quads for Lower Colonias and San Geronimo.

Finding the trail: From Santa Fe drive north on Interstate 25 for about 16.5 miles to the Glorieta/Pecos Exit. Exit here, go left, and cross over I-25 to NM 50. Turn right onto NM 50 and drive 6 miles to the town of Pecos. At the 4-way stop in Pecos, go straight. You are now on NM 223. Continue on NM 223 for just over 3 miles before turning right onto County Road B44A, also FS 83, a gravel road. Continue on FS 83 for almost 6 miles past the small settlement of Lower Colonias. FS 83 bears left here; continue on FS 83 for almost another 4 miles to where FS 83 meets a 3-way intersection at the top of Ruidoso Ridge. Park here.

Sources of additional information: Santa Fe National Forest, Pecos Ranger District, P. O. Drawer 429, Pecos, New Mexico 87552-0429; (505) 757-6121.

Notes on the trail: From the 3-way intersection where you parked ride straight ahead, continuing on FS 83. About 1 mile in, you will pass a road heading off to your right and then another to your left; keep heading straight towards Barillas Peak. After you cross Sebadilla Creek the road begins to climb more steeply. At 6.5 miles from the start, FS 626 heads downhill to the right. Take this road to make a circuit of Barillas Peak. Go right on FS 626 and continue for another 2.5 miles to the next fork, where you will bear left heading up a steep hill. This spur road will take you to the top of the peak and once again becomes FS 83. Go left as you head back down on the spur road to get onto the main FS 83 and to return the way you came. If you do not wish to make the 3-mile circuit of Barillas Peak, simply stay left on FS 83 at the fork with FS 626 and head straight to the top.

RIDE 19 *GLORIETA MESA*

This ride is an easy ten-mile out-and-back cruise across the mostly flat, wide-open country of Glorieta Mesa. Side roads heading off in all directions make for some good adventuring should you want to lengthen this ride. This route follows hard-packed dirt roads that can become deeply rutted and marred by muddy potholes after a big rain. Riders of all abilities will enjoy getting out on these roads, maybe not for a hard-core workout, but just to enjoy rolling through some gorgeous high desert country.

Grazing cattle dot expansive grasslands rimmed with stately ponderosa pines. The mesa itself slopes gently away from a well-defined band of cliffs along its eastern edge. Sweeping views across this open mesa top are wonderful as are the views to the east from the edge of the mesa. This is a great place just to get out, explore, and work on conditioning.

General location: Glorieta Mesa is located about 10 miles southeast of Santa Fe in the Santa Fe National Forest.

Elevation change: After driving up the west side of the mesa, you will reach the trailhead at 7,300' above sea level. You will ride across open, rolling terrain atop the mesa at elevations between 7,300' and 7,500'. The highest points on the mesa run along its eastern edge and run as high as 7,900'. Elevation gain is under 1,000'.

Season: This is a good place to ride almost year-round so long as the roads are dry and free of snow. There will be several months during midwinter when these roads will probably be impassable due to mud or snow.

Services: All services are available in Santa Fe.

Hazards: Watch out for jeep traffic (which is usually light), hunters during hunting season, and thunderstorms.

Rescue index: There are several homes and ranch houses at the base of the mesa

RIDE 19 *GLORIETA MESA*

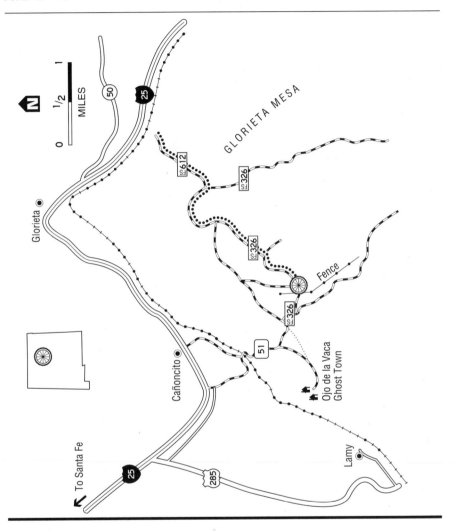

and at the settlement of Cañoncito where you might find help in the case of an emergency. Other help can be found in Pecos or in Santa Fe.

Land status: Santa Fe National Forest, Pecos Ranger District.

Maps: The Santa Fe National Forest map is adequate here. For more detail, get the USGS 7.5-minute quad for Glorieta, Ojo de la Vaca, and Pecos.

Finding the trail: From Santa Fe drive north (this section of Interstate 25 actually heads east and south) 7.5 miles to the exit for Lamy and Vaughn. Exit here

The wide open, rolling terrain of Glorieta Mesa is a great place for riders of all abilities to get out and do some cruising.

and go left underneath I-25 to the frontage road. Turn right onto the frontage road and continue for about 2 miles to the intersection of County Road 51. Go right onto County Road 51, which becomes a rough dirt road, heading back under the freeway. After crossing some railroad tracks turn right and head up onto the mesa. Continue on this road for 3.5 miles to where the road forks. Bear left onto Forest Service Road 326. Drive another mile on FS 326 to a fence line and a sign marking National Forest land. Park here.

Sources of additional information: Santa Fe National Forest, Pecos Ranger District, P. O. Drawer 429, Pecos, New Mexico 87552-0429; (505) 757-6121.

Notes on the trail: From your parking place follow FS 326 as it rolls across the top of Glorieta Mesa. The many side roads you'll encounter take off in all directions; they are fun to follow but riders can get confused without USGS maps here. Just over 4 miles from where you started, make a left turn onto FS 612. You will encounter a short, steep, rocky section that levels off quickly. Not quite a mile from here are the edge of the mesa and some fantastic views. Turn around and go back the way you came.

Taos Area Rides

The town of Taos is situated 7,100 feet high on a plateau against the western flank of the Sangre de Cristo Mountains of northern New Mexico. A small town of only about five thousand residents, Taos boasts a fascinating history, a spectacular natural setting, and a unique blend of cultures. The tall peaks of the Sangre de Cristo Mountains behind the town are cloaked green in summer, golden in fall, and white in winter, and have many deep, winding canyons coursed by rivulets of sparkling water. Out in the valley a rumbling ribbon of green water at the bottom of the Rio Grande River Gorge tirelessly sculpts and polishes the black lava rock of its canyon. Summers are warm in Taos—mid- to low 90s are common—but the nights are always cool at this elevation. Winters are snowy but never bitterly cold. Taos Ski Valley holds legendary status among ski aficionados for its powder snow that can accumulate over 500 inches deep in one season. Skiers, rafters, fishermen, bikers, those seeking the beauty of wide open spaces as well as an interesting cultural experience—will all find what they are looking for in this little mountain town. Any trip to New Mexico, especially a biking trip, would be seriously lacking without a visit to Taos.

The Taos Indians tell a legend of how an eagle led their ancestors to settle in this valley over 800 years ago. Today, the Taos Indians still inhabit the land they settled and still occupy the original stone pueblo built here by their ancestors. The Taos Pueblo is thus considered to be one of the oldest continually inhabited communities in the country. The Taos Indians have always been known for their fierce independence and self-determination. Several Taos Indians were leaders in the planning and execution of the Pueblo Revolt of 1680 that drove the Spanish completely out of the New Mexico territory for 12 years. The Taos Indians, as well as the rest of the Pueblo Indian people, were eventually vanquished and paid dearly for their insurrection. In the century that followed, however, the Pueblo people and Spanish settlers worked together to protect themselves from raiding Comanche, Apache, and Ute Indian tribes.

The first European to enter the Taos Valley was Hernando de Alverado, who came to the Southwest as part of Coronado's expedition in the year 1540. Settlement of the Taos Valley by the Spanish was first attempted by Fray Pedro de Miranda, who built a mission church at the Taos Indian Pueblo in 1617. For more than 15 years the mission served Indians and settlers both, but tensions began to grow as the numbers of settlers increased and the priests became more determined in their efforts to convert the land's native inhabitants. In 1631 Miranda, and several others, were killed by the Indians, who now demanded that all settlers and churchmen move to what is today the site of the town of Taos. The Taos Pueblo Indians are known for their huge trade fairs, that in the past drew Indian tribes from all over the West and the Great Plains. Taos became an important gathering place for the exchange of Native American goods as well as skills, crafts, and ideas. By the early 1800s these fairs had begun to draw American trappers and mountain men. Everything from corn and beans to horses, cattle, and guns was traded between the white man and the Indian in mutual respect. It was at this time that a young Kit Carson entered the Taos Valley. He married twice here, in between expeditions that took him all over the West, exploring and fighting hostile Indians for the U.S. government. Carson, who figures prominently in the history of Taos, eventually retired and died here. His house in Taos is now the site of the Kit Carson Museum.

As early as 1845 writers and artists had discovered the valley; in 1880, painters Joseph Henry Sharp, Irving Course, Bert Phillips, and Ernest Blumenschein founded the Taos Society of Artists. When this group began to send work to art centers on the East Coast, critics quickly took notice. A quarter of a century later, Taos was drawing the likes of Georgia O'Keeffe, Ansel Adams, and D. H. Lawrence. Today Taos supports a thriving community of accomplished artists and writers.

The dramatic landscape of the Taos Valley was created by both the rifting Rio Grande Valley and the uplifting of the Rocky Mountains. Taos is situated at the most rapidly subsiding point in the Rio Grande Rift Valley. In a rift valley, a narrow block of the earth's crust has dropped between two parallel fault zones; the depression formed is then discovered and followed by running water. The Sangre de Cristo Mountains on the east side of the valley and the Tusas and Brazos mountains to the west, are all made up of granite and metamorphic rock. All part of the Rocky Mountains, these ranges were split into two prongs by the rifting valley. Volcanic activity is often associated with rifting faults because they are so deep, reaching all the way down to the earth's mantle. The lava flows that cover the Taos Plateau oozed out over the landscape from countless cinder cones and fissures and several shield volcanos in the north. These basalt flows are exposed in layers in the 700-foot-deep river gorge in beautiful formations called columnar joints, a term that refers to the pattern created in the rock during cooling. Black boulders of basalt that have fallen into the river have been polished by the tumbling waters of the Rio Grande and throw an eerie light about in the canyon.

Silvery sagebrush covers the broad sloping flats of the Taos Plateau, accented by pinyon and juniper growing in drainages and near natural windbreaks. Down in the Rio Grande River Gorge you'll find ponderosas growing straight and tall in the shelter of the canyon's walls. Out here you can sometimes spot pronghorn antelope or a coyote dashing through the sage, perhaps chasing a cottontail or a black-tailed jackrabbit. Pinyon and juniper dominate the foothills, giving way to ponderosas and then to mixed pine, spruce, fir, and aspens at the higher elevations of the Sangre de Cristo Mountains. The canyons of the Sangre de Cristos harbor willows, various deciduous trees, and several types of cottonwoods, some of which grow to reach a very old age and enormous proportions. The colors in these canyons and peaks in the fall are spectacular, embellishing an already fantastic landscape. In the lower reaches close to town you will most likely see mule deer and white-tailed deer, wild turkeys, porcupine, and coyote. You might get lucky and catch a glimpse of a bobcat or a gray fox, but both are pretty shy. In the higher and more remote areas of the wilderness surrounding Taos you'll be sharing the forest with elk, black bear, and mountain lion.

Because of its high elevation and more northern latitude, Taos has a shorter riding season than most of the Southwest. Here, spring, summer, and fall storms can drop temperatures drastically in a short time so it is a good idea to ride with an extra lightweight layer for warmth and a weatherproof shell if storms are in the forecast. This area also gets pummeled by violent summer thunderstorms that come from the south, packing a lot of electrical fireworks. Most of the national forest lands surrounding Taos are hunted in the fall and spring, so be sure and check with local Forest Service people for hunt locations and times as well as road conditions and weather forecasts before you head out. Also, remember that even though you are at higher elevations where it is nice and cool you are still in the desert where the threat of dehydration is always present. Carry lots of fluids, don't drink from open water sources, and don't let thirst regulate your intake. Here are the addresses and phone numbers you'll need to start planning a trip to Taos:

Taos Chamber of Commerce
Paseo del Pueblo Sur 1139
P.O. Drawer I
Taos, New Mexico 87571
(800) 758-3873
(505) 758-3873

Carson National Forest
Camino Real Ranger District
P.O. Box 68
Penasco, New Mexico 87553
(505) 587-2255

Carson National Forest
Questa Ranger District
P.O. Box 110
Questa, New Mexico 87556
(505) 586-0520

Carson National Forest
Supervisor's Office
P.O. Box 558
208 Cruz Alta Road
Taos, New Mexico 87571
(505) 758-6200

Native Son Adventures
P.O. Box 6144
Paseo Del Pueblo Sur 813A
Taos, New Mexico 87571
(505) 758-9342

Gearing Up Bike Shop
P.O. Box 6335
Taos, New Mexico 87571
(505) 751-0365

RIDE 20 *CEBOLLA MESA*

This ride is an easy seven-mile out-and-back ramble across Cebolla Mesa, terminating at the edge of the Rio Grande River Gorge. Beginning and intermediate riders in good physical condition, as well as more experienced riders, will enjoy this ride. This route follows hard-packed dirt roads that can be very rutted in spots. If the ground is saturated, the dirt roads out here can become a muddy bog. Allow one to two hours to complete this ride, with time spent peering over the gorge and hiking down to the river.

The silvery sagebrush–covered expanse of the Taos Valley floor stretches away in all directions out here. From Cebolla Mesa, you'll see sweeping views across the Taos Plateau, up to the Sangre de Cristo Mountains, and across to the Brazos and Tusas mountains in the west. Views down into the river gorge are breathtaking. There is a fairly steep, mile-long trail from the Cebolla Campground that will take you down to the river for a swim or a picnic.

General location: Cebolla Mesa is located 15 miles north of Taos within the Carson National Forest.
Elevation change: At the intersection of Forest Service Road 9 and NM 522 the elevation is 7,820' above sea level. From there you will descend very gradually to the edge of the Rio Grande River Gorge, at 7,200'. Total elevation gain, on your ride back, is 620'.
Season: This is a good ride to do any time of year provided the ground is dry and not covered with snow.
Services: All services are available in Taos.
Hazards: If it is rainy or wet out here, the road turns into a greasy mud bog—you'll have about as much traction as if you were trying to ride in butter. This stuff is sticky too, and will take hours to get off your bike. Avoid riding out here if the ground is saturated.
Rescue index: The campgrounds out by the river and the roads that take you

RIDE 20 *CEBOLLA MESA*

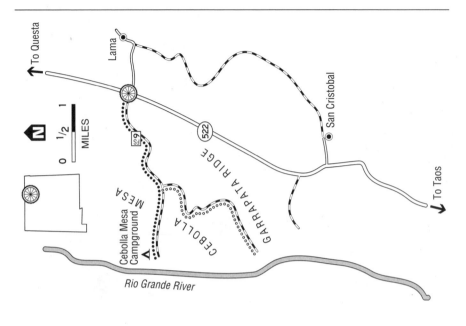

out here receive a fair amount of use during the summer months. Help may be sought at the small towns of San Cristobal or Arroyo Hondo, which you will pass on your way out here. Other help can be found in Taos.

Land status: Carson National Forest, Questa Ranger District.

Maps: The Carson National Forest map shows this route, but without a lot of detail. Use the USGS 7.5-minute quad for Arroyo Hondo.

Finding the trail: From the town of Taos drive about 15 miles north on NM 522. Look for a sign for Cebolla Mesa Campground and a pullout on the left (west) side of the road directly across from the road to the settlement of Lama. Here on the left-hand side of NM 522 you will find the beginning of FS 9. Park your car at this pullout or drive over the cattle guard and park off the road.

Sources of additional information: Carson National Forest, Questa Ranger District; address and phone are listed in the introduction to this section.

Notes on the trail: Follow FS 9 as it rolls down and out across Cebolla Mesa. You will encounter one major fork in the road where you will want to stay right. Follow the signs for Cebolla Mesa Campground.

There are several lesser used roads heading off in various directions out here

A view of the Sangre de Cristo Mountains behind Taos from Cebolla Mesa.

that you might want to try. Because this is such open country, with views to everywhere, it is hard to get really lost.

At about 1.5 miles there will be a fork in the road and a sign marking the road to Cebolla Mesa Campground; the other road leads out to Garrapata Ridge and the edge of the gorge about two miles south of Cebolla Campground. Try this route option if you want to lengthen your ride.

RIDE 21 *DUNN BRIDGE*

This ride follows a route that begins at the settlement of Arroyo Hondo, crosses the Dunn Bridge, and emerges on top of the rolling mesa west of the Rio Grande. The 16-mile out-and-back route that I have specified here is easy to moderate, and there are many trail options to explore this side of the river if you want to lengthen or shorten the trip. Beginning and intermediate riders in good physical condition will find it a challenge to climb up the west side of the river, but will enjoy cruising along the hilly roads once they reach the mesa top. You'll find both

RIDE 21 *DUNN BRIDGE*

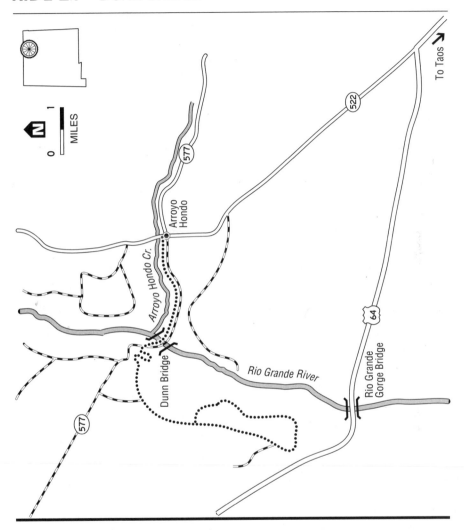

maintained gravel and hard-packed dirt roads, some of which have deteriorated into double-track, having been abandoned or rarely used.

You will wind around through the village of Arroyo Hondo before following the Arroyo Hondo River down to where it meets the Rio Grande. Having crossed the Rio Grande by way of the Dunn Bridge, you will climb up on the other side of the gorge where you will have spectacular views of the Sangre de Cristo Mountains and of the entire Taos Valley. Clump grasses, sagebrush, and

A view of the Rio Grande River and river gorge from the Dunn Bridge.

chamiso dominate this landscape. You may want to take a dip in the river when you reach Dunn Bridge in preparation for your push back up to Arroyo Hondo and your car.

General location: Arroyo Hondo, where this ride begins, is 9 miles northwest of Taos.

Elevation change: At Arroyo Hondo the elevation is 7,010' above sea level. From there you will drop down to the level of the river at 6,400', and then climb back up onto the western side of the plateau to 7,120 feet. Total elevation gain is 1,330'.

Season: This route is rideable any time of year provided the ground is not covered with snow or super-saturated by rain.

Services: All services are available in Taos.

Hazards: The roads are not marked out here, but open views prevent you from getting really lost. There can be a fair amount of car traffic on NM 577, which crosses the bridge and takes you up onto the western side of the river; be alert and wear something bright.

Rescue index: NM 577, the main road that takes you out of Arroyo Hondo, across the bridge, and up onto the western side of the river is moderately well used throughout the year. Flag a ride here or seek help at the settlement of Arroyo Hondo or on US 64 on the western side of the river.

Land status: This ride covers ground allotted to the Arroyo Hondo Land Grant and the Bureau of Land Management (BLM).

Maps: Although this route is not in the National Forest, it shows up on the Carson National Forest map. Also use USGS 7.5-minute quads for Arroyo Hondo and Los Cordovas.

Finding the trail: From Taos drive north 9 miles on NM 522 to the village of Arroyo Hondo. Park at the intersection of NM 522 and NM 577 at the center of the village.

Sources of additional information: Although this ride is not within the national forest, the Carson National Forest ranger will have information and suggestions concerning this ride; address and phone are listed in the introduction to this section.

Notes on the trail: Ride west on NM 577, following Arroyo Hondo Creek down to the Rio Grande River and the Dunn Bridge. Cross over the bridge and then climb the switchbacks up the west side of the gorge. When you get to the top you will see NM 577 stretching away in a straight line for miles and miles—don't go that way. Instead, look for a rough, unused dirt road that heads west. This road will soon bend around and head south, following the direction of the river. Two miles from where you crested the west side of the gorge there will be a fork in the road. Here you can stay right or go left. The left-hand road parallels the other road just to the east and, after making a 45-degree turn to the right, rejoins it in about 2 miles. Make a loop and head back on this road.

You can explore the many roads that head off in all directions on the west side of the gorge without getting too lost. Adjusting the length and time of your ride out here is easy. If you are interested in knowing all your choices here I suggest supplementary topographical maps.

RIDE 22 *GALLINA CREEK TRAIL*

The Gallina Creek Trail is a moderate to mildly strenuous ten-mile out-and-back trip up a beautiful canyon. The first part of the route follows an old mining road, which gets washed out in places and is loose and gravelly in others. This road deteriorates into a double-track that is hard-packed dirt with a grassy median where it drops in closer to the creek bottom. Riders in good physical condition with intermediate riding skills will take at least two hours to complete this 20-mile round-trip.

Pinyon and juniper cover these foothills of the Sangre de Cristo Mountains. You will be able to see Gallina Peak to the north and east and catch a glimpse up into the Wheeler Peak Wilderness from the ridge before dropping into Gallina

RIDE 22 *GALLINA CREEK TRAIL*

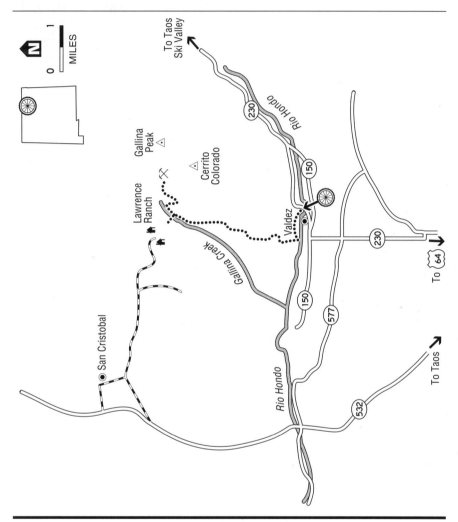

Creek Canyon. Gallina Creek Canyon is beautifully edged with cottonwoods and other deciduous trees that provide precious shade on your ride up. The remnants of an old mine can be found in the drainage just below Gallina Peak up the east fork of this road. The west fork ends at the boundary of the Lawrence Ranch, owned by the family of D. H. Lawrence.

General location: Gallina Creek Trail begins 6 miles north of Taos, at the settlement of Valdez.

Small graveyards like this one at the beginning of the Gallina Creek Trail are common in New Mexico.

Elevation change: At Valdez the elevation is 7,250'. From there you will climb to an elevation of approximately 8,600'. Total elevation gain is 1,350'.

Season: Early spring through late fall this route should be dry and free of snow.

Services: All services are available in Taos.

Hazards: The soft, gravelly trail surface here can make this climb technical. The road can be very rutted and loose, so use caution on the way down.

There were several new roads cut into the hillside heading off in different directions that I found confusing. It is a good idea to carry topos and a compass on this ride.

Rescue index: This is a pretty popular mountain bike ride so you may see a few riders. Otherwise this road receives moderate to light use. Help may be sought at the settlement of Valdez where you began this ride or back in Taos.

Land status: This route travels lands in the Arroyo Hondo Land Grant and in the Carson National Forest.

Maps: The Carson National Forest map shows this route but without much detail. Use the USGS 7.5-minute quad for Arroyo Seco.

Finding the trail: From Taos, drive north out of town on US 64 and in four miles go right at the forked intersection onto NM 230, which heads due north. Continue on NM 230, crossing over NM 150 (the road that heads up Arroyo Hondo Canyon to the Taos Ski Valley) down into a small valley and the settlement of Valdez. You will pass by a cluster of houses that constitute the town of Valdez before coming to a right-hand elbow turn. Just above the turn in the road you will see a trail heading up a bank and around a chainlink fence. This is the start of this ride. Parking is a problem here. Park along the road before or after the elbow turn, being sure to keep clear of driveways and mailboxes.

Sources of additional information: Carson National Forest, Questa Ranger District; address and phone are listed in the introduction to this section.

Notes on the trail: From the fence, the trail heads due west for just about a half a mile before making a right-hand turn and heading north. You will pass an old cemetery and an abandoned tennis court. This is an old road and, although it is easily recognizable, several new roads have been cut in here and may confuse you, so use your compass and supplementary maps to double-check your heading. Continue heading north, climbing up the side of a ridge and eventually dropping into wooded Gallina Creek drainage.

At about mile 4 the road forks; you can go right, continuing up the Gallina Creek drainage to the old mine ruins, about another mile, or go right, across the creek bed and the next drainage to the boundary of the Lawrence Ranch. Or just go straight, for an out-and-back.

RIDE 23 *DEVISADARO LOOP*

The Devisadaro Loop is a short but extreme little ride that requires a serious pair of legs, big lungs, and a good amount of technical skill. Advanced and intermediate riders in excellent physical condition will enjoy the challenge of this steep, five-mile single-track loop with short, rocky sections that are sometimes loose. Allow two hours to complete this ride, with some time spent taking in the view from Devisadaro Peak.

Pinyon and juniper cover this mountain as they do all the foothills of the Sangres. Excellent views of the entire Taos Valley are to be had from here.

General location: The Devisadaro Loop is located 4 miles southeast of Taos, within the Carson National Forest.
Elevation change: Where this ride starts at the El Nogal Picnic Area the elevation is 7,200' above sea level. From here you will climb to the top of Devisadaro Peak to an elevation of 8,300'. Total elevation gain is 1,100'.
Season: This loop should be rideable early spring through late fall provided the trail is free of snow and not super-saturated.

RIDE 23 *DEVISADARO LOOP*

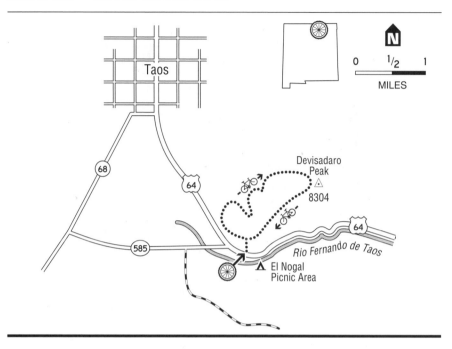

Services: All services are available in Taos.

Hazards: This trail is steep and very loose in spots; this is a good time to wear a helmet. Be on the lookout for hikers and other bikers, and give yourself enough time to slow down should you happen to see someone on the trail.

Rescue index: You are close to Taos; seek help there in an emergency.

Land status: The trail is in Carson National Forest, Camino Real Ranger District.

Maps: The Carson National Forest map shows this route, but without much detail. Use the USGS 7.5-minute quad for Taos.

Finding the trail: From Taos drive southeast out of town on US 64 to your first pullout on the right just as you enter the canyon at El Nogal Picnic Area. Park here.

Sources of additional information: Carson National Forest, Camino Real Ranger District, or Supervisor's Office in Taos; phone and address are listed in the introduction to this section.

Notes on the trail: The ride begins directly across US 64 from the picnic ground. Begin climbing, bearing left when you get to the point where the loop rejoins

A view to the south toward Maestas Ridge from Devisadaro Peak.

the trail. You will be riding this loop in a clockwise direction: if you look back over your shoulder here you will see where the trail comes down over a steep hill behind you. You can't get lost, so fasten your seat belt and hang on!

RIDE 24 *OJITOS TRAIL*

The Ojitos Trail, referred to by locals as the "Whoop-dee-doos" trail, features a fun series of berms across an old jeep road and takes you to the end of Ojitos Canyon. This straight out-and-back route will give a round-trip distance of about seven miles. Several great options for exploring off this route, however, will lengthen this ride. It will take riders with intermediate riding skills in good physical condition about two hours to complete this trail—more, if you want to stay and play on the berms. The short, steep humps that continue for about a quarter-mile section of this ride will test your technical skill and your nerve. Trials riders and BMX riders will love this part. This route also includes abandoned jeep roads and single-track.

RIDE 24   OJITOS TRAIL

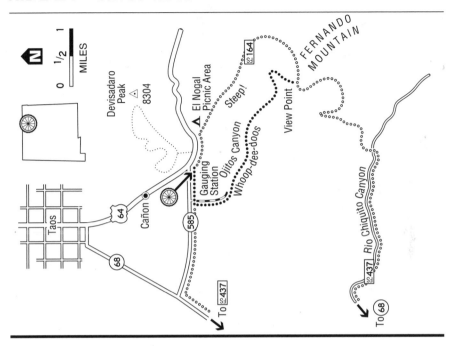

You are in the pinyon- and juniper-covered foothills of the Sangre de Cristo Mountains here. If you ride this area in the fall, stop along the trail every now and then to gather a handful of pinyon nuts—they're tasty and good energy food!

General location: The Ojitos Trail is located 3 miles from the center of Taos at the mouth of Fernando de Taos Canyon, in the Carson National Forest.

Elevation change: At the point where the road leaves US 64, just before the Gaging Station, the elevation is approximately 7,200' above sea level. Where you enter Ojitos Canyon the elevation is 7,400'. When you reach the main intersection on this trail, signaling the end of the Ojitos Canyon Trail, the elevation is 8,800'. Total elevation gained on the Ojitos Trail is 1,600'.

Season: This ride will be clear of snow and dry by early spring. It should stay rideable until late into the fall.

Services: All services are available in Taos.

Hazards: You can catch big air off of some of these rollers, so check your speed and adjust to your skill level. Don't forget to wear your brain bucket!

Rescue index: You are not far from Taos on this ride, but the route does not receive a lot of traffic. In case of an emergency, head back to town.

A rider playing on the "whoop-dee-doos" on the Ojitos Trail.

Land status: Carson National Forest, Camino Real Ranger District.

Maps: The Carson National Forest map does not show this ride. You'll need USGS 7.5-minute quads for Taos and Rancho de Taos.

Finding the trail: From Taos take US 64 south to the settlement of Cañon. Continue on US 64 until you pass NM 585, a graded dirt road taking off on the right. Just after this intersection there will be a gaging station and a big turnout area. Park here.

Sources of additional information: Carson National Forest, Camino Real Ranger District; address and phone are listed in the introduction to this section.

Notes on the trail: From the pullout head back to the graded dirt road you passed driving in, NM 585. Follow NM 585 for three-tenths of a mile, heading due west, to a dirt road taking off on your left. This is the start of the Ojitos Trail. Follow this road as it bends around and heads east, up Ojitos Canyon. Two and a half miles into this ride the road will deteriorate into a double-track and begin to climb out of the canyon. In another three-quarters of a mile you will come to an intersection. At this point you can either turn around and head back down for some serious fun on the "whoop dee doos," or continue on to explore some single-track.

You can take a left at the intersection of trails marking the end of the Ojitos Trail, riding up to the ridge of Fernando Mountain, eventually reaching FS Trail 164. You can go left again here and head down this extremely rough and hair-raising single-track to where it comes out on US 64 at the El Nogal Picnic Area, just a short distance up the road from where you left your car. You might also choose to go right at the end of the Ojitos Trail, and explore this single-track that climbs for a short distance before descending into Rio Chiquito Canyon. You can ride down Rio Chiquito Canyon on FS 437 to Rancho de Taos and NM 68. Go right on NM 68, then right on NM 585, which will take you back to your car.

RIDE 25 *GARCIA PARK LOOP*

The loop described here is 14 miles long. There are several routes up to Garcia Park, so you can adjust the length of the ride to suit yourself. Riders in good physical condition with intermediate riding skills will take three to four hours to complete the 14-mile loop. The hard-packed dirt road surfaces become quite rough, with deep ruts, and sections of this road get pretty washed out from time to time as well.

The Rio Chiquito is a beautiful drainage with many large cottonwoods and excellent camping sites along the way. Garcia Park is a high, sunny meadow laced with wildflowers in summer and rimmed with golden aspens in fall. The alpine forests up here are deep and luxuriant—unmistakably the Rocky Mountains. Views into the Wheeler Peak Wilderness Area are fantastic.

General location: The loop up to Garcia Park is southeast of Taos in the Carson National Forest.
Elevation change: Elevation at the point where the Rio Chiquito Road (Forest Service Road 437) leaves NM 518 is approximately 7,100' above sea level. At the fork in FS 437 heading up to Garcia Park, elevation is 8,900'. Elevation at Garcia Park is 10,000'. Elevation at Borrego Crossing is 9,600', and at Puertocito it is 9,956'. At Valle Escondido it is 8,200'. Total possible elevation gain is 2,900'.
Season: Late spring through fall this route should be clear of snow and relatively dry.
Services: All services are available in Taos.
Hazards: The roads in this part of the Sangre de Cristo Mountains receive a good deal of car and jeep traffic in the summer. A bright T-shirt or helmet cover

RIDE 25 *GARCIA PARK LOOP*

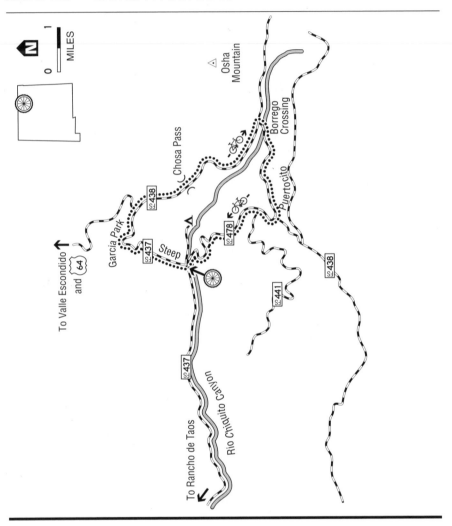

will help to alert motorists and hunters to your presence. This part of the Sangre de Cristo Mountains is hunted in the fall and spring; be sure to check with the district ranger for hunting season areas, schedules, and recommendations.

At this elevation the days cool off quickly and storms can drop temperatures in a hurry. Carry a weatherproof shell and a thin layer for warmth any time of year. **Rescue index:** The roads in this area receive a good deal of tourist traffic from hunters and campers during the dry season. Still, you are in the wilderness here. The closest phones are in the small town of Valle Escondido or Taos.

The sunny, open meadow of Garcia Park.

Land status: Carson National Forest, Camino Real Ranger District.

Maps: The Carson National Forest map shows this entire route in adequate detail. For more detail, use USGS 7.5-minute quads for Rancho de Taos, Osha Mountain, and Shadybrook.

Finding the trail: Drive south out of Taos on NM 68 to Rancho de Taos. Here, take NM 518 south for about 2 miles until you reach a sign for FS 437 (Rio Chiquito Road). Go left on FS 437 and follow it for about 11 miles to its intersection with FS 478. Park here.

Sources of additional information: Carson National Forest, Camino Real Ranger District; address and phone are listed in the introduction to this section.

Notes on the trail: From the intersection of FS 437 and FS 478 begin riding uphill on FS 437, bearing left in half a mile. At this point FS 437 begins climbing more steeply. Three miles from where you left your car you will enter the open grassy meadow that is Garcia Park. Here, you will encounter a fork in the road; bear right onto FS 438. FS 438 will take you downhill until you hit Borrego Crossing. Cross over the stream and continue on FS 438, now heading uphill, to an area known as the "Puertocito" (an open area at the intersection of several trails); turn right. In just under a mile, where FS 441 forks off to the left, stay right on what is now FS 478. FS 478 now heads down some steep, rocky switchbacks before leveling off and returning to the intersection with FS 437 where you left your car.

Optional routes for this ride include riding up and back down the Rio Chiquito Road (FS 437), riding up and down from Valle Escondido via FS 437, or getting dropped off at Valle Escondido and riding up on FS 437 and back into town on NM 518. Another option is to ride up Rio Chiquito, down to Valle Escondido, and then down the pavement of US 64 to Taos—close to 40 miles. Be especially careful on US 64 heading downhill.

If you are in excellent physical condition and looking for an all-day outing, you can do this loop right from town, following the roads you would drive in on. From Taos it is 28 miles round-trip.

You can also ride up to Garcia Park from Valle Escondido. To get to Valle Escondido, drive east out of Taos on US 64 up Fernando de Taos Canyon about 13 miles. FS 437 takes off out of the town of Valle Escondido heading uphill and will take you all the way to Garcia Park.

Rio Chiquito Canyon is a moderate climb where the road up from Valle Escondido is steeper and shorter. These routes show up on all the maps and are well marked. Have fun!

RIDE 26   *MAESTAS RIDGE*

Riders in excellent physical condition with intermediate to advanced skills will love this 26-mile loop. Extended climbs and a total elevation gain of 3,000 feet will make this ride strenuous for most. Route surfaces include hard-packed dirt roads that become rough four-wheel-drive jeep roads in certain sections. Some portions of this ride are fairly steep and rocky. This is an all-day affair: allow six hours to complete the loop.

The ride up to Maestas Ridge offers many excellent views into the Wheeler Peak Wilderness Area and of Wheeler Peak itself. You will ride up in alpine forests of mixed conifers and aspen and then emerge onto the ridge before dropping down into the really pretty Rio Grande del Rancho drainage. This ride makes for a wonderful day of riding. Enjoy!

General location: The beginning of the Maestas Ridge ride is located about 10 miles south of Taos in the Carson National Forest.

Elevation change: At the point where this ride begins, at the start of Forest Service Road 440, the elevation is approximately 7,500' above sea level. From there you will reach a high elevation along the ridge of just over 10,250'. Total elevation gain is 2,750'.

Season: Because of its high altitude, this ride is a late spring, early summer,

RIDE 26 *MAESTAS RIDGE*

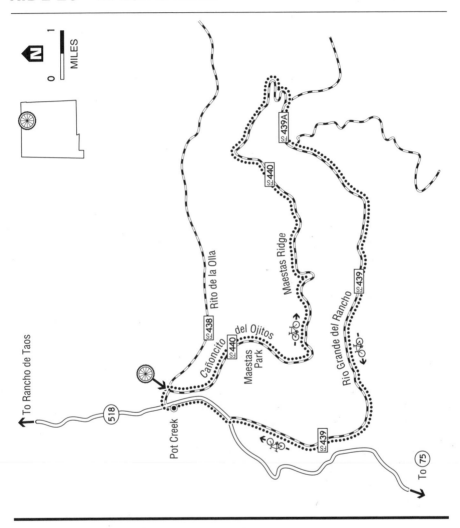

or midfall excursion. In early summer, you may still find much of this route saturated and muddy due to snow melt.

Services: All services are available in Taos.

Hazards: This is a long day, so be sure you come prepared. Bring extra water, plenty of high-energy snacks, sunscreen, a warm layer, and your tool kit.

During the midsummer months, you will most likely encounter some jeep traffic on these roads—but not much. The bulk of traffic through here is in the fall during hunting season. Be aware of hunting season schedules and areas anytime you are riding in the national forest in the spring and fall.

Rescue index: You may see a few other folks on this ride, but you are still fairly deep in the wilderness here. You may find help and a phone at the settlement of Pot Creek, that you will pass just before reaching the trailhead. The best thing you can do to prevent serious injury when mountain biking is to wear your helmet. Also, come prepared; dehydration, exposure, and lack of food can combine to create a number of very dangerous situations very quickly.

Land status: Carson National Forest, Camino Real Ranger District.

Maps: The Carson National Forest map shows this route well. You can also use USGS 7.5-minute quads for Ranchos de Taos, Tres Ritos, Shadybrook, and Cerro Vista.

Finding the trail: From Taos, drive south on NM 518 past Ranchos de Taos. In about 7 miles from Rancho de Taos turn left onto FS 438. A hundred yards from the turn you will find FS 440 taking off to your right. Park here.

Sources of additional information: Carson National Forest, Camino Real Ranger District; address and phone are listed in the introduction to this section.

Notes on the trail: FS 440 begins to climb immediately. Following Cañoncito del Ojito you will reach Maestas Park and Maestas Spring approximately 2.5 miles from the start. At this point the trail begins to climb up to the ridge. Several roads take off on both sides, but FS 440 is the most heavily used and will remain obvious. Between miles 4.5 and 5.5 you will be at the highest point along Maestas Ridge. From here, you will gradually descend for the next 5 miles until you encounter an intersection (about 10.5 miles from the start). Go right here onto FS 439A and climb steeply for a short distance. Continue down the other side of the ridge on FS 439A over some steep, rocky switchbacks. Go right when you reach the Rio Grande del Rancho drainage. Descend all the way down this canyon until you reach NM 518. Turn right here, and ride 1.5 miles back to where you left your car at the intersection of FS 438 and FS 440.

The many, many roads taking off from the Maestas Ridge Road offer ample opportunity for exploring and creating your own rides. If you are interested in doing any adventuring in this area, use the supplemental topographical maps.

RIDE 27 *PICURIS PEAK*

The ride up to Picuris Peak is a 16-mile up-and-back affair that riders of intermediate to advanced ability in good to excellent physical condition will find difficult to strenuous. This route follows a road that is sometimes hard-packed dirt and sometimes loose and rocky. Expect to encounter sections that are washed

RIDE 27   *PICURIS PEAK*

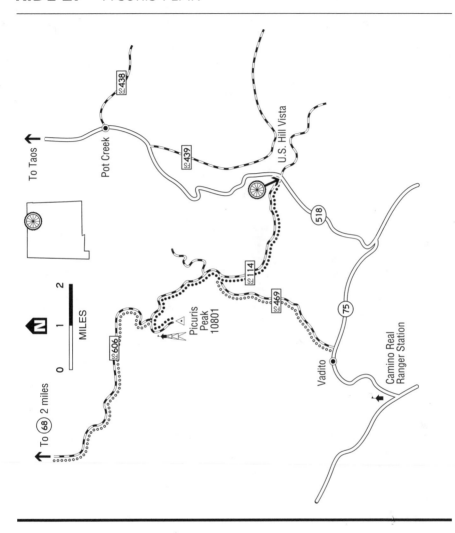

out and rutted. The last mile and a half up to the peak is a grueling push at an altitude of 10,000 feet! Allow four hours to complete this ride.

Because Picuris Peak is somewhat isolated you will enjoy fantastic, 360-degree views from the top. The Taos Valley stretches away to the north, the Jicarita Peaks and the Truchas Peaks rise like a fortress to the south. About two miles from the start of this ride you will cross the historic Camino Real, or "Royal Highway," that served as the original highway to Taos for traders, settlers, and Indians traveling north and south for several hundred years.

The Sangre de Cristo Mountains of New Mexico are famous for their aspen trees that turn a flaming yellow in autumn.

General location: The ride up to Picuris Peak begins about 12 miles south of Rancho de Taos and 15 miles south of Taos. Picuris Peak is on the border of the Carson National Forest and the Cristoval de la Serna Land Grant.

Elevation change: Where this ride begins, at the intersection of NM 518 and Forest Service Road 114, the elevation is about 8,450' above sea level. From here you will climb 2,200' over the next 8 miles to the meadow just below the peak at an elevation of 10,801'. Total elevation gain is 2,350'.

Season: Late spring through fall the road up to Picuris Peak will be dry and free of snow. It can be pretty beastly pushing up this mountain in the middle of summer: plan on riding in the early or late hours of the day to avoid the heat.

Services: All services are available in Taos.

Hazards: Don't get caught up here during one of those hellacious summer thunder and lightning storms: you are very exposed and there is no shelter to be found. If you see threatening-looking thunderclouds approaching you would be wise to beat a hasty retreat off this mountain.

Rescue index: This road receives light use from sightseers, hikers, hunters, and bikers during the dry season. Your best bet for finding help in an emergency is at the Camino Real ranger station in Camino Real, about 7 miles farther south on NM 518 from where this ride begins.

Land status: Carson National Forest, Camino Real Ranger District and Cristoval de la Serna Land Grant.

Maps: The Carson National Forest map adequately depicts this route. You can also use USGS 7.5-minute quads for Tres Ritos, Peñasco, and Taos Southwest.

Finding the trail: From Taos drive south on NM 68 to Ranchos de Taos. Go left onto NM 518 heading south about 13 miles to the intersection with FS 114. Park here.

Sources of additional information: Carson National Forest, Camino Real Ranger District; address and phone are listed in the introduction to this section.

Notes on the trail: This ride is very straightforward. Ride FS 114 all the way to the top of Picuris Peak, being careful *not* to bear right when you reach the fork with FS 469 on your way down. There are a couple of side roads off of this main route, but the road up to the peak will remain obvious.

The most interesting option here is to ride down the western side of Picuris Peak on FS 606. This road leaves almost a mile from the meadow just below the peak and heads back down FS 114 on the left-hand side of the road. After a series of switchbacks FS 606 heads west, then northwest, and ends up about 13 miles south of Taos on NM 68, just north of the settlement of Rio Vista. You could pick up the car you dropped there earlier, or have a shuttle waiting for you.

You can also approach Picuris Peak via FS 469 from the settlement of Vadito. As before, after driving out of Taos on NM 68, turn south on NM 518, pass FS 114, and continue to where NM 518 intersects NM 75. Go right on NM 75 and head west for approximately 3 miles to Vadito. FS 469 heads north from NM 75 in the town of Vadito.

RIDE 28 *BERNARDIN LAKE*

This is an especially interesting ride because you start at the point where a landslide has blocked the road. The ride up to Bernardin Lake from the slide is only seven miles round-trip, but there are many side roads and trails to explore here. Trail surfaces include an abandoned dirt road and about a mile of single-track. Beginning and intermediate riders in fair to good physical condition are well suited to this ride. It should take only two hours to complete, with time spent at the lake cooling your toes.

Clearing the road of this landslide that came down a couple of years ago is not high priority for the Forest Service, whose scant funds are needed elsewhere. The formerly well-used Forest Service Road 438 up Rio de La Olla Canyon is

RIDE 28   *BERNARDIN LAKE*

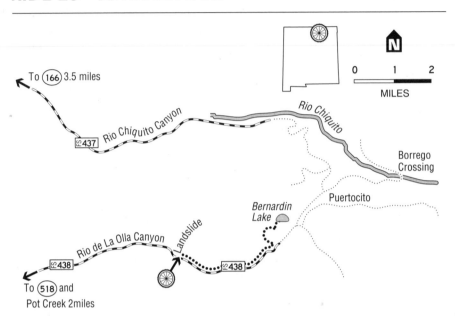

To (166) 3.5 miles

Rio Chiquito

Rio Chiquito Canyon

FS 437

Borrego
Crossing

MILES
0   1   2

Bernardin
Lake

Puertocito

Rio de La Olla Canyon

Landslide

FS 438

FS 438

To (518) and
Pot Creek 2 miles

now closed to vehicles a little more than halfway up. Rio de La Olla Canyon is gorgeous and there are many good swimming holes in the creek that you can try on your way down.

General location: The beginning of FS 438 and Rio de La Olla Canyon are approximately 7 miles south of Rancho de Taos.

Elevation change: At the landslide on FS 438 the elevation is approximately 8,650' above sea level. The trail up to Bernardin Lake leaves the main road at 9,425', and the lake is reached at 9,780'. Total elevation gain is 1,130'.

Season: This area is free of snowpack and dry enough to ride by mid- to late spring through fall.

Services: All services are available in Taos.

Hazards: You won't have to worry about cars on this ride, but you should be aware of hunters during hunting season.

Rescue index: You are fairly deep into the Carson National Forest here. In the event of an emergency you will have to get back down FS 438. You can find a phone at the small settlement at Pot Creek or at Rancho de Taos, north on NM 518.

The Sangre de Cristo Mountains are dotted with small lakes like Bernardin Lake.

Land status: Carson National Forest, Camino Real Ranger District.

Maps: The Carson National Forest map is good for finding your way along this trail and others in the area as well as showing how to get to them. You can also use USGS 7.5-minute quads for Shadybrook.

Finding the trail: From Taos drive south to Rancho de Taos, where you can pick up NM 518. Drive south on NM 518 another 7 miles to the settlement of Pot Creek. In Pot Creek, find FS 438 and turn left here. Drive up FS 438 for 6 miles to the landslide. Park here.

Sources of additional information: Carson National Forest, Camino Real Ranger District; address and phone are listed in the introduction to this section.

Notes on the trail: Begin by riding across the toe of the slide to where FS 438 continues. Follow FS 438 up for about 3 miles to where a trail takes off to your left. This is the trail up to Bernardin Lake. Note: it may or may not be marked. Turn left, and go half a mile to Bernardin Lake. Have a seat and look around, enjoy a snack, and then head back down the way you came.

If you're up for a little more of a workout you can continue on FS 438 past the turnoff up to Bernardin Lake. Half a mile past the turn bear right onto FS

153, which continues up the Rio de La Olla drainage. This road will eventually take you up and over a ridge to where it will join FS 76, a few miles from the communities of Black Lake and Angel Fire.

If you bear left half a mile past the turnoff to Bernardin Lake, you can continue up FS 438. In 2 miles you will come to the Puertocito and an intersection. FS 438 branches to the right and takes you down to Borrego Crossing. FS 478 takes you up and over a ridge and eventually heads down into Rio Chiquito Canyon.

If you spend some time looking at a map and perhaps talking to a Forest Service ranger, you can put together lots of great routes. Combine parts of this ride with sections of the Garcia Park Loop (Ride 25) for some interesting options. Good luck and happy adventuring!

RIDE 29 *GALLEGOS PEAK*

The ride up to Gallegos Peak and back is a difficult, but rewarding, 13-mile out-and-back excursion that will take intermediate to advanced riders in excellent physical condition four hours to complete. The route up to Gallegos Peak (10,528 feet) follows a dirt road that is rocky and very steep for several longish sections, making portions of this ride strenuous.

The views and scenery on this ride are fabulous. Just below the peak is a beautiful meadow that dances with wildflowers in the spring and early summer, and then again in the fall after the seasonal rains. From the top of Gallegos Peak you can see Little Jicarita Peak (12,835 feet) and Truchas Peak (13,103 feet) to the south, both of which are located inside the Pecos Wilderness Area. This is a fun, sometimes hair-raising descent; use caution and make sure that helmet strap is snug under your chin.

General location: The ride starts from NM 518, about 15 miles south of Taos.
Elevation change: At the intersection of NM 518 and Forest Service Road 442, the starting point of this ride, the elevation is approximately 8,500′. From there you will climb to Gallegos Peak at an elevation of 10,528′. Total elevation gain is 2,028′.
Season: There will be snowpack left on this route until midspring. You can expect snow to return to these elevations sometime in November.
Services: All services are available in Taos.
Hazards: Vehicle traffic on this route is light but may increase during hunting season. Check with forest rangers for hunting season schedules and areas if you are riding in spring or fall.

Several extremely steep pitches on this route are rocky and can get washed out, so some sections may require a portage.

RIDE 29 *GALLEGOS PEAK*

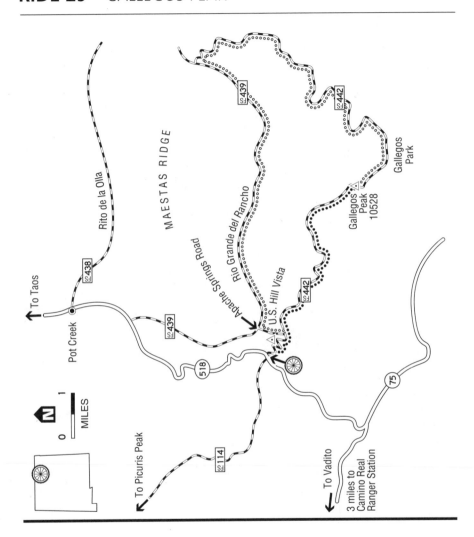

Rescue index: This is not a heavily trafficked area. Your best bets for finding help in an emergency are at the Camino Real Ranger Station in Camino Real, reached by taking NM 518 south to NM 75 and heading west for approximately 5 miles, or at the small settlement of Pot Creek, or back in Taos.

Land status: Carson National Forest, Camino Real Ranger District.

Maps: The Carson National Forest map is adequate for finding this route and other routes in the area. You can also use the USGS 7.5-minute quad for Tres Ritos.

Riders setting out for Gallegos Peak.

Finding the trail: From Taos drive south on NM 68 to Ranchos de Taos, where you will pick up NM 518. Drive about 13 miles south on NM 518 to the intersection with FS 442. This is also where you'll find U.S. Hill Vista. Park here.

Sources of additional information: Carson National Forest, Camino Real Ranger District; address and phone are listed in the introduction to this section.

Notes on the trail: Begin this ride by climbing up the steep switchbacks of FS 442. You will climb, climb, climb on FS 442 until approximately 1.5 miles from the peak, where the pitch mellows somewhat. About 6.5 miles from the start you will reach Gallegos Peak, the highest point along this route. Have a look around, and when you're good and rested you can head on back the way you came.

There are several very interesting route options here. The best option from Gallegos Peak is to continue on FS 442, following the ridge that leaves the peak and runs northeast for approximately 8 miles to the intersection with FS 439. Turn left on FS 439 and ride down the gorgeous Rio Grande del Rancho drainage for just over 7 miles to where you can pick up the Apache Springs Road on the left. This road will take you back to FS 442.

For the really adventurous, there is a single-track trail heading down the ridge to the west of Gallegos Peak. As many as 5 single-track trails then branch off this ridge trail and head south, down various drainages to where they all intersect NM 75. Once down to NM 75 you will need to head east to NM 518 to get back to your car. Supplementary maps are a must if you wish to try out some of these single-tracks. Although they are passable to mountain bikes, progress can be difficult when rocks and boulders and overgrowth block them.

RIDE 30 *AMOLE CANYON*

Amole Canyon is listed in this group of rides not so much as a specific trail but as an area where mountain bikers who are just starting out can get off-road, try some new riding skills, and work on their conditioning. This area has been developed as a nordic ski area and features a network of trails where riders can create their own routes or simply go exploring. The southernmost loop is 3.1 miles long, the loop just to the north is 6.1 miles, and the most northern loop is 7.2 miles.

Amole Canyon trails roll gently through piney woods on the hard-packed dirt of old logging roads. You will find neither major obstacles in the trails nor daunting pitches. This is a good place to let the kids see what they can do.

General location: Amole Canyon is off NM 518 about 15 miles south of Taos in the Carson National Forest.

Elevation change: The beginning of Amole Canyon is approximately 8,100' above sea level. Amole Loop, to the south, reaches a high elevation of 8,400', and both the Lower and Upper loops reach elevation highs of almost 9,200'. It is possible to gain 1,000' when riding in this area.

Season: This area should be dry and free of snow by midspring. After heavy rains these trails can become pretty muddy. Stay off the trails if they get really muddy to keep from creating bad ruts.

Services: All services are available in Taos.

Hazards: These trails pose few hazards. While most of the trails are unmarked, it is hard to get lost out here.

Rescue index: You are never far away from your car or help when riding in Amole Canyon. The nearest help will be found by going south on NM 518 and then west on NM 75 to the small town of Vadito, or by heading to the Camino Real Ranger Station another 2 miles south.

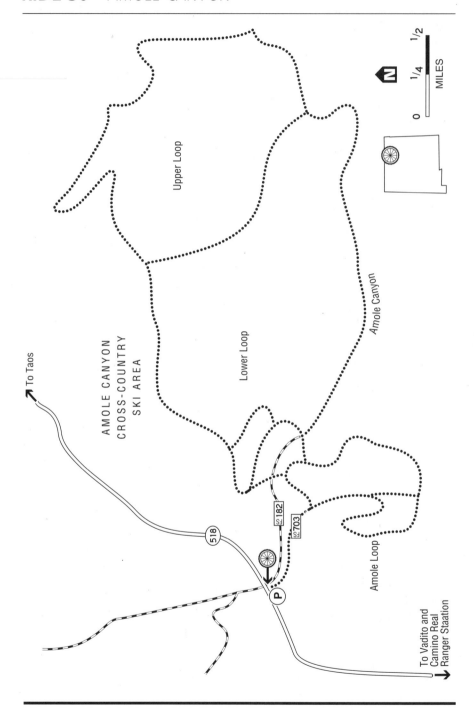

Upper Loop

Amole Canyon

Lower Loop

To Taos

AMOLE CANYON
CROSS-COUNTRY
SKI AREA

SD182

SD703

518

P

Amole Loop

To Vadito and
Camino Real
Ranger Staation

MILES

0 1/4 1/2

N

Land status: Carson National Forest, Camino Real Ranger District.

Maps: The Carson National Forest map shows the general location of Amole Canyon, but does not give much detail. Use the USGS 7.5-minute quad for Tres Ritos.

Finding the trail: From Taos, drive south on NM 68 to Ranchos de Taos, where you pick up NM 518. Drive 15 miles south on NM 518 to the Amole Canyon Nordic Ski Area. Park at the entrance to the ski area.

Sources of additional information: Carson National Forest, Camino Real Ranger District; address and phone are listed in the introduction to this section.

Notes on the trail: From where you park your car ride about a mile up the main road (also Forest Service Road 703) to a fork in the road. If you bear right you will ride the southernmost loop. You will come to a gate; continue past it. A short steep hill and some berms toward the end of this loop will bring you back to the main ski area road at the point where you first branched right. Descend a short distance on the entrance road and bear right onto a trail (also known as Comales Sheep Driveway) that will take you up Amole Canyon to the Lower and Upper loops.

RIDE 31 *SOUTH BOUNDARY TRAIL*

The South Boundary Trail is a five-star mountain biking adventure for advanced and intermediate riders who have the physical stamina for a full day's ride at high altitudes. The South Boundary Trail—so called because at one time it defined the boundary between the Taos and Rio Grande del Rancho land grants—is a 20-mile trek across the Sangre de Cristo Mountains one-way. Almost the entire length of this route is single-track riding, with sections of Forest Service roads that have been closed to motor vehicles.

The best way to ride the South Boundary Trail is to get a shuttle to drop you off at the trailhead just outside the town of Angel Fire, on the eastern slope of the Sangre de Cristo Mountains, and then ride to Taos. Going in this direction you start higher and get most of the climbing out of the way in the first five miles of the ride. This lets you enjoy almost 15 miles of rolling single-track that descends all the way to the Taos Valley.

This is an incredible tour of the Sangre de Cristo Mountain Range that takes you across ridges, valleys, and several peaks, through gorgeous conifer forests and incredible stands of aspen. This ride is at its very best in the fall when the aspens along this route turn every shade of yellow, gold, and fiery orange. Besides being a wonderfully scenic tour of New Mexico's Rocky Mountains, this is also one of the state's very best mountain bike rides.

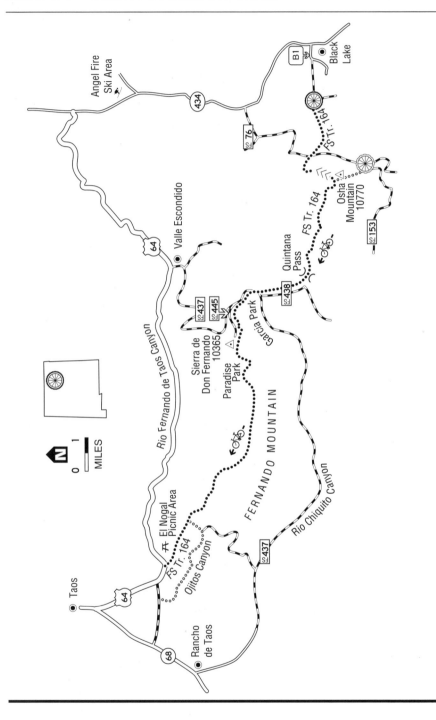

General location: The South Boundary Trail runs in a northwesterly direction from where it begins in Angel Fire and traverses the Sangre de Cristo Mountains to come out in Taos. The entire South Boundary Trail is within the Carson National Forest.

Elevation change: At the start of the South Boundary Trail the elevation is approximately 8,700' above sea level. From here you will climb up and over Osha Mountain, at an elevation of 10,770'. You will reach Quintana Pass at an elevation of 9,600', continuing on to Garcia Park, at an elevation of 10,000'. You will then climb gradually to Paradise Park, at an elevation of 10,365', and then descend from there all the way to El Nogal Campground, at an elevation of 7,200'. You will gain over 2,000' on this ride.

Season: Because of its very high elevations, the season for riding the South Boundary Trail is relatively short. Portions of this trail will not be free of snow and dry until summer. Snow returns to these peaks by the end of October or beginning of November, and sometimes sooner.

Services: All services are available in Taos. Most services, except for those that are bike-related, are available in Angel Fire.

Hazards: This is a long day; riders need to honestly assess their fitness and endurance levels before attempting this ride. Come prepared! You'll want to bring plenty of water, lots of high-energy snacks, a layer for warmth, a weatherproof shell, and your tool kit. Be sure to bring your maps and a compass, too. A medium-sized fanny pack or a standard-size pannier should hold all this.

Watch out for those violent summer thunderstorms up here—you will be very exposed at certain points along the trail. Thunderstorms in these mountains build up in a matter of hours. Leave your bikes at a distance and seek shelter under low bushes or small trees should lightning get close—do not cluster together underneath a tall tree. Check with rangers for local forecasts before you go. If you get an early start, you can get off the most exposed portions of the trail before afternoon.

Rescue index: Help is not close by on this adventure. The best way to prevent any kind of emergency situation is to be prepared. You may want to contact rangers and give them your riding schedule and perhaps establish a contact time for after your ride. At about the halfway point on this ride you can head down Forest Service Road 437 to reach the town of Valle Escondido on US 64. Other help can be found in Angel Fire or in Taos.

Land status: Carson National Forest, Camino Real Ranger District.

Maps: The Carson National Forest map shows the South Boundary route adequately, but topographical maps will give more detail. Use the USGS 7.5-minute quads for Osha Mountain, Shadybrook, and Rancho de Taos.

Finding the trail: From Taos, drive east on US 64 and then south on NM 434. Go past Angel Fire Ski Basin and continue to the small town of Black Lake. Go right onto County Road B1, which heads due west just north of the town of Black Lake. Where this road forks, bear right and continue for just under 2 miles

The South Boundary Trail is a fantastic mountain biking adventure that offers miles of single-track riding.

to where the road makes a sharp left-hand turn. This is your drop-off point. You will see a firebreak heading up from the elbow of this turn. This is the beginning of the South Boundary Trail, also listed as FS Trail 164.

Sources of additional information: Carson National Forest, Camino Real Ranger District; address and phone are listed in the introduction to this section.

Notes on the trail: The South Boundary Trail is fairly well marked at this point with brown plastic fiber stakes. (The Forest Service is currently working to erect permanent markers.) The trail follows a number of Forest Service roads and trails with different numbers, but the whole route is designated on maps as FS Trail 164.

You will begin riding up the firebreak at your drop-off point. The steep single-track will climb for just about 2 miles to where it meets FS 76. The South Boundary Trail (FS Trail 164) crosses over FS 76 and keeps climbing steeply until you reach Osha Mountain in another 1.6 miles. This section of trail is the toughest part of this ride, very steep and rocky in places. Descend the west side of Osha Mountain, rolling along for the next 3 miles until you reach Quintana Pass. As you descend over the western side of Quintana Pass find FS 438 on the right. Bear right here and head to Garcia Park. This section of FS 438, between Quintana Pass and Garcia Park, is closed to motorized vehicles.

As you enter Garcia Park you will encounter FS 437—a well-used road that comes out of Rio Chiquito Canyon and descends into the town of Valle Escondido. Go right onto FS 437 and ride for just over a mile to where FS 445, a rough jeep road, takes off on the left-hand side of the road. Go left here and head up to Paradise Park. At Paradise Park there are berms across the road to keep out motorized vehicles. Continue over and around these berms on FS 445, which soon deteriorates into a single-track. This is still the South Boundary Trail, or FS Trail 164, heading down the ridge of Fernando Mountain. You now have approximately 6 miles of descending single-track down to Ojitos Canyon Road on the left and a single-track on the right. Bear right down the fairly radical single-track descent to El Nogal Campground on US 64, at the mouth of Rio Fernando de Taos Canyon.

On this very last section of the ride, you can choose a milder descent: At the point where the single-track down to El Nogal Campground bears right and the Ojitos Canyon Road goes off to the left, you can go down the Ojitos Canyon Road instead of heading down the very hairy, rocky, and steep single-track. This is a really fun descent down Ojitos Canyon, but it will add another 3 miles to your ride.

A shorter ride with a different starting point eliminates the first 4 miles of difficult single-track climbing. From NM 434, drive 2 miles past Angel Fire, and turn right on FS 76 (this will be 3 miles before you reach the town of Black Lake). Take FS 76 approximately 5.5 miles to where FS 153 branches off on the right-hand side of the road. Begin riding here. You will ride FS 153 for about a quarter-mile, then bear right onto an old road that heads north toward Osha Mountain. This road eventually degenerates into a single-track that meets up with the South Boundary Trail (FS Trail 164). Continue on your way from there.

Red River Area Rides

The little town of Red River, located at the most northern point of what is referred to as "the Enchanted Circle," is surrounded by some of the biggest mountains in New Mexico and boasts some of the state's best scenery. The Enchanted Circle is an 85-mile loop that circles Wheeler Peak—at 13,161 feet, the highest peak in the state—and the Taos Pueblo Indian Reservation. Within this loop you will find fantastic alpine settings, expansive vistas, and some incredible opportunities for mountain biking. Also included in this section are two rides in the Valle Vidal region. The Valle Vidal lies just ten miles to the northeast of Red River as the crow flies, but must be reached by car via the town of Costilla, just a mile from the Colorado border. The Valle Vidal is fantastically wild and beautiful country, home to some of this state's healthiest populations of wildlife.

Red River actually came to life as a vacation and recreation spot back in the late 1800s when miners came over the pass from Elizabethtown to fish or play in the river and to stay at one of the town's resorts. People still come to Red River during all seasons to enjoy many outdoor activities, including mountain biking. Red River Ski Area, built in 1958, has five chair lifts and, at an elevation of 8,700 feet, receives enough snow to keep skiers on the hill until sometime in April. The Enchanted Forest Cross-Country and Ski Touring Center is a very popular nordic resort that offers eighteen miles of groomed trails for classic and skating-technique-type skiers, and provides lessons in telemark and backcountry skiing.

In summer, after these mountains finally shed their coat of snow, there is a whole new raft of recreational sports for the adventurous to try. Campers and hikers use this area as a launching point for their excursions into the state's highest and wildest regions. Fishermen come to ply the waters of the Red River, its many tributaries, and the many alpine lakes in the mountains nearby. Roads left behind by miners bit by bit by the gold bug traverse many of the canyons, ridges, and hillsides of this area, allowing mountain bikers to penetrate deep into the wilds of the Sangre de Cristo peaks. Although some consider Red River to be kind of a tacky tourist stop, those who are willing to look beyond the gaudy T-shirt and curio shops will find a spectacular mountain wonderland awaiting them.

You are in the Rocky Mountains here, mountains that have been created by uplifting fault blocks. Wheeler Peak and the peaks to the north of it are mainly composed of granite and metamorphic rocks. Some of this older Precambrian rock has actually been twisted as it was thrust upward and is pushed eastward over younger, sedimentary rocks. The Moreno Valley just south and east of Red River is a double-faulted valley like the Rio Grande Valley, but it is not yet classified as a rifting valley because the faults that created it do not reach down to the earth's mantle. Gold was discovered in the rocks of this valley in 1866, leading to a boom that helped to establish some of the small communities that still survive here. Elizabethtown, now in ruins, was once one of the area's busiest spots. At one time it had five stores, six saloons, two hotels, and several dance halls. Most of these structures were destroyed in a fire in 1903. Today you will find only stone foundations and some piles of old metal scrap where Elizabethtown once stood.

The open, grassy hillsides around Red River and the high alpine meadows throughout these mountains host a riot of summer wildflowers in June and July. Many of these flowers will bloom again in September after the monsoonal thunderstorms have once again soaked the ground with rain. These mountainsides are cloaked in mottled green in summer, with aspens, pine, and spruce. In fall, a relatively short season at this altitude, the aspens distinguish themselves by turning a million shades of yellow, gold, and orange. You can expect to spot all the creatures that normally dwell in an alpine environment. Deer, elk, the rare bighorn sheep, and an occasional moose roam these hills during the summer months, as do porcupine, marmots, and the seldom-seen black bear.

THE VALLE VIDAL

The Valle Vidal is a 100,000-acre tract of wilderness that was once maintained exclusively for the country's rich and famous as a private hunting preserve. In 1982 the land was donated to the National Forest Service by the Pennzoil Company, which had given up hopes of finding oil in the region and recognized the area as some of the most productive wildlife habitat in the Southwest. Although the Valle Vidal does contain vast timber and grazing land, as well as some valuable minerals, it is managed solely for the benefit of the wild creatures that are able to carry on relatively free from the disruptive hand of man. A herd of Rocky Mountain elk over 2,000 strong makes these mountains and valleys their home, and is considered to be the Valle Vidal's most precious resource. South and west sections of the Valle Vidal Unit of the Carson National Forest are often closed until the first of July to protect calving elk cows. Other sections of the Valle Vidal may be closed at any time to protect the wildlife.

The Valle Vidal Unit is nested between several different blocks or ranges of the Rocky Mountains. These mountains are the source of Costilla Creek, Comanche Creek, and Ponil Creek, all of which boast healthy populations of native trout. The Culebra Range extends south from Colorado to form the western boundary of the Valle Vidal. The Cimarron Range forms the eastern boundary of this wild landscape and includes the broad, flat-topped Ash Mountain. The crowning jewel of the Cimarron Range is Baldy Peak, which rises to an elevation of 12,441 feet and can be seen rising from the higher ridges and peaks on the southern horizon. Oritz Peak (11,209 feet), Van Diest Peak, and Tetilla Peak belong to the Sangre de Cristo Mountains and form the southwest boundary of the Valle Vidal Unit.

This area is quite remote and not easily accessible. When you go be sure you have enough fuel, water, food, proper camping equipment, and a bike in good working condition, with all the tools and spare parts you might need. Checking in with the district ranger in Questa for information about weather, road conditions, closed wildlife areas, and the hunting season is a must before you start. There is a Forest Service facility at the Shuree Picnic Area in the Valle Vidal, but do not count on getting your information there. Contact the Carson National Forest's Questa Ranger District office in Questa for information and suggestions for a trip to the Valle Vidal (address and phone follow).

The best way to get to the Valle Vidal Unit of the Carson National Forest is to come from the northwest by way of the town of Costilla, just south of the New Mexico/Colorado border. From the town of Costilla you will drive east on a gravel road, designated as both NM 196 and Forest Service Road 1950, some 20 miles before entering the Valle Vidal. This is a gorgeous drive and the best choice for getting in here. The other way to get to the Valle Vidal is to come from the southeast. From US 64, pick up FS 1950 and drive north for some 25 miles up Cerrososo Canyon to get to the Valle Vidal. Getting into and riding in the Valle Vidal is a true wilderness adventure that takes some planning and preparation, but is worth the energy it takes to get there.

Any bikers who venture into the mountains surrounding Red River or the wildlands of the Valle Vidal will be richly rewarded for their efforts. All of the rides in this section are at elevations at or above 8,000 feet, which will add a factor of difficulty. If you've come from another part of the country you may want to give yourself a few days riding at slightly lower altitudes to acclimate to high elevation before attempting the rides in this section. Here are a few addresses to help you start planning a trip to Red River and the Valle Vidal:

Red River Chamber of Commerce
P.O. Box 668
Red River, New Mexico 87558
(505) 754-2366

Carson National Forest
Supervisor's Office
P.O. Box 558
208 Cruz Alta Road
Taos, New Mexico 87571
(505) 758-6200

Questa Ranger District
Carson National Forest
P.O. Box 110
Questa, New Mexico 87556
(505) 586-0520

Late afternoon on the way up to Old Red River Pass.

Sitzmark Sports
416 West Main Street
Red River, New Mexico 87558
(505) 754-2456

RIDE 32 *OLD RED RIVER PASS*

This ride is a great ten-mile loop that you can do right out of town. You will gain just over 1,000 feet in the first four miles of this ride that follows paved and graded dirt roads. Beginning and intermediate riders in good physical condition will find this loop fairly easy. Plan on taking at least two hours to complete the loop up to Old Red River Pass and back to town.

The length and location of this ride make it a good introduction to the area.

RIDE 32 *OLD RED RIVER PASS*

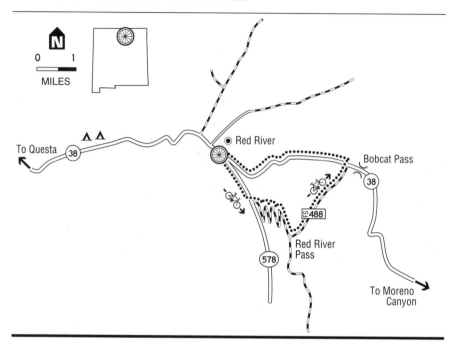

This route also offers the chance to work on acclimating to these higher elevations without committing to a full day's ride. From Old Red River Pass you will
be looking south and east into the Moreno Valley. Behind you will be a good
view of the Red River Valley. Farther to the south and west rises Gold Hill, at an
elevation of 12,711 feet and Wheeler Peak, elevation 13,161 feet.

General location: Old Red River Pass is located 2 miles southeast of the town
of Red River inside the Carson National Forest.
Elevation change: From where you begin this ride at the town of Red River the
elevation is approximately 8,700' above sea level. From there you will climb to
a high at the pass of 9,854'. Total elevation gain is 1,155'.
Season: Because of the high elevations around Red River, this route will not be
open and free of snow until late spring or summer.
Services: Water, gas, groceries, and lodging can be found in Red River. Mountain bikes may be rented and basic repairs attended to at Sitzmark Sports on
Main Street in Red River.
Hazards: The biggest hazard you will face on this ride is cars filled with rubber-
necking sightseers. The road over Old Red River Pass is a favorite of theirs.
Usually they're looking at the scenery, not at you, so be careful. You'll also en-

counter plenty of car traffic on the paved routes that take you out and back from the dirt road.

Rescue index: You are never far from help on this ride. Flagging down a car on the road is probably the quickest way to get help. More help and phones can be found back in Red River.

Land status: Carson National Forest, Questa Ranger District.

Maps: The Carson National Forest map shows this route with adequate detail. You can also use USGS 7.5-minute quads for Red River and Red River Pass.

Finding the trail: You will begin this ride from the town of Red River. You can leave your car there; there is no need to drive anywhere.

Sources of additional information: Carson National Forest, Questa Ranger District; address and phone are listed in the introduction to this section.

Notes on the trail: From the town of Red River ride south on NM 578 from the fork of NM 578 and NM 38 and go up Red River Canyon. It is just under 2 miles to where Forest Service Road 488 leaves on the left-hand side of the road. This is the old pass road. You will start climbing as soon as you are on this dirt road. You will climb up five switchbacks and then some before reaching the pass itself. Continue on FS 488, heading downhill to where FS 488 hits NM 38 just below Bobcat Pass. Go left on NM 38 and ride up the pavement for just over 3 miles back into the town of Red River.

RIDE 33 *4TH OF JULY CANYON*

This ride is just over 12 miles long and follows a loop route over graded dirt, rougher hard-packed dirt, and paved roads. Beginning and intermediate riders in good shape will love this ride, which gains a little over 1,000 feet in four miles. Allow two to three hours to complete this ride.

Great views of the Red River Valley, Moreno Valley, Gold Hill, and Wheeler Peak can be had from atop Old Red River Pass. You will then enjoy a rolling descent that takes you through beautiful alpine forests with still more excellent views to 4th of July Canyon. This is a fun one. Pedal on.

General location: This ride begins in the town of Red River and runs south within the Carson National Forest.

Elevation change: From where you begin this ride at the town of Red River the elevation is approximately 8,700' above sea level. From here you will climb to a high elevation of 9,854' at Red River Pass. Total elevation gain is 1,155'.

Season: This route will not be free of snow and dry until late May or early June.

Services: All basic services and some bike services are available in Red River, but specialized bike repairs will have to be taken care of in Taos.

RIDE 33 *4TH OF JULY CANYON*

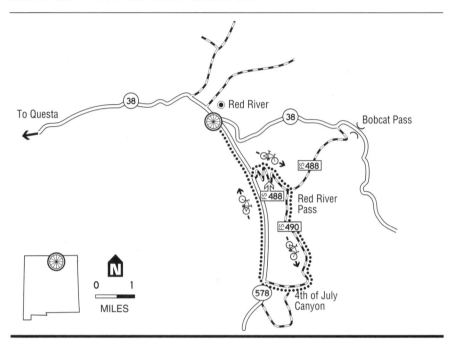

Hazards: Cars driven by sightseers along this route can pose a hazard. A bright piece of clothing helps alert motorists to your presence.

Rescue index: You are not far from help on this ride. You can flag down help on the road or back in Red River.

Land status: Carson National Forest, Questa Ranger District.

Maps: The Carson National Forest map is fine for this route. You can also get USGS 7.5-minute quads for Red River and Red River Pass.

Finding the trail: This ride begins in the town of Red River, so no trail-finding by car is necessary.

Sources of additional information: Carson National Forest, Questa Ranger District; address and phone are listed in the introduction to this section.

Notes on the trail: From the town of Red River ride south on NM 578 up Red River Canyon. From the fork of NM 578 and NM 38 in town it is just under 2 miles to where Forest Service Road 488 leaves on the left-hand side of the road. This is the old pass road. You will start climbing as soon as you are on this dirt road. You will climb up five switchbacks and then some before reaching the pass itself. From the pass look to your right to find FS 490. Take FS 490 heading

The road down through 4th of July Canyon is covered with yellow aspen leaves in autumn.

south, following it as it descends before making a right-hand turn down 4th of July Canyon. You will intersect NM 578 approximately 1 mile from where you made the right-hand turn down 4th of July Canyon. Go right on NM 578 and ride the pavement 4.5 miles back to the town of Red River.

RIDE 34 _MIDNIGHT MEADOWS_

The ride up to Greenie Peak and Midnight Meadows is a somewhat demanding tour of the beautiful country to the north of Red River. Trail surfaces on this 19-mile loop include unmaintained dirt jeep roads that are rough and rocky and sometimes deteriorate to a double-track, and a stretch of moderately well maintained dirt road. Riders with intermediate riding skills in good to excellent shape are best suited to this ride, which will take at least four hours to complete.

You will ride through several really pretty meadows, including Midnight Meadows, on your way up to Greenie Peak, the highest point in this ride. Beautiful alpine settings abound as you head down to Cabresto Creek. The old Midnight Mine is just a half mile up the Cabresto Creek Road when you reach the road at Lagunita Saddle, and the Anchor Mine is another mile beyond that. The last leg of the ride is a mellow climb up Bonito Canyon back to the saddle where you leave your car.

General location: The starting point for this ride is approximately 5.5 miles northwest of the town of Red River, within the Carson National Forest.
Elevation change: At the point where you leave your car and begin riding, the elevation is approximately 9,600'. A high elevation is reached on this ride at the summit of Greenie Peak, at 11,249'. Total elevation gain is 1,650'.
Season: Due to high elevations this route will not be dry and free of snow until early summer. Check with the forest ranger for more specific information.
Services: Almost all service needs, including bike rental, can be taken care of in Red River. Any bicycle repair service needs will have to be addressed in Taos.
Hazards: You will encounter some vehicle traffic on the Cabresto Creek Road. Be aware of locations and times of scheduled hunting seasons. Also, you are very exposed as you approach Greenie Peak; at the peak itself, keep an eye on those dark clouds if they're moving your way, and retreat if lightning gets close.
Rescue index: This is wild country—you won't see a lot of other people or cars. Your best bet for finding help in an emergency is back in the town of Red River.
Land status: Carson National Forest, Questa Ranger District.
Maps: The Carson National Forest map shows this entire route, whereas the older topo maps don't. You can get USGS 7.5-minute quads for Red River, Red River Pass, Latir Peak, and Comanche Point.

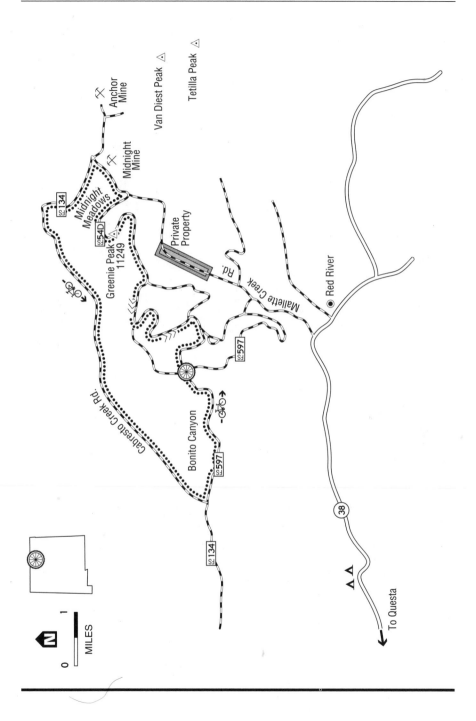

Starting downhill from high in the Sangre de Cristo Mountains.

Finding the trail: From Main Street in Red River drive northeast on the Mallette Creek Road (Forest Service Road 597) for approximately 5.5 miles to a three-way intersection at a saddle. You will find a sign for Greenie Peak and Midnight Meadows here. Park your car.

Sources of additional information: Carson National Forest, Questa Ranger District; address and phone are listed in the introduction to this section.

Notes on the trail: The Midnight Meadows Trail leaves on the right-hand side of the road at the saddle. This trail—really a road—forks immediately; bear right and head downhill. You will head downhill for just over a mile before turning left and heading uphill on the Greenie Peak Road. You will now begin climbing steeply. You will pass many side roads taking off on both sides of the main route—ignore them. After one last really steep climb you will enter a small meadow where you will come to an intersection. Go left up to Greenie Peak. From the peak you will go right, downhill, on what is now FS 54D. Just under a mile from the top you will enter Midnight Meadow. You will descend through the meadow, hitting the Cabresto Creek Road at mile 8 of this ride. You will then turn left and head down Cabresto Creek Canyon for just over 6 miles to where

FS 597 leaves on the left, heading up Bonita Canyon. Ride up Bonita Canyon for another 4.5 miles to the saddle where you left your car.

RIDE 35 *MIDDLE FORK LAKE*

The ride up to Middle Fork Lake is short but gains 1,500 feet in just three miles. The trail surface is hard-packed dirt with only a few steep and rocky sections. Riders who are in good to excellent physical condition, and who consider themselves intermediate in their skill level, will enjoy this climb up to a beautiful alpine lake that rests in the shadow of Wheeler Peak at an elevation of 10,845 feet above sea level. Allow two hours for this six-mile round-trip ride, plus some time for enjoying your surroundings once you get there.

This is a really pretty spot. Pack a picnic, bring the camera, and plan on cooling your heels in the lake for a little while. You may even want to attempt a short hike into the Wheeler Peak Wilderness from here. Enjoy!

General location: The ride up to Middle Fork Lake begins at the end of NM 578, 6.5 miles south of the town of Red River.

Elevation change: Where this ride begins at the end of NM 578, the elevation is approximately 9,345' above sea level. From here you will climb to a high elevation at Middle Fork Lake of 10,845'. Total elevation gain is 1,500'.

Season: The high elevations reached along this route make it best suited for riding in late spring through fall.

Services: Most needs can be taken care of in Red River. For specialized bike repair, go to Taos.

Hazards: You may encounter some off-road vehicle (or jeep) traffic along this route. There will also probably be some hikers on the trail. Please show them courtesy—keep your speed controlled on this descent.

Rescue index: In an emergency you will need to seek help back down the road on NM 578 or in the town of Red River.

Land status: Carson National Forest, Questa Ranger District.

Maps: The Carson National Forest map is fine for finding this route. You can also use the USGS 7.5-minute quad for Wheeler Peak.

Finding the trial: Drive out of Red River on NM 578, heading south for approximately 6.5 miles to where the pavement ends. Park here.

Sources of additional information: Carson National Forest, Questa Ranger District; address and phone are listed in the introduction to this section.

Notes on the trail: From the end of NM 578 ride up the dirt road that follows Middle Fork Creek. This is Forest Service Road 58. Just over a mile from where

RIDE 35 *MIDDLE FORK LAKE*

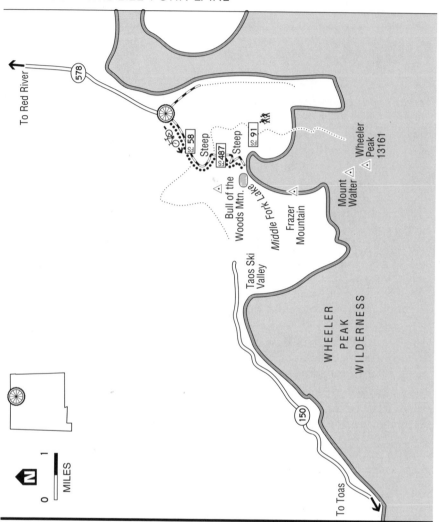

you began riding the road forks; go right, over a bridge that crosses the creek, and continue up what is now FS 487. The road is rougher now and begins to climb more steeply. Two miles into this ride, FS Trail 91 branches off, heading to the top of Wheeler Peak, which is a great trail to hike but not to bike. Continue straight on FS 487. Now, for the last push up to the lake. You made it! Okay, now you can relax. Head back down the way you came.

RIDE 36 *GOOSE LAKE*

The loop up to Goose Lake and back will have intermediate and advanced riders sweating on the way up, and hooting on the way down. While you will climb up on a dirt road, you will descend on a single-track trail for over seven miles. A good amount of physical fitness and stamina is a must for this ride, which takes you up to an elevation of 11,600 feet. The loop up to Goose Lake and back is just about 16 miles long. Plan on taking three to four hours to ride this loop, more if you want to spend time at the lake.

Once you reach the lake you'll probably want to spend an hour or so snacking on your goodies and enjoying the view. That's Gold Hill just to the north, at an elevation of 12,711 feet. Strap on that helmet once you're rested, make sure it's snug, and get ready for a wild descent. Yahooooo!

General location: The ride to Goose Lake leaves directly from the town of Red River and heads south, into the Carson National Forest.

Elevation change: The elevation in Red River, where this ride starts, is approximately 8,630' above sea level. From here you will climb to a high elevation, reached at Goose Lake, of 11,600'. Total elevation gain is 2,970'.

Season: The high elevations of this country make riding much before May impossible due to snow. Once the snow has melted, however, this route should stay clear of snow until late October or early November.

Services: Almost all your needs can be taken care of here in Red River. Take care of special bike repairs in Taos.

Hazards: The road up to Goose Lake receives a fair amount of four-wheel-drive traffic during the summer months. The single-track descent down Goose Creek is not heavily used—it is sometimes overgrown and hard to follow. Not to worry, it's there, following the creek all the way to the bottom.

Rescue index: You might flag down a four-wheeler in the event of an emergency, or head back down to Red River.

Land status: Carson National Forest, Questa Ranger District.

Maps: The Carson National Forest map is fine for finding this route and the other trails in this area. You can also use the USGS 7.5-minute quad for Red River.

Finding the trail: Ride or drive east out of Red River on NM 578. About .7 miles from the eastern edge of town you will find Forest Service Road 486 heading south. This is the beginning of the ride.

Sources of additional information: Carson National Forest, Questa Ranger District; address and phone are listed in the introduction to this section.

Notes on the trail: At the intersection of NM 578 and FS 486, go right onto FS 486, over a bridge that crosses the Red River, and begin climbing. The first

RIDE 36   *GOOSE LAKE*

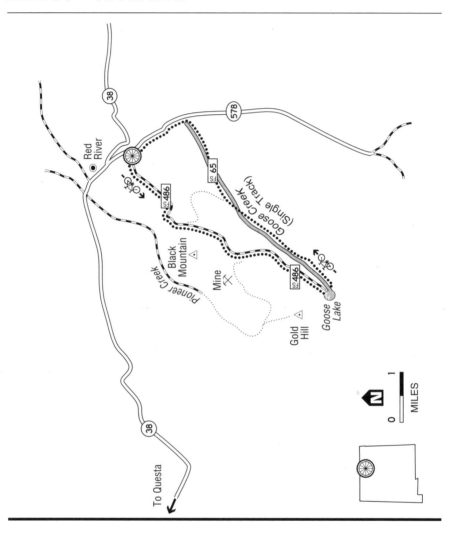

section of this climb is steeper than the rest. There will be several side roads heading off either side of the main route; stay on FS 486. You will reach the lake 8 miles from where you began. Take a break and get ready for this descent. The trail down Goose Creek leaves from the far side of the lake by the outhouse. This is FS Trail 65. In a short distance you will come to a fork in the trail; head left down along the drainage. This is the way to your single-track adventure. As you approach, the Red River will jog left, then right, under a bridge. When you reach NM 578, go left and ride back to town.

If you are not up for this single-track descent, you can ride the road back down the way you came. Another interesting option would be to get a shuttle back to Red River from the Taos Ski Valley. From Goose Lake you can ride one of several trails down to the Taos Ski Valley. While you are not adding a lot of mileage to your ride doing this, you will have a lengthy car ride to get back to Red River. Check with the forest ranger and look at some maps before you attempt this.

RIDE 37 *COSTILLA PASS*

This is a great ride for beginning and intermediate riders, or for anyone interested in a tour of some of New Mexico's most pristine wildlands. Elevations along this ride, however, will require good physical fitness. The whole route is 13 miles, with 9 miles of it forming a loop. The trail will take you up the main drainage of the Valle Vidal to Costilla Pass, and then down the Comanche Creek drainage on four-wheel-drive roads that receive very light use and are for the most part a double-track. Allow three to four hours to complete and fully enjoy this ride.

This is simply some of the prettiest country to be found in New Mexico. The loop is in an elk calving ground that usually remains closed until sometime in July. The Forest Service keeps people out of this area during the spring to ensure that the cows are not disturbed or frightened into abandoning their calves while the calves are still nursing and vulnerable to predators. If you keep your voices low and ride in the early morning and evening hours, you have the best chance of catching these regal animals out and about. Views all along this route are great— you'll probably want to pack along a camera for this one. To the south you can look into the Moreno Valley, behind you is the Valle Vidal. Tetilla Peak is just to the west of you, and Van Diest Peak is a little farther to the north.

General location: Costilla Pass is located in the Valle Vidal Unit of the Carson National Forest on the northern edge of New Mexico.
Elevation change: From where this ride begins at the gate just off of Forest Service Road 1950, the elevation is 9,250' above sea level. From there you will roll along gently, but gain in elevation, until you reach Costilla Pass at an elevation just under 10,000'. Total elevation gain is 750'.
Season: Because of the high elevations this route won't be dry and free of snow until late spring. If this area is closed for elk calving in the spring, put off your ride until midsummer or fall.
Services: Basic services can be found in either Red River, Questa, or Costilla. Bike-related services will have to be taken care of in Taos, Santa Fe, or Albuquerque.
Hazards: The biggest hazard out here is running out of fuel, food, and water. Be

RIDE 37 *COSTILLA PASS*

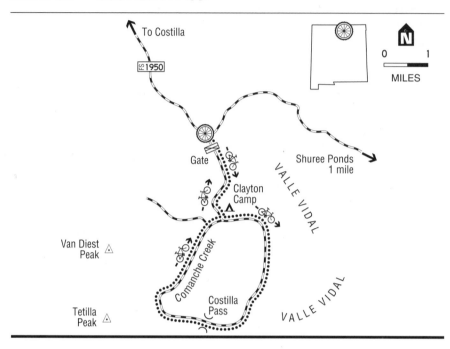

sure to plan ahead. Thoughtful preparation will save time and energy and ensure a safe and enjoyable trip.

It is strongly suggested that you contact the Forest Service to check on weather and road conditions, wildlife closure areas, and hunting season schedules before heading out. A ranger will be able to give you both valuable and interesting information about your trip.

Rescue index: This is very remote country. During the summer and fall months you will probably be able to find a Forest Service ranger at the ranger outpost at Shuree Picnic Area in the Valle Vidal. Check in with the district ranger in Questa to find out if someone will be out there. If not, you may want to establish contact times with the district ranger. Once again, the best protection against any kind of emergency is careful planning and preparation.

Land status: Carson National Forest, Questa Ranger District, Valle Vidal Unit.

Maps: The Carson National Forest map is fine for finding both rides in this area. You can also get the USGS 7.5-minute quads for Red River Pass and Comanche Point.

Finding the trail: From the town of Red River drive west on NM 38 almost 13 miles to the town of Questa. Go left on NM 522 and drive north for another 20 miles to the small town of Costilla. Once in Costilla you will go right on NM

Costilla Pass is included in the Valle Vidal Unit of the Carson National Forest, one of the most remote areas in northern New Mexico.

196, which remains paved for 11 miles before turning to gravel and becoming FS 1950. Continue driving east on what is now FS 1950 for another 8 miles until you reach a fork in the road at Comanche Point. Bear right here, continuing on FS 1950, for 4.5 miles to where a dirt road takes off to the right. Turn onto this dirt road and follow it for about a half mile to a small dirt parking area. Park here.

Sources of additional information: Carson National Forest, Questa Ranger District; address and phone are listed in the introduction to this section.

Notes on the trail: You will ride out of the parking area past a gate on a double-track road that heads up along Comanche Creek. Just under 2 miles from where you started you will reach a fork in the road; go left, around another gate, and continue on past Clayton Camp. (If the gate is locked you can still go around.) At this point the road becomes somewhat overgrown and hard to see. Bear right at the next fork you encounter, following the road that parallels the Valle Vidal. Just under 8 miles from where you began you will reach Costilla Pass. Take a break, have a look around, and have a snack. When you're ready to get back on your bike, head northwest off the pass. You will pass a gate on the left and several forks heading off to your left; ignore them. Bear right, taking the road that descends following Comanche Creek drainage all the way to where it comes out at Clayton Camp. Go left and head back to your car from here.

RIDE 38 *ROCK WALL LOOP*

This ride makes an 18-mile loop in the center of the Valle Vidal Unit that best suits intermediate riders in good condition. The section of this road listed as Forest Service Road 1910 that cuts down across the Rock Wall Formation is quite rocky and will require some technical riding skills. The rest of the route is easily negotiable dirt roads. Allow three to four hours to complete this loop.

The gorgeous country, views, and wildlife you are likely to see on this intermediate route make it a ride that even the most advanced riders will enjoy. You will be cruising through alpine forests of mixed conifers, glades of aspen, and lush meadows that grow thick with wildflowers. Camping and riding right from your campground is a good option on this ride.

General location: This loop ride is located in northern New Mexico in the Carson National Forest within an area called the Valle Vidal Unit.

Elevation change: Where this ride begins at the Shuree Picnic Area the elevation is 9,287' above sea level. From here you will descend to an elevation of almost 8,200' at the intersection of Forest Service Road 1950 and FS 1914. From here you will climb gradually over the next 11 miles back to your starting elevation. Total elevation gain is just over 1,000'.

Season: This is a late spring through early fall adventure due to elevations and road conditions.

Services: The Valle Vidal is in a remote area of northern New Mexico. You will find no services of any kind on the way out here or at the campground once you arrive. Plan carefully and come prepared; it is 20 miles by dirt road to the nearest convenience. Bring plenty of water, food, fuel, and camping supplies, should you decide to stay. Basic needs can be met in Costilla to the north, or in Cimarron if you are approaching the Valle Vidal from the south. Any bike services needed will have to be found in Taos.

Hazards: Checking in with the Forest Service station in Questa is an absolute must before heading out this way. From the rangers there you can get information on hunt areas and schedules as well as weather forecasts and road conditions. They will also be able to tell you which areas may be closed for wildlife.

This is remote country, so come prepared! Once you leave the pavement it is 20 to 25 miles to your destination, and you will find no hotels, convenience stores, or bike shops along the way.

Rescue index: During the summer and fall months you may be able to find a Forest Service ranger at the ranger outpost at Shuree Picnic Area in the Valle

RIDE 38 *ROCK WALL LOOP*

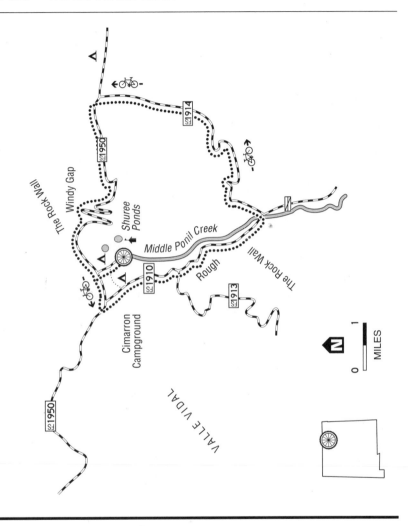

Vidal. Check in ahead of time with the district ranger in Questa to find out if someone will be out there. If not, you may want to establish contact times with the district ranger.

Land status: Carson National Forest, Questa Ranger District, Valle Vidal Unit.

Maps: The Carson National Forest map shows this route in adequate detail. You can also get USGS 7.5-minute quads for Ash Mountain, Van Bremmner Park, and Bald Mountain.

Finding the trail: From the town of Red River drive west on NM 38 almost 13 miles to the town of Questa. Go left on NM 522 and drive north for another 20 miles to the small town of Costilla. Once in Costilla you will go right on NM 196, which remains paved for 11 miles before turning to gravel and becoming FS 1950. Continue heading east on what is now FS 1950 for another 8 miles until you reach a fork in the road at Comanche Point. Bear right, continuing on FS 1950 another 9 miles to the campground and picnic area at Shuree Ponds. Park here.

Sources of additional information: Carson National Forest, Questa Ranger District; address and phone are listed in the introduction to this section.

Notes on the trail: Find a trail that heads west and south about 200 yards from the Shuree Picnic Area ranger's outpost; this is a shortcut across to Cimarron Campground. If you can't find this trail, go back to FS 1950 and take your first left, which is FS 1910. Once on FS 1910 you will be heading south and east, down a steep, rocky road that parallels Middle Ponil Creek. You are cutting down across a formation known as the Rock Wall. Approximately 4 miles from Cimarron Campground you will come to a fork. There will be a gate on the right fork; bear left onto the road that turns and begins to head northeast, up and out of the creek drainage. This is FS 1914. You will climb for about 1 mile before descending for the next 5.4 miles to where FS 1914 joins FS 1950. Go left onto FS 1950 and continue for the next 6 miles, climbing uphill, through several switchbacks that take you up and over the Rock Wall, through Windy Gap, and back to the campground at Shuree Ponds. Whew! You made it!

Grants Area Rides

The town of Grants, New Mexico, is an inconspicuous gas and fast food stop along Interstate 40 about halfway between Albuquerque and the Arizona border. While there is not a whole lot to see in Grants itself, the town serves as the jump-off point to northwestern New Mexico's best attractions and some really gorgeous country. Spring, summer, and fall are comfortable seasons for riding around Grants, where elevations start around 6,500 feet. Winters are blustery across this wide-open country; you'll run into snow anywhere in the plateau country or Zuni Mountains above 7,000' after the first of December. Mount Taylor (11,000 feet) keeps its coat of snow far into summer and puts it back on again by late October or early November. This mountain's shining white volcanic peak is a beacon that can be seen for miles in all directions and is an important landmark of religious significance for both Navajo and Pueblo Indian peoples.

The Grants area was first settled by Europeans in 1872 but did not make it on the map until the Grant brothers, from Ontario, Canada, founded a railroad stop here in 1881. Before the town was officially christened in 1935, the stopover was known as "Grants Camp." One of the largest uranium mines in the world opened up in the mountains outside of Grants in the 1950s after a discovery of some strange yellow rocks made by a Navajo sheepherder. By 1970 the Grants mining district had become the source of half of all the uranium oxide mined in the United States. The economy of the area fluctuates with the world's demand for uranium ore, which today has scaled back considerably. The New Mexico Museum of Mining in Grants is on the site of an operating uranium mine. Tours of the mine, its tunnels, vertical passageways, and equipment, are given each day by former miners to interested visitors.

The fantastic Anasazi ruins at the Chaco Culture National Historical Park; the ancient lava flows, ice caves, and strange rock formations at El Malpais National Monument; the inscriptions at El Morro; and the Zuni and Acoma pueblos are sights worth seeing and exploring just outside of Grants. Mount Taylor, the San Mateo and Zuni mountains, and the sprawling plateaus around town are all part of the beautiful, empty country surrounding Grants that is well suited to exploring by mountain bike. In this section you will find eight rides sprinkled in and around several of these natural and man-made wonders.

Grants and surrounding country sit at the margin of the southeast corner of the Colorado Plateau and so exhibit the characteristics of sedimentary deposition and vulcanism associated with the plateau's geology. Sandstones, mudstones, limestones, and shales that were deposited during Cretaceous, Jurassic, and Triassic periods record eras when shallow seas, beach dunes, deserts, and marshes alternately covered this area. These layers of rock lie exposed in cliffs on either side of I-40 between the Arizona border and Grants. Throughout this region, however, the orderly layers of deposition have been broken or covered by volcanic intrusions and eruptions. The Zuni Uplift, an intrusion of granite that created an enormous oval-shaped dome, is surrounded by broken and eroding cliffs of sandstone that together form the Zuni Mountains. In other places softer mudstones have eroded beneath more resistant sandstones to create a jumble of broken rock slabs.

The San Juan Basin is an enormous area some 150 miles across, extending from the southern tip of the San Juan Mountains in Colorado all the way to I-40 and Grants. This basin, which has been subsiding since Tertiary times, is the reason for the rich deposits of uranium found around Grants and north of I-40 extending west. As water trickles down through porous volcanic rock, ash, or sedimentary rock, it picks up uranium particles. They are then deposited in organic materials, along a vegetated floodplain or in a reed-filled riverbed, for instance. Water runoff carrying uranium may have come from the San Juan Mountains to the north, from the intrusive rocks of the Zuni Mountains to the south, or from ash contained in Morrison Formation sandstones.

Most of the mesas and plateaus of northwestern New Mexico are capped by an erosion-resistant layer of basalt. Much of the basalt that is spread over the country to the north of Grants and I-40 came from Mount Taylor, which grew to its enormous size by erupting for over two million years. The amount of debris around Mount Taylor suggests that explosions destroyed the volcano more than once. The volcano continued to rebuild itself until it stopped erupting two million years ago. There is evidence of volcanic activity throughout New Mexico, but the Malpais lava fields south of Grants are perhaps some of the most interesting.

It is not uncommon to see pronghorn antelope grazing out on the open stretches of grassy plain at the edge of a plateau or between the flows of black rock around Grants. White-tailed deer are numerous in the pinyon and juniper country atop the plateaus and are hunted extensively during the fall. If you keep your eyes open, chances are you'll catch a coyote darting through the brush, or maybe a gray fox. Cougars and bobcats like this rocky plateau country, but they'll more than likely see you long before you see them. Ponderosas thrive in the sandy volcanic soils throughout much of the Zuni Mountains and across these plateaus above 7,500 feet. Above 8,000 feet, fir, spruce, and other pines take over, which, along with glades of aspen, like the cooler temperatures, thinner air, and precipitation of the higher elevations.

EL MALPAIS NATIONAL MONUMENT

The El Malpais (Spanish for "bad country") National Monument, a newly established park, includes cinder cones and lava flows that were active as recently as 1,000 years ago. Pueblo Indian legends tell of the "fire rock" that buried the fields of their ancient ancestors. Some of these flows date back as far as 1 million years. The lava flows that cover this region came from a handful of volcanos located about 25 miles south of Grants. The lava that these cones produced now intermittently covers over 300,000 acres. This land, previously designated as a conservation area, was granted national monument status in 1987.

The many shapes and textures of the lava make it look as if it came to a standstill only a few years ago. In some places, the lava lies flat and still bears the design of its fluid past. In others, it is twisted and ropy, revealing the taffylike consistency it had at the time it was stretched just before it finally cooled. Some of the flows show squeeze-ups, domes, and pressure ridges that cracked when molten lava flowing beneath the surface pushed through. Gas bubbles and vesicles created by escaping gases are frozen in the rock, as are the very strange lava tubes. Lava tubes are actually tunnels created by lava flowing through rock that hardened around it. In some instances these tubes collapsed, creating other strange formations.

Stop in at the El Malpais Visitor Center in Grants on the corner of Santa Fe and Patton streets to learn more about the volcanic history of this region before you head out there to ride. This type of landscape is unique to continental America and is something everyone should see.

CHACO CULTURE NATIONAL HISTORICAL PARK

The Anasazi ruins at Chaco Canyon are some of the most valuable and intriguing remnants of our continent's ancient cultures anywhere in the United States. Chaco Culture National Historical Park is a must-see stop for visitors with even a passing interest in the archaeology of ancient civilizations. Located 30 miles from the nearest paved road and 60 miles from the nearest store, the ruins can be found in a modest setting among the shallow canyons and low mesas of the Chaco Plateau. Here, well inside the Navajo Reservation, lie the remnants of what was once the social, religious, economic, and cultural center of the most advanced society that populated this continent before European settlement. Within the park at Chaco Canyon there are as many as 11 expertly masoned stone cities. These stone cities, or pueblos, are centered around the largest and most magnificent of the ruins, Pueblo Bonito. There may have been as many as five thousand inhabitants of this canyon at one time. Here they built well-designed irrigation systems and farmed the valley floor, growing corn and squash. Archaeologists have identified as many as 75 pueblo dwellings, some as far as 100 miles away, connected by an intricate and laboriously constructed road system that radiates from the ruins in Chaco Canyon.

The ruins at Chaco were found in 1849 by a group doing topographical surveys. Due to their size and remoteness they were not fully excavated by archaeologists until the turn of the century. In 1907 Chaco was established as a national monument and then expanded in 1980 to include 33 sites outside the canyon and given national historical park designation. Over the years the surrounding area, known as the San Juan Basin, has been heavily drilled for oil that percolated up through the porous sandstones and now lies trapped just below the surface. Drilling continues today for oil and gas across hundreds of miles of the San Juan Basin and on the Chaco Plateau, now crisscrossed by thousands of miles of dirt roads.

Although it is recognized that the Anasazi were the group responsible for the ruins at Chaco, they and their culture are referred to as Chacoan because of the level of their achievements. Evidence suggests that the Anasazi first occupied the canyon sometime between A.D. 1 and A.D. 450, during the Early Basket Maker Period. They did not become firmly established in the canyon and start building housing structures and farming until sometime between A.D. 500 and 750. Over the next 500 years the Chacoan Anasazi moved out of their pit houses into single-story, flat-roofed stone structures; by the end of the period they were building homes like apartment buildings, one on top of the other. During this time they also began to use cotton textiles, perfected the design and manufacture of distinctive Anasazi black-on-white pottery, and refined methods of irrigation.

By A.D. 1100 the Chacoans had reached their zenith in what is referred to as the Classic or Great Pueblo Period. Highly sophisticated structures now stood four stories high, with several great kivas each, the focus of a deeply religious people who practiced elaborate rituals throughout their daily life. By this time Chaco was the center of an enormous trade network stretching far south into Mexico. Copper bells, Pacific seashells, and brightly feathered macaws were among the goods that Chacoans exchanged with cultures of the tropics. The enormous storage bins for grain among the ruins at Chaco could hold far more than what could be grown on their narrow canyon floor. This seems to suggest that Chaco existed as a control center that managed the supply and distribution of foodstuffs to outlying groups, carefully rationing grain during slim years.

By A.D. 1200 Chaco was almost entirely abandoned for reasons that are still unknown. Archaeologists have developed—and hotly debated—several very interesting theories about why this sophisticated culture that flourished for so long suddenly vanished. The answer to this mystery is probably found in a combination of theories.

One of the most prominent theories maintains that the decline of Chaco roughly coincided with a prolonged drought in the San Juan Basin. This drought, combined with decreased farm productivity due to depleted soils, could have sent individuals in search of wetter, more productive, regions. Another theory correlates the decline of the Chaco Culture with the movement of Athapascan-speaking tribes into the area. Athapascan-speaking people are thought to have migrated down from the north to become the progenitors of the Navajo, Apache, Paiute, Ute, and Comanche peoples. The Anasazi, although quite advanced, were thought to be a very peaceful people who may not have been prepared for the warlike ways of these more primitive newcomers.

The most intriguing theory of all suggests that Chaco was an outpost of the

Toltec empire of southern Mexico, which fell to hostile tribes during a time of stress just about the same time as Chaco was abandoned. The most likely explanation is that Chaco was suffering like any overcrowded city with limited technology. Unrest, hostilities, both internal and external, disease, depleted soils, and the effects of a few years of drought would be enough to cause almost complete social disintegration.

We know the Anasazi left, but where did they go? Scholars generally agree that these people filtered southward to the Rio Grande Valley and surrounding areas. The Acoma, Hopi, and Zuni peoples all claim Anasazi ancestry to some degree, and the Hopi use a clan system similar to one used by the ancients. Several of the 19 different pueblos built throughout northern New Mexico were constructed shortly after the time that Chaco was supposedly abandoned—strong evidence that today's Pueblo Indians are in some way connected to the Anasazi of long ago. Still, the fact remains that when the Chacoans left their canyon they left behind their knowledge of architecture, masonry, and irrigation systems, knowledge that was never matched by their descendants.

Northwestern New Mexico offers as much variety to riders as anywhere in the state. From the rolling lava fields of El Malpais National Monument to the top of Mount Taylor there are many excellent opportunities for mountain biking, camping, and sightseeing. All you need is your bike, some camping gear, and a little get-up-and-go to thoroughly enjoy an adventure in this corner of the Land of Enchantment. Here are a few addresses you will need to start planning your trip to the Grants area:

Greater Grants Chamber of Commerce
100 North Iron Street
Grants, New Mexico 87020
(505) 287-4802

Cibola National Forest
Supervisor's Office
2113 Osuna Road NE, Suite A
Albuquerque, New Mexico 87113-1001
(505) 761-4650

Cibola National Forest
Mt. Taylor Ranger District
1800 Lobo Canyon Road
Grants, New Mexico 87020
(505) 287-8833

El Malpais National Monument
P.O. Box 939
Grants, New Mexico 87020
(505) 285-4641

Chaco Culture National Historical Park
Superintendent's Office
Star Route 4
Box 6500
Bloomfield, New Mexico 87413
(505) 988-6727 or 6716

RIDE 39 *CERRO RENDIJA*

This ride takes you out into the lunar landscape of El Malpais National Monument, going out to Cerro Rendija and making an 8-mile loop around it, for a total of 16 miles. The route follows a dirt road that is cinder-covered in places, and rocky where it crosses over lava flows. Intermediate and beginning riders in good condition should allow three hours to complete the ride. The first couple of miles of this trail wind through a checkerboard of park and unmarked private property, so please stay on the road through this section.

This ride begins on County Road 42, just to the west and north of Bandera Crater, on the Continental Divide. For the first two miles you will be riding right on the Divide through healthy groves of aspen. On your right the water flows toward the Colorado River and on your left it flows toward the Rio Grande. Also on your left you'll see the lava that flowed from Bandera Crater, responsible for some of the biggest flows within the monument. At the most eastern point in this loop you will find trails leaving on the right-hand side of the road, heading out to some lava tubes—caves that were created by molten lava flowing through tubes of rock that cooled around it. You may want to throw a small flashlight into your fanny pack for checking out these strange black tubular caves.

CR 42 provides access to some of the best sights in the monument, including Big Lava Tubes, the Braided Cave, and Chain of Craters. Before you head out be sure to stop in at the Visitor Center in Grants to find out more about these formations and where they are located.

General location: The ride out and around Cerro Rendija is approximately 25 miles southwest of Grants, within the El Malpais National Monument and El Malpais National Conservation Area.

Elevation change: The turnoff where you leave your car and begin riding is the highest point in the ride, at 7,720'. From there you will roll along very gently, losing and gaining modest increments of only 100'. The lowest point on the ride, 7,584', is reached at the southeast corner of the loop. Total elevation gain is 136'.

Season: Riding at this elevation and on these surfaces will be great almost year-round, provided there is not a lot of wind and blowing snow during the winter months. It can get pretty hot out here in the summer.

RIDE 39 *CERRO RENDIJA*

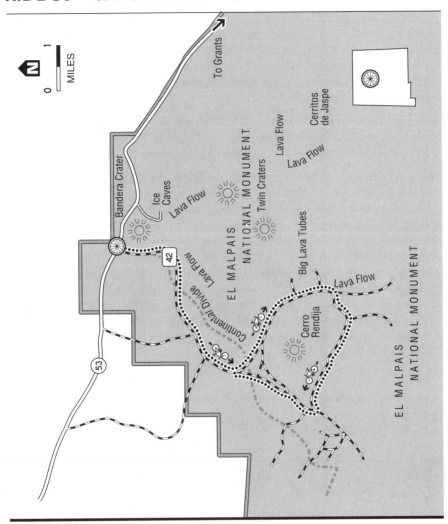

Services: Basic services can be taken care of in Grants, but those requiring bike parts or knowledgeable service will have to be sought in either Albuquerque or Santa Fe. There is no water at the trailhead so make sure you bring plenty of your own.

Hazards: You are very exposed out here should one of those wild lightning storms move in. Take shelter or hurry on back to the car.

Rescue index: In the event of an emergency you may find help at the Ice Caves parking lot a mile east from where you began this ride off of NM 53.

Land status: El Malpais National Monument, National Park Service, El Malpais Nation Department of the Interior.

Maps: The Cibola National Forest map for the Mt. Taylor Ranger District is fine for finding this ride and others in this section. You can also use USGS 7.5-minute quads for Paxton Springs and Cerro Hueco.

Finding the trail: From Grants take NM 53 south for approximately 24 miles until you see the sign for the Ice Caves. Continue past the sign and turn off for the Ice Caves for another mile to CR 42 on the left-hand side of the road. Turn left onto this road and park.

Sources of additional information: El Malpais National Monument; address and phone are listed in the introduction to this section. The El Malpais Visitor Center is located in Grants at the corner of Santa Fe and Patton streets.

Notes on the trail: Ride heading south on CR 42. You will be rolling along the Continental Divide for about 2 miles before descending off the Divide to the west. Continue heading south for approximately 2.5 miles to where you come to a fork. Bear left at this fork, heading up and over the Divide, along the northern flank of Cerro Rendija and the western edge of a lava flow. Along this stretch keep an eye out for the trails leading to the lava tubes. Once back on the main road you came out on you will head south and west. Ignore the next two roads taking off on the left. You will soon be heading in a northwesterly direction. At the next intersection you encounter you will go right again; you are now heading north. While there are many side roads in this area, the main road should remain obvious. If you become confused, bear left; soon you will loop back to CR 42. Pedal back to your car from there.

RIDE 40 *QUARTZ HILL*

This ride is a short, seven-and-a-half–mile loop around Quartz Hill. Beginning and intermediate riders who are in good physical shape will take only a couple of hours to complete this ride. The route follows an old abandoned mining road that is not much more than a double-track. Several short, steep, rocky sections will add a touch of difficulty to this ride that otherwise rolls along, providing many fun, short, climbs and descents.

On this ride you will traverse both Zuni and Bonita canyons. Along the way you will find lava flows that made their way into Zuni Canyon and the remnants of two old mine works. This is beautiful rolling country, favored by the tall, red-barked ponderosa pine. Breathe deep and enjoy these beautiful surroundings while you pedal on.

RIDE 40 *QUARTZ HILL*

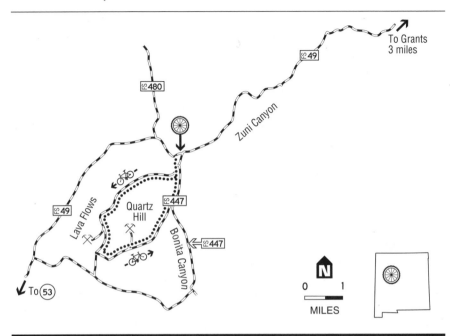

General location: The Quartz Hill loop ride is located approximately 11 miles southwest of Grants in the Zuni Mountains, which are included in the Cibola National Forest.

Elevation change: Where this ride begins at the intersection of Forest Service Road 49 and FS 447, the elevation is 7,400' above sea level. You will reach a high elevation of 8,000' at the southern end of this loop. Total elevation gain is just under 600'.

Season: Spring, summer, and fall are all going to be great times to be riding out here, though it might get a little warm during midsummer. You could also ride out here in the winter provided the route is dry and free of snow.

Services: Basic services can be taken care of in Grants. Bike services, parts, and accessories will have to be found in Albuquerque or Santa Fe.

Hazards: Check with a Forest Service ranger about hunting season areas and schedules before you head out this way. It's always a good idea to wear a piece of bright clothing if you are out here in hunting season.

Rescue index: While you may run into other folks on the trail, this is pretty remote country. In an emergency you'll have to head back to Grants to find help and a phone.

Land status: Cibola National Forest, Mt. Taylor Ranger District.

Maps: The Cibola National Forest map shows this route and how to get there in good detail. You can also use the USGS 7.5-minute quad for Paxton Springs.

Finding the trail: From Grants drive south on NM 53 and go left onto Forest Service Road 49 (Zuni Canyon Road) right after it crosses under the freeway. Follow this paved road for approximately 4.5 miles to where it turns to gravel. Continue heading south and west on this road for another 6.5 miles until you come to the intersection where FS 447 takes off up Bonita Canyon to your left. Park at this intersection.

Sources of additional information: Cibola National Forest, Mt. Taylor Ranger District; address and phone are listed in the introduction to this section.

Notes on the trail: Bear left onto FS 447 and ride down Bonita Canyon. About 300 yards from this intersection there will be a double-track road heading up to your right, the second right after the intersection where you parked. Turn right here and climb up into Zuni Canyon. At approximately 3.5 miles you will pass a right-hand road that goes to one of the old mine areas along this route. Continue past this turn and on up the next steep rocky section. You will soon reach the saddle between Zuni and Bonita canyons. Bear left and continue to climb for another short distance to where a left-hand fork branches off to another mine site. From here you will descend across rolling terrain into Bonita Canyon. You will reach FS 447 in Bonita Canyon approximately 6.5 miles from the start. Go left on FS 447 and head back to your car at the intersection with FS 49.

RIDE 41 *CERRO COLORADO*

The loop around Cerro Colorado in the Zuni Mountains is an 11-plus-mile ride following dirt roads that become double-track in sections. Both beginning and intermediate riders will enjoy this slightly longer ride that rolls along gaining only about 700 feet. Allow two to three hours to complete this loop.

This rolling pinyon- and juniper-covered country is subtle and beautiful. The ride up Limekiln Canyon offers a tour of one of the bigger drainages in this part of the Zuni Range. Several lava flows encountered at the most northern and western portions of this loop are reminders that below the planet's crust the earth lives and breathes.

General location: The loop around Cerro Colorado is 12 miles south and west of Grants inside the Cibola National Forest.

Elevation change: Where this ride begins at the intersection of Forest Service Road 49 and FS 448 the elevation is approximately 7,500'. The ride's highest elevation is 8,250'. Total elevation gain is 750'.

RIDE 41 *CERRO COLORADO*

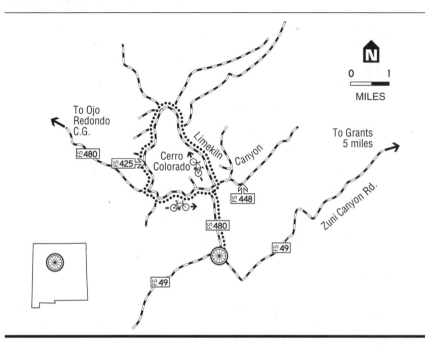

Season: Because of elevation and latitude, this is great riding spring, summer, and fall. You could try riding out here in winter provided you have some warm clothes to ride in and the trail isn't covered with snow.

Services: Bike needs and services will have to be taken care of in either Albuquerque or Santa Fe. All other services can be found in Grants.

Hazards: Be aware of vehicle traffic along FS 480. Campers use this road to get to Ojo Redondo Campground.

Rescue index: You won't find any pay phones or convenience stores out here. In an emergency you'll need to find help back in Grants.

Land status: Cibola National Forest, Mt. Taylor Ranger District.

Maps: The Cibola National Forest map shows this route, how to get out there, and other trails in the area in good detail. You can also use the USGS 7.5-minute quads for Paxton Springs and Mount Sedgwick.

Finding the trail: From Grants drive south on NM 53 and go left onto FS 49 (Zuni Canyon Road) right after it crosses under the freeway. Follow this paved road for approximately 4.5 miles to where it turns to gravel. Continue heading south and west on this road for another 7.5 miles until you come to where FS 480 forks off to the right. Turn onto FS 480 and park.

Riding through the ponderosas of the Zuni Mountains.

Sources of additional information: Cibola National Forest, Mt. Taylor Ranger District; address and phone are listed in the introduction to this section.

Notes on the trail: Begin riding by heading up FS 480. Go 2 miles to where FS 480 makes an abrupt turn to the left. Take the road that forks off to the right from the elbow of this turn. This is the road that takes you up Limekiln Canyon, referred to by some as Limekiln Canyon Road. Bear left at the next 2 intersections, continuing up Limekiln Canyon for 2.5 miles. At this point you will go left, heading downhill into a valley. You will cross this valley and intersect FS 425. Go left onto FS 425 and follow it for approximately 3 miles to where it intersects FS 480. Go left onto FS 480 and follow it past the turn you made off the elbow and back to where you left your car.

RIDE 42 *MOUNT SEDGWICK*

This loop is just over nine miles long, and includes a spur that takes you up to Mount Sedgwick, the highest point in the Zuni Mountains. Beginning and intermediate riders in good condition who are acclimated to higher altitudes will find this ride moderately difficult—the hardest part of the ride being the spur that takes you up to the peak. This route follows dirt roads that are in good condition for the most part. Allow two hours to complete this loop.

Elevations are high on this ride: you will find yourself riding through the mixed conifers and aspens common to alpine environments. Several meadows boast a riot of wildflowers in early summer and after the monsoonal storms of fall. Ojo Redondo Campground is a good place to establish a basecamp for riding several of the routes in this section.

General location: Mount Sedgwick is located 20 miles west of Grants within the Cibola National Forest.

Elevation change: Where this ride begins at the Ojo Redondo Campground the elevation is approximately 8,800' above sea level. You will reach a high point of 9,256' atop Mount Sedgwick. From there you will descend to a low point in the ride in Diener Canyon, at 8,400'. Total elevation gain is 800'.

Season: Because of the slightly higher elevations on this ride there will be more foul weather and snow up here in the winter. Best times to ride this loop will be spring, summer, and fall.

Services: Gas, food, lodging, and all basic needs can be found in Grants. Bike services, however, will have to be taken care of in Albuquerque or Santa Fe.

Hazards: Don't end up on top of Mount Sedgwick when one of those nasty afternoon thunderstorms blows in. Also, keep an eye out for traffic along this route; the four-wheelers like to drive this loop.

Rescue index: You may find help among fellow campers at Ojo Redondo Campground or at Post Office Flat Ranger Station off Forest Service Road 480 along this route. Other help and a phone can be found back in Grants.

Land status: Cibola National Forest, Mt. Taylor Ranger District.

Maps: The Cibola National Forest map is good for finding your way out to the campground and following the route up to Mount Sedgwick. You can also use USGS 7.5-minute quads for Post Office Flat and Mount Sedgwick.

Finding the trail: From Grants drive south on NM 53 and go left onto FS 49

RIDE 42 *MOUNT SEDGWICK*

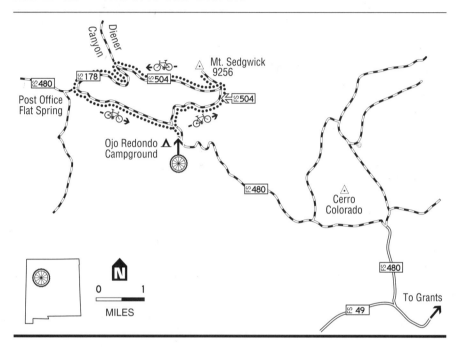

(Zuni Canyon Road) right after it crosses under the freeway. Follow this paved road for approximately 4.5 miles to where it turns to gravel. Continue heading south and west on this road for another 7.5 miles until you come to where FS 480 forks off to the right. Turn right onto FS 480 and drive for 8 miles to Ojo Redondo Campground. Park here.

Sources of additional information: Cibola National Forest, Mt. Taylor Ranger District; address and phone are listed in the introduction to this section.

Notes on the trail: From the campground go out and left onto FS 480 and ride for half a mile to where FS 504 takes off on the right just past an old cabin. Go right onto FS 504 and continue for 2 miles to FS 504A, which leaves from the right-hand side of the road. Turn here and go up a steep, rocky section of road to the top of Mount Sedgwick. Head back down this fast, wild descent back to FS 504; turn right and continue heading downhill until FS 504 hits FS 178 in Diener Canyon. Go right onto FS 178 and ride up this graded dirt road to where it intersects FS 480 at Post Office Flat. Go left onto FS 480 and ride another 2.5 miles to Ojo Redondo Campground.

RIDE 43 *LOBO LOOP*

This longer loop ride gains significantly in elevation, making it best suited to intermediate and advanced riders in excellent physical condition. The 20-mile loop covers sections of pavement, graded dirt road, and rough, four-wheel-drive roads. Allow at least four hours to complete this ride.

This ride takes you up through the rolling foothills of the San Mateo Mountains at the base of Mount Taylor. Starting low in pinyon and juniper country around 7,000 feet, you will climb up through ponderosa pine forests into the mixed conifers and aspens of alpine altitudes. Views to the south out over Horace Mesa and to the north and east up to Mount Taylor are stunning.

General location: The start of this loop ride is 8 miles northeast of Grants in the Cibola National Forest.

Elevation change: At the point where this ride begins at the Coal Mine Canyon Campground the elevation is 7,444' above sea level. From here you will climb up onto Horace Mesa at an elevation of 8,200' and continue to climb gradually until you reach a high elevation on this ride of 8,941'. Total elevation gain on this ride is just about 1,500'.

Season: Spring, summer, and fall will be the best times for this ride. You can ride late into the fall provided the ground is dry and free of snow.

Services: All basic services can be taken care of in Grants, but for bike services go to Albuquerque or Santa Fe.

Hazards: This is a long ride, so be sure to bring lots of water and a cache of high-energy snacks. Be aware of hunting season schedules and areas; this is a popular place during deer hunting season.

Rescue index: Help might be found at Coal Mine Canyon Campground, where this ride begins; at Lobo Canyon Picnic Area; out on the paved Lobo Canyon Road; or the district ranger station a mile outside of Grants on Lobo Canyon Road.

Land status: Cibola National Forest, Mt. Taylor Ranger District.

Maps: The Cibola National Forest map shows this loop and other routes nearby in good detail. You can also use USGS 7.5-minute quads for Lobo Springs and San Mateo.

Finding the trail: From 1st Street in Grants drive north out of town on NM 547, also the Lobo Canyon Road. Just 1.5 miles out of town you will come to the district ranger station. Stop in and get information for your trip here. Continue up NM 547 for another 9.5 miles to Coal Mine Canyon Campground. Park here.

Sources of additional information: Cibola National Forest, Mt. Taylor Ranger District; address and phone are listed in the introduction to this section.

RIDE 43 *LOBO LOOP*

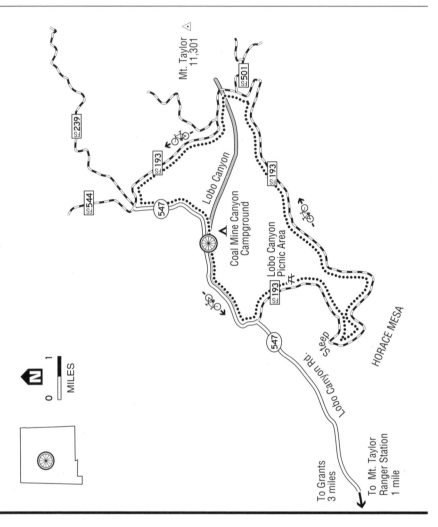

Notes on the trail: From Coal Mine Canyon Campground head back down the paved Lobo Canyon Road for approximately 2.5 miles to where Forest Service Road 193 takes you into Lobo Canyon Picnic Area. Ride through the picnic area and continue on FS 193 heading out and gently rolling along until you make a short steep climb up onto Horace Mesa. Climb up the rolling terrain atop the mesa for the next six miles to where FS 501 enters FS 193 from the right-hand side of the road. Don't turn here; this is the highest point in the ride. Bear left to continue on FS 193 and cross the top of Lobo Creek drainage. Descend gradually for the next three miles until you reach NM 547 (Lobo Canyon Road) at the point where its pavement ends and it becomes the dirt road FS 239. Turn left and ride 2.5 miles down the pavement to Coal Mine Canyon Campground where you left your car.

RIDE 44 *MOUNT TAYLOR LOOP*

Advanced and intermediate riders who are in excellent physical condition will love this route that ascends Mount Taylor on a well-maintained dirt road and then drops off the southern slope of this 11,301-foot peak via Gooseberry Springs single-track. In just under 19 miles you will gain and lose 3,100 feet of elevation. This is a full day's adventure that will take most riders at least five hours to complete. Plan on taking some time at the summit of Mount Taylor to enjoy the view.

This ride features some incredible single-track riding, as well as a substantial amount of climbing, and will rate as one of the best rides to be found anywhere in New Mexico. The views up here stretch away to the horizon in all directions. As you make your way up you will rise through ponderosa pine to alpine forests. Autumn lights the aspens on the slopes of Mount Taylor with hues that range from orange to gold to pale yellow. Wind your way up the gentle apron of this giant; as you finally stand gasping at its summit, trying to take in the enormity of the land and sky before you, it's not hard to understand how this mountain has earned a place of importance in the religions of the Navajo, Hopi, and Pueblo people.

General location: The loop that takes you up to the top of Mount Taylor begins approximately 13 miles northeast of Grants inside the Cibola National Forest.
Elevation change: Where the surface of the Lobo Canyon Road switches from pavement to dirt, the point at which this ride begins, the elevation is 8,213' above sea level. From here you will climb up the side of the volcano, riding up La Mosca Canyon to reach La Mosca Peak at an elevation of 11,036'. The highest point is reached by riding a short distance from here to the top of Mount Taylor at an elevation of 11,301'. Total elevation gain on this ride is 3,088'.
Season: The high elevations of this route make it a summer and early fall adventure. You are likely to run into bad weather up here during the monsoon season and later in the fall, so come prepared.
Services: Food, gas, lodging, maps, and camping supplies are available in Grants. Biking services will have to be sought in Santa Fe or Albuquerque.
Hazards: This is a long, hard day of riding, requiring an honest assessment of physical fitness for yourself and those in your group. Do not attempt this ride unless you are reasonably well acclimated to higher altitudes and are in good

RIDE 44 *MOUNT TAYLOR LOOP*

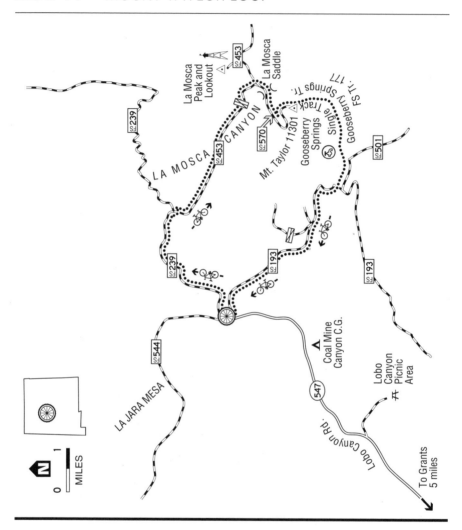

to excellent physical condition. Bring plenty of fluids and a good cache of high-energy snacks. Remember—don't let thirst or hunger regulate your intake of food and fluids. Stop to drink and snack often; you'll feel much better for it by the end of the day.

You are very exposed once you reach the summit of Mount Taylor. Should you see dark rumbling clouds approaching, retreat from these high, open ridges and peaks.

Rescue index: In an emergency your best bet for finding help will be at the district ranger station just outside of Grants on NM 547. Help may also be found at the lookout tower on top of La Mosca Peak.

Land status: Cibola National Forest, Mt. Taylor Ranger District.

Maps: The Cibola National Forest map is good for finding this route and how to get there, but does not show surrounding landmarks with much detail. For that, use USGS 7.5-minute quads for Mount Taylor, Lobo Springs, San Mateo, and Cerro Pelon.

Finding the trail: From 1st Street in Grants drive north out of town on NM 547 (Lobo Canyon Road). Just 1.5 miles out of town you will come to the district ranger station. Stop in here for information and suggestions. Continue heading up NM 547 for another 11.5 miles to where the pavement ends. At this point NM 547 becomes a dirt road, Forest Service Road 239. The point where NM 547 ends and the dirt FS 239 begins is also the point where FS 193 branches off to the right. This is the road on which you will be completing this loop. Park here.

Sources of additional information: Cibola National Forest, Mt. Taylor Ranger District; address and phone are listed in the introduction to this section.

Notes on the trail: Ride up FS 239 as it wraps around the northwestern flank of Mount Taylor. Approximately 3.5 miles from the start FS 453 takes off on the right. Go right onto FS 453 and climb, following this road as it bends around following La Mosca Canyon all the way up to where it emerges onto La Mosca Saddle, just over 8 miles from the start. At this point FS 453 branches off to the left (north), taking you up to La Mosca Peak and lookout. It is a short, steep trip up to the lookout—but worth the effort. Just after FS 453 forks left you will come to another fork; bear right here, heading uphill onto FS 570. Continue climbing on FS 570 for another 2 miles to a saddle just below Mount Taylor. Here, the single-track FS Trail 77 (Gooseberry Springs Trail) leaves from the right-hand side of the road and heads up to the summit of Mount Taylor. This single-track trail climbs steeply (not much farther now) for about a third of a mile to the summit. Take a break, relax, have a drink and a snack and prepare for the ride down. FS Trail 77 heads down through the meadow to the south below you. Follow this single-track, which starts to become a double-track, for approximately 3 miles to where it intersects FS 501. Go right onto FS 501 and continue for just over half a mile to the intersection with FS 193. Go right again onto FS 193 and head downhill for just over 5 miles to the intersection of FS 193 and FS 239 where you left your car.

RIDE 45 *WIJIJI RUIN*

No technical riding skills or advanced level of fitness is required for this ride. It is a wonderful tour into this region's ancient past that all ability levels will enjoy. The route from the Chaco Culture National Historical Park Visitor Center out to Wijiji Ruin follows both a paved road and an old double-track dirt road, just over seven miles out-and-back. The dirt road is closed to vehicles but remains very rutted. If the ground is saturated this road becomes a muddy bog that should be avoided. Allow an hour's riding time. Obtain a backcountry permit for visiting Wijiji Ruin at the Visitor Center before heading out this way.

The trail to Wijiji Ruin is the old Sargent Ranch Road that works its way up the north side of Chaco Wash between Wijiji and Chacra mesas. Edward Sargent was a wealthy sheepman from Chama who brought large herds here to graze during the winter months. Indians of mixed Pueblo and Navajo heritage, who had been grazing their animals and farming in this canyon for some two hundred years prior to Sargent's arrival, were less than happy to share the canyon with him. Livestock stealing and murder resulted and, throughout the years that both laid claim to the area, violence continued.

Chaco Canyon and Wijiji Ruin are within what Navajos consider their homeland and figure in many of their legends and stories of the past. One legend tells of a mysterious woman who came from the Pueblo people and brought with her the secret of weaving, which she gave to the Navajo people. At one time Wijiji Ruin had 92 first-floor rooms and 2 enormous kivas. Archaeologists surmise that Wijiji was built in a single effort in the early 1100s. This ruin is noted among the ruins at Chaco for its uniformly sized rooms and symmetrical layout. Sagebrush, chamiso, and other desert shrubs fill the canyon bottom here where once rows of corn and squash were planted and tended by the Anasazi.

General location: Chaco Culture National Historical Park is located 70 miles north of Interstate 40 and 90 miles from Grants. The last 20 miles of road getting into Chaco is a dirt road that can be rutted and very rough.

Elevation change: Elevations in and around the Chaco Canyon area are surprisingly high. The canyon floor is just over 6,000' above sea level, with the mesa tops nearby reaching up to 7,000'. The ride out to Wijiji Ruin traverses the canyon bottom with little or no elevation change.

Season: As long as this old road is dry this trail can be ridden year-round, but spring and fall will be best for riding in this area as winters are cold and blustery and summers are hot.

Services: There are no services within 60 miles, so be sure you have plenty of food, fuel, and supplies before heading out this way. Drinking water is available

RIDE 45   *WIJIJI RUIN*

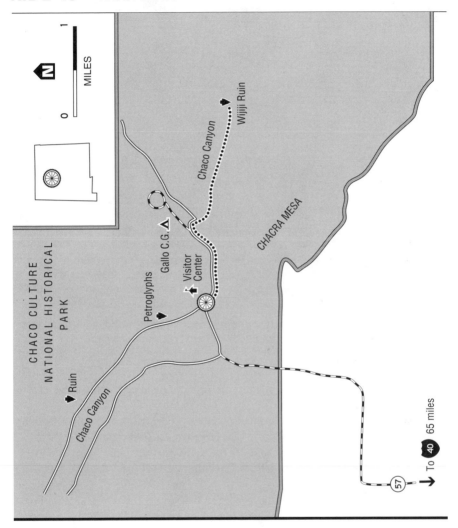

at the park Visitor Center and at Gallo Campground, the only campground in the park.

Hazards: Mud is going to be your biggest problem if it is wet. Some of the ruts that form in these tracks after the road has become washed out are kind of tricky. Watch for cars along the road and hikers along the trail.

Rescue index: In an emergency get out to the main road and head back to the Visitor Center where you'll find plenty of park personnel. Also, help may be

The buildings at Chaco Canyon were the most beautifully constructed of the many thousands of Anasazi buildings now in ruins found throughout the Southwest.

found at the park superintendent's private residence directly behind the Visitor Center.

Land status: Chaco Culture National Historical Park is under the jurisdiction of the National Park Service and the U.S. Department of the Interior.

Maps: Park maps of this trail and all the trails throughout Chaco are available at the Visitor Center. Use USGS 7.5-minute quads for Pueblo Bonito and Sargent Ranch.

Finding the trail: From Grants drive west on I-40 to the town of Thoreau. From Thoreau take NM 371 heading due north. Continue on NM 371 for approximately 35 miles. Just past the town of Crowpoint, go right onto NM 57. In another 15 miles you will reach the turnoff to Chaco Canyon. This is a left-hand turn onto a dirt road that will take you another 20 miles to the park. Once inside the park proceed directly to the Visitor Center for information, maps, and a backcountry permit for visiting Wijiji Ruin. Leave your car at the Visitor Center.

Sources of additional information: The Visitor Center at Chaco Culture National Historical Park has several excellent exhibits, a good selection of books and films, and knowledgeable people to help you learn more about the ruins at Chaco Canyon.

Notes on the trail: From the Visitor Center ride out of the parking lot and go left toward Gallo Campground. Just past the left-hand turn to the campground, approximately 1.5 miles from the Visitor Center, you will go right at the trailhead to Wijiji Ruin and the beginning of the old Sargent Ranch Road. Follow this road out to the ruin, leaving your bike at the provided bike rack on the road before you head over to the ruins. Head on back the way you came.

RIDE 46   *KIN KLIZHIN RUIN*

The ride out to Kin Klizhin, or Black House Ruin, on paved and hard-packed dirt roads, does not require much in the way of technical skills but requires an intermediate level of physical fitness and stamina because of its length. From the Visitor Center it is 24 miles out-and-back, requiring at least four hours riding time.

As you roll westward toward the very farthest edge of the park you will be looking out over broad, flat mesas and across expansive valley floors. This is gentle country, not the dramatic setting that many of the ruins the Anasazi left behind are found in. Black House Ruin, or Kin Klizhin, as it is called by the Navajo, is an "outlier" community of the Chacoan Anasazi that is built high on a lone hill with excellent views and a road that connected it to life in the canyon. Kin Klizhin is one of the great houses built during the Classic Pueblo Period, distinguished by its tower kiva, massive construction, and banded masonry. The flats surrounding Kin Klizhin were most probably covered with fields of corn, beans, and squash fed by water that was carefully channeled and stored behind dams like the one that can be seen at this ruin.

General location: Chaco Culture National Historical Park is located 70 miles north of Interstate 40 and 90 miles from Grants. The last 20 miles of road getting into Chaco is a dirt road that can be rutted and very rough.

Elevation change: At the Visitor Center the elevation is 6,185' above sea level. From there you will roll along very gently, reaching a high point of 6,286'. Total elevation gain is 101'.

Season: If roads are dry and free of snow this route will be rideable year-round. Spring, summer, and fall are the best times to ride out here, although midsummer can get pretty hot.

Services: Although water is available at the Visitor Center and at the campground there are no other services within 60 miles of here. Be sure you have plenty of fuel, food, and supplies with you before heading out this way.

RIDE 46 *KIN KLIZHIN RUIN*

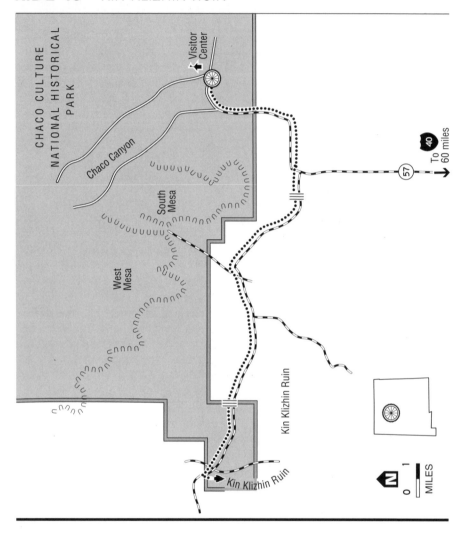

Hazards: Mud along this route is a hazard if the weather has been wet and the ground is saturated. Also, be aware of traffic along this route—pickup trucks fly along these dirt roads.

Rescue index: Your best option for finding help in an emergency is back at the Visitor Center or at the park superintendent's private residence nearby.

Land status: Chaco Culture National Historical Park is under the jurisdiction of

Riding along the low mesas and sandstone cliffs of the Chaco area.

the National Park Service and the U.S. Department of the Interior. Although the park is surrounded by Navajo tribal land, the park itself is federally owned land. **Maps:** Park maps detailing how to ride out to Kin Klizhin are available at the Visitor Center. Use USGS 7.5-minute quads for Pueblo Bonito and Kin Klizhin. **Finding the trail:** From Grants drive west on I-40 to the town of Thoreau. From Thoreau take NM 371 heading due north. Continue on NM 371 for approximately 35 miles. Just past the town of Crowpoint, go right onto NM 57. In another 15 miles you will reach the turnoff to Chaco Canyon. This is a left-hand turn onto a dirt road that will take you another 20 miles to the park. Once inside the park proceed directly to the Visitor Center for information and maps. A backcountry permit is not required for this ride. Leave your car here.

Sources of additional information: The Visitor Center at Chaco Culture National Historical Park has several excellent exhibits, a good selection of books, and knowledgeable people to help you learn more about the ruins at Chaco Canyon.

Notes on the trail: From the Visitor Center ride out of the park heading south. Approximately 3 miles from the Visitor Center the road makes a 90-degree turn and heads south as NM 57. Take the dirt road that heads west off the elbow of this turn. You will continue heading west on this road for the next 6 miles across the private property of the Navajo people—please be respectful and do not camp on their land. You will then cross back into the park, ride across Kin Kilzhin Wash, pass a turnoff to your left, and take the next left turn. You will reach the ruin 12 miles from where you started. After you've had a good look around, head on back the way you came.

Jemez Mountains Area Rides

The Jemez Mountains of north-central New Mexico have some excellent mountain biking to offer just over an hour's drive from both Santa Fe and Albuquerque. The Jemez Mountains are really the remnant of an exploded volcano. Ridges and valleys radiate away from the Valle Grande, an enormous flat-bottomed valley that is really a caldera. The closest towns to the Jemez backcountry are Los Alamos and Jemez Springs. Los Alamos sits 7,173 feet up on the eastern flank of the Jemez and is the birthplace of the infamous "Fat Man," America's first atomic bomb. The settlement of Jemez Springs, in Jemez Canyon, is a funky little mountain community, featuring a 150-year-old bath house, a monastery and retreat, a Zen Center, and fourteenth-century Indian ruins. "Jemez" (pronounced 'hey-mez') is the Spanish interpretation of an Indian word that simply means "people." There are many good camp spots up here—check in with the ranger in Jemez Springs for information—as well as lodging possibilities in Jemez Springs, Los Alamos, and La Cueva.

History here begins with the Anasazi, who settled the incredibly rugged southeastern section of the Jemez Mountains, now included in Bandelier National Monument. This monument covers some 36,000 acres of plateaus, cliffs, and canyons and contains hundreds of ruins and pictographs. Many of these sites have yet to be thoroughly studied and excavated due to their remote and rugged location. Some 75 miles of hiking trails provide the only access to a good many of the ruins at Bandelier National Monument. The soft volcanic tuff of this region allowed the Anasazi to attach wall and floor supports directly to canyon walls. In some cases natural caverns were further hollowed out to create living space in the cliff walls themselves.

The Jemez Pueblo Indians, possibly descendants of the Anasazi who lived at Bandelier, built the pueblo that is now in ruins inside Jemez State Monument in Jemez Canyon. The Jemez people first encountered Europeans when Fray Alonso de Luga came to this region in 1598 with Onate's expedition. He returned to the Jemez Pueblo in 1622 and, with the help of the tribe's women (it was shameful for the men to do such work), built the Misson de San Jose, a classic example of Spanish church architecture from this period. The mission is also among the ruins at the monument.

The Jemez people at first welcomed the Spanish priests, but when they destroyed the pueblo's kivas, it placed a seed of bitter resentment among the Indians. When news of the Pueblo plot to rise against their oppressors came, the Jemez joined in the plan with their cousins to the north, and fought fiercely in the revolt of 1680. While many other Pueblo tribes surrendered, the Jemez Pueblo continued their resistance when the Spanish returned in 1692. In 1696, with the help of the nearby Zia Pueblo Indians, the Spanish planned one final assault against the Jemez. The Jemez, however, caught wind of the attack and fled to the west, into Navajo country, before the assault came. This explains the close relationship and shared blood between the Navajo and Jemez Pueblo Indians today. The modern-day Jemez Pueblo live on two separate reservations, one at the mouth of Jemez Canyon, the other on the western flank of the Jemez Mountains.

Worlds away from the ancient cultures of the Anasazi and Pueblo Indians is the story of the scientific revolution that took place in the mid-twentieth century in the town of Los Alamos. Los Alamos was originally the site of a secluded boarding school that educated boys in the classics and the joys of the outdoors. The school closed in 1942 and was selected soon after to become the site of the secret laboratories where scientists would gather to develop the world's first atomic bomb. Unknown to all but the highest government officials, the group at Los Alamos labored for two years until July of 1945 when "Fat Man" was dropped from a tower in the desert northwest of Alamagordo. The resulting flash confirmed to the world that the United States now had the power of mass destruction. Three weeks later Nagasaki and Hiroshima were flattened and the world saw the grisly ironies of human progress. Nuclear weapons research continues at the laboratories at Los Alamos, but the town of Los Alamos now has many other services and businesses that support a thriving community of people, many of whom came here for the mountain scenery.

The Jemez Mountains are a fan of ridges and valleys that once formed the slopes of a massive volcano. Scientists believe this volcano may have risen more than 14,000 feet into the air at one time. This volcano, like most of the volcanos in New Mexico, grew up on a fissure where magma from the earth's mantle escaped to the surface through a rift fault. About a million years ago the pressure that had been building for eons was finally released in two massive explosions. Over 100 times the amount of debris contained in the Mount St. Helens explosion was thrown into the air. Evidence of these eruptions can be found for hundreds of miles in all directions. Without the debris or pressure to support the remaining walls, the volcano collapsed, or subsided, creating the enormous Valle Grande. The Valle Grande is a giant caldera: a round, cliff-rimmed valley almost 14 miles across. Views from rim to rim are obstructed by pressure domes—low, mounded hills in the middle of the caldera that arose shortly after the eruption and subsidence. The remaining slopes of the volcano walls were covered with layers of ash that came down in boiling incandescent clouds of gas and fine rock particles. As the ash cooled it settled, and welded together, creating the porous light-colored rock called tuff that you see everywhere in these mountains. The cliffs along the edges of the canyons in the Jemez come in shades of pink, purple, white, yellow, and sometimes even orange, and are all welded tuff. In some places you will find odd pinnacles and tent formations, formed by gas escaping through the ash before it had cooled. The bizarre-looking formation of Soda Dam was, and still is, being formed by heated calcium carbonate–laden water cooling at the surface. The numerous hot springs throughout the Jemez Range are the legacy of its volcanic past.

The lower reaches of the Jemez are forested by pinyon and juniper that give way to dense stands of ponderosa pine and mixed conifer in the higher plateaus and ridges. Broad, sunny meadows frequently carpet the gullies and valleys of the Jemez. These grassy bottoms often hold clear running streams home to healthy populations of rainbow trout. In the fall, stands of aspen in these mountains and valleys turn a fantastic gold tinted by orange. Cottonwoods that grow in the gullies and near the streams here echo the season's change with brilliant yellows of their own.

Almost the entire Jemez Mountain Range falls within the jurisdiction of the Sante Fe National Forest. Currently the bulk of this national forest land is managed to bring profit from natural resources, mostly through cattle grazing and logging, which some say have taken too heavy a toll on the land. Management of the Jemez Mountains' natural resources has drawn criticism from an outspoken group of recreationalists who live nearby and come to ride and play in these mountains. If you find yourself anywhere in our national forests with questions and concerns about logging or grazing practices you have witnessed, contact the appropriate National Forest Service people and give them your input; remember, these are public lands and they belong to all of us.

All the hazards of riding at elevation in the mountains exist here. Check in with the ranger in Jemez Springs for current information on weather and road conditions as well as for hunting seasons and posted areas in these mountains. Thunderstorms fed by a warm moist monsoonal flow from the south can become a menace certain times of the year in New Mexico. If this type of weather pattern is present and thunderstorms are predicted for the afternoons, plan your ride for early in the day. A thin layer for warmth, like a polypropylene long underwear top, and a weatherproof shell are easy to carry and are considered a necessity by experienced riders venturing into the high country where days cool off fast and storms can grow ugly, lash out, and pass on, all within a couple of hours.

Here are a few places to write or call to plan your trip in and around the Jemez:

Los Alamos Chamber of Commerce
2132 Central Avenue
P.O. Box 460
Los Alamos, New Mexico 87544
(505) 662-8105

Santa Fe National Forest
Supervisor's Office
P.O. Box 1689
Santa Fe, New Mexico 87504
(505) 988-6940

Santa Fe National Forest
Jemez Ranger District
Jemez Springs, New Mexico 87025
(505) 829-3535

Trail Bound Sports
771 Central Avenue
Los Alamos, New Mexico 87544
(505) 662-3000

RIDE 47 *EAST FORK CROSS-COUNTRY AREA*

The East Fork Cross-Country Area has been included in this section not as a specific ride but as a good area for inexperienced riders to get off-road and do some exploring. Spend an hour or an afternoon cruising one of the five easy trails in the East Fork area that have been designed for use by cross-country skiers in winter. There are many options for creating your own loops on trails that are abandoned logging roads. This is a good place to get out, stretch your legs, work on your conditioning, and acclimate to the higher elevations of the Jemez.

You will be riding across mostly level terrain in this area, through the thick stands of ponderosa pine that thrive in the volcanic soils of these mountains. As you explore the trails at the northern edge of this area you will eventually encounter a gorge cut into the tuff by the east fork of the Jemez River. This area is bordered to the south by NM 4.

General location: The East Fork Cross-Country Area is located in the Santa Fe National Forest, approximately 7 miles east of the La Cueva Ranger Station.
Elevation change: Elevations range between 8,200' and 8,600' above sea level in this area. Modest increments of only 400' will be gained and lost on this ride.
Season: Because of the altitude of this ride it will not be dry and free of snow until mid- to late spring.
Services: Groceries, gas, and accommodations are available in Jemez Springs. Bike services are available in Albuquerque, Santa Fe, or Los Alamos.
Hazards: If the ground is saturated you will not only get muddy but you will also damage the trail surface with deep ruts that can remain for months and even years. It's best to stay off these trails when the ground is soaked.
Rescue index: You are not far from help in the East Fork area; the small settlement of Vallecitos de Los Indios is directly across NM 4 off Forest Service Road 10. Other help can be found at the La Cueva Ranger Station at the intersection of NM 4 and NM 126.
Land status: Santa Fe National Forest, Jemez Ranger District.

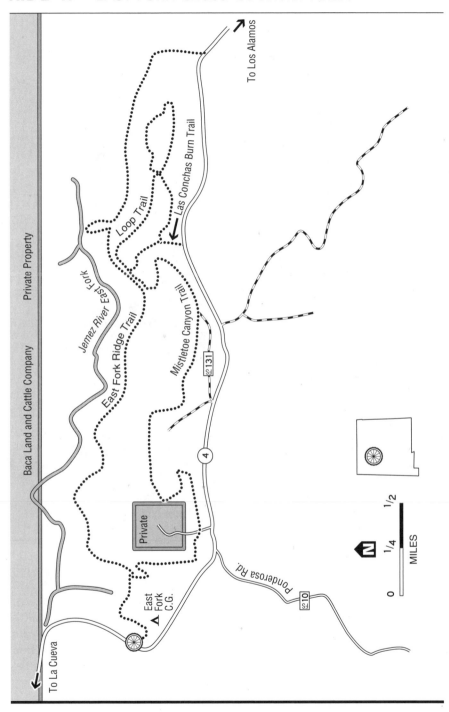

To Los Alamos

Las Conchas Burn Trail

Loop Trail

Jemez River East Fork

East Fork Ridge Trail

Mistletoe Canyon Trail

FS 131

Private Property

Baca Land and Cattle Company

Private

East Fork C.G.

Ponderosa Rd.

FS 10

To La Cueva

N

0   1/4   1/2

MILES

Trails groomed for cross-country skiers during winter are great for mountain bikers in summer.

Maps: The Santa Fe National Forest map shows the East Fork area but not with any detail. Use the USGS 7.5-minute quad for Redondo Peak.
Finding the trail: From Albuquerque, drive 40 miles north to the small town of San Ysidro, located at the intersection of NM 44 and NM 4. From San Ysidro drive north for another 27 miles to the small settlement of La Cueva. From here you will bear right on NM 4 heading east. You will continue in this direction for 6.5 miles until you see the signs for the East Fork Recreation Area on the left-hand side of the road. Drive in and park here.

Sources of additional information: Santa Fe National Forest, Jemez Ranger District; address and phone are listed in the introduction to this section.

Notes on the trail: At the parking lot for the East Fork Recreation Area you will find the trailheads for the East Fork Ridge Trail and the Mistletoe Canyon Trail. These two trails traverse almost the entire length of the East Fork Recreation Area. By heading east on either one of these trails you will intersect the East Fork Overlook Trail, FS 131, and the Las Conchas Burn Trail. Create your own route, do a little adventuring, and have some fun!

RIDE 48 *JEMEZ CANYON OVERLOOK*

This is a great, short out-and-back ride for beginners, kids, or anyone who has a couple of hours and wants to get out and have a look around in some beautiful country. From the Jemez Canyon Overlook parking lot you will roll along a mostly level mesa top for a total distance of seven miles. You will be riding on a hard-packed dirt road that sometimes becomes a double-track. Allow one to two hours to complete this route.

You may want to plan on bringing a picnic for this ride. There are some fantastic views to the south down Jemez Canyon along the way, as well as a pretty meadow at the far end of this out-and-back excursion. It would be hard to get lost on this one. Enjoy!

General location: The Jemez Canyon Overlook is just 2.5 miles southeast of the settlement of La Cueva in the Santa Fe National Forest.
Elevation change: At the Jemez Canyon Overlook the elevation is approximately 8,200' above sea level. You will gain and lose under 200' of elevation on this ride.
Season: This route should be dry and free of snow by midspring. Snow won't return to these elevations until sometime in November.
Services: Groceries, gas, and accommodations are available in Jemez Springs and La Cueva. Bike services are available in Albuquerque, Santa Fe, or Los Alamos.
Hazards: You won't encounter a lot in the way of vehicle traffic out here, but keep an eye on the weather in case one of those dark, really mean-looking summer thunderstorms should start rumbling.
Rescue index: You don't get too far out into the woods on this ride. In an emergency seek help at the ranger station in La Cueva, just 2.5 miles back at the intersection of NM 126 and NM 4.
Land status: Santa Fe National Forest, Jemez Ranger District.

RIDE 48 *JEMEZ CANYON OVERLOOK*

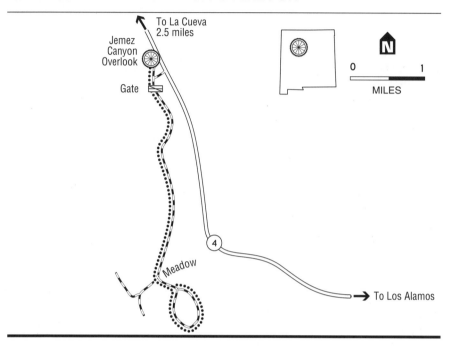

Maps: The Santa Fe National Forest map does not show this route. Use the USGS 7.5-minute quads for Redondo Peak and Jemez Springs.

Finding the trail: From the town of San Ysidro, located at the intersection of NM 44 and NM 4 about 40 miles north of Albuquerque, drive north for approximately 27 miles to the settlement at La Cueva. From here, bear right on NM 4, heading east. Drive approximately 2.5 miles east from La Cueva to the Jemez Canyon Overlook parking area on the right side of the road. Park here.

Sources of additional information: Santa Fe National Forest, Jemez Ranger District; address and phone are listed in the introduction to this section.

Notes on the trail: From the overlook parking area head south on an old dirt road paralleling NM 4. You will encounter a fork in the road in the first half a mile of this ride. Bear right at this fork, staying on top of the mesa. You will encounter a gate soon after. Go through it and close it behind you. Now roll along until you reach a broad grassy meadow. Bear left at the fork at the edge of the meadow and ride the short loop at the far side of the meadow. This loop has a couple of steep sections where you can try out your riding skills and test your strength. When you're done playing around, find a spot to sit down and snack on your munchies, then head back the way you came.

The many long mesas of the Jemez, which offer so many wonderful views, radiate like fingers from the sunken caldera at their center called Valle Grande.

RIDE 49 *SAN JUAN MESA LOOP*

The ride across San Juan Mesa is an 18-mile loop that beginning and intermediate riders will find only moderately difficult. The length and elevation gained in this ride will require a good amount of physical fitness, however. The route surface includes hard-packed sandy dirt roads that can become loose in sections. Riders should also expect to find sections of road that are both rutted and washboarded. Allow three to four hours to complete this ride.

The trail begins in healthy pinyon and juniper stands that surround the town of Vallecitos de Los Indios, then climbs into sweet-smelling ponderosa forests. From along the ridge you can glimpse through the trees and catch images of other ridges silhouetted blue and green against one another in the distance.

General location: San Juan Mesa is located within the Santa Fe National Forest, approximately 7.5 miles east of the junction of NM 4 and NM 126 at La Cueva and south of the settlement called Vallecitos de Los Indios.

Elevation change: Where this ride begins at the settlement at Vallecitos de Los Indios the elevation is approximately 8,000' above sea level. From there you will climb out of a valley and then make a short descent before climbing up the ridge of San Juan Mesa to a high elevation of approximately 9,500'. Total elevation gain is 1,500'.

Season: This route probably won't be dry and free of snow until mid- to late spring. The snow will return again sometime in November.

Services: Groceries, gas, and accommodations are available in Jemez Springs and La Cueva. Bike services are available in Albuquerque or Santa Fe.

Hazards: Be aware of car traffic along this route, especially when you are riding up the canyon on Forest Service Road 269. Summer and fall thunderstorms can rip loose up here, so be aware of forecasted weather.

Rescue index: You are pretty well removed from any sizeable communities up here. In an emergency head back to the small settlement of Vallecito de Los Indios. If you are farther along than halfway on this route, head all the way south on FS 269 to the small town of Ponderosa. You can find a forest ranger at the ranger station at Jemez Springs.

Land status: Santa Fe National Forest, Jemez Ranger District.

Maps: The Santa Fe National Forest map shows this route well and is adequate for finding most of the rides in this section. You can also use the USGS 7.5-minute quads for Redondo Peak, Ponderosa, and Jemez Springs.

Finding the trail: From the town of San Ysidro, located at the intersection of NM 44 and NM 4 about 40 miles north of Albuquerque, drive north for approximately 27 miles on NM 4 to the intersection at the small settlement of La Cueva. From here, bear right on NM 4 heading east. Continue in this direction for approximately 8 miles to the town of Vallecitos de Los Indios. Park here.

RIDE 49   *SAN JUAN MESA LOOP*

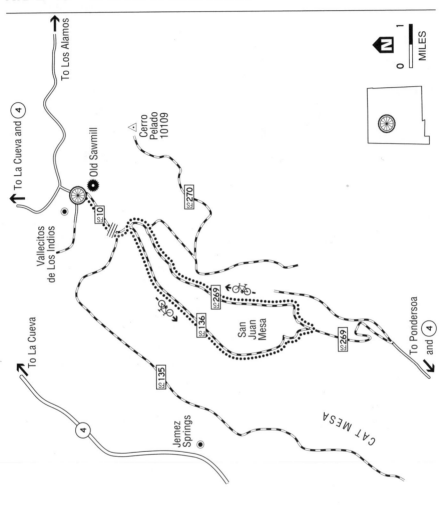

To Los Alamos

To La Cueva and (4)

Old Sawmill

Cerro
Pelado
10109

FS 270

Vallecitos
de Los Indios

FS 10

FS 269

To Pondersoa
and (4)

To La Cueva

FS 136

San
Juan
Mesa

FS 269

FS 135

4

Jemez
Springs

CAT MESA

MILES

Sources of additional information: Santa Fe National Forest, Jemez Ranger District; address and phone are listed in the introduction to this section.

Notes on the trail: Begin by riding up and out of Vallecitos de Los Indios on FS 10, heading south. The road will cross a cattle guard and descend for about half a mile, at which point you will turn right onto FS 136. This road will take you along the ridge of San Juan Mesa. You will gently descend and then loop around to join FS 269, which will take you back up the mesa. FS 269 rejoins FS 10 at

The ruins of Mission San Jose de los Jemez in Jemez Canyon, which was burned during the Pueblo Revolt of 1680.

about mile 15; turn left here, climbing back up to the top of a hill. From there descend back down into the town of Vallecitos de Los Indios where you left your car.

There are many, many old logging routes in the Jemez and countless possibilities for creating your own routes. If you are interested in doing some exploring on your own, supplementary maps and a compass are a necessity.

This loop can also be ridden from the south, from the settlement at Ponderosa. Just over a mile north of the Jemez Pueblo, FS 290 heads east from NM 4 to the small town of Ponderosa. Just past the middle of town, FS 269 heads west off the main road. Follow this road for approximately 3 miles until you reach the intersection, a fork in the road, of FS 269 and FS 490. Park here, and begin your loop by going west on FS 269.

RIDE 50 *PALIZA CANYON LOOP*

This ride is a fun 12-mile loop that intermediate riders in good physical condition will find moderately difficult to strenuous. The route up Paliza and down Borrego Canyon is on hard-packed sandy roads. While the portion of this ride that goes up Paliza Canyon is graded, the way down Borrego is a very rough jeep road at best. At points it seems as though this road has been almost completely reclaimed by a creek that runs down the drainage. Deep ruts and ditches have been carved by the stream and remain filled with water most of the year. Allow three hours to complete this ride.

Paliza Campground is a gorgeous spot in a stand of old ponderosas. The arms of these giants rustle in the wind, and a creek burbles nearby. Through the branches you will see light-colored bands of volcanic tuff capping the canyon walls. Aspens and mixed conifers appear near the top of this ride. Lots of tricky ditches and water crossings will keep you entertained. Good fun.

General location: The Paliza Canyon loop is within the Santa Fe National Forest, approximately 8.5 miles from the intersection of NM 4 and NM 290.
Elevation change: From where this ride begins at Paliza Campground the elevation is 7,200' above sea level. You will climb up Paliza Canyon to reach a high point of 8,660'. Total elevation gain is 1,460'.
Season: This ride will probably be dry and ready to ride by early spring.
Services: Groceries, gas, and accommodations are available in Jemez Springs and at La Cueva. Bike services are available in Albuquerque, Santa Fe, or Los Alamos.
Hazards: Rocky sections and ditches can sneak up on you here. Portions of Forest Service Road 271 receive heavy traffic; a bright piece of clothing or helmet cover will alert motorists to your presence.
Rescue index: Your best bet for finding help quickly in an emergency is back in the settlement of Ponderosa. You can find a Forest Service ranger in Jemez Springs.
Land status: Santa Fe National Forest, Jemez Ranger District.
Maps: The Santa Fe National Forest map is adequate for finding this ride. You can also use the USGS 7.5-minute quads for Ponderosa and Bear Springs Peak.
Finding the trail: Drive 40 miles north of Albuquerque to San Ysidro. From the intersection of NM 44 and NM 4, drive approximately 6.5 miles to the intersection of NM 4 and NM 290. Go right onto NM 290 and continue to the town of Ponderosa. After you pass through town, the main road turns to dirt and becomes FS 10. Drive up FS 10 until you reach Paliza Campground. Park here.

Sources of additional information: Santa Fe National Forest, Jemez Ranger District; address and phone are listed in the introduction to this section.

RIDE 50 *PALIZA CANYON LOOP*

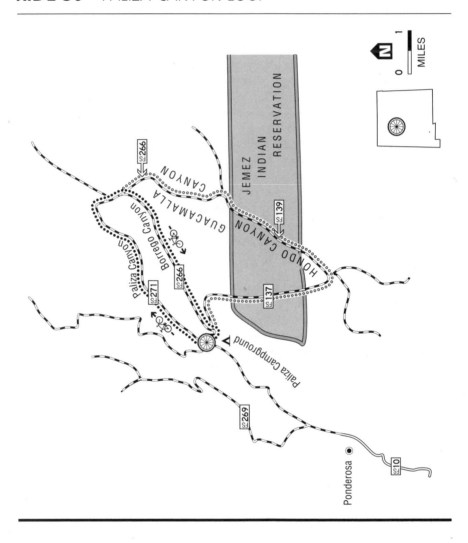

Notes on the trail: From Paliza Campground, head back out to FS 10, turn right, and continue for approximately half a mile. Turn right here on FS 271, and begin climbing up Paliza Canyon. Continue on FS 271 over several short descents and climbs to a sunny, open meadow about 4.5 miles from the start of this ride. The meadow will be on your right and is bisected by a double-track jeep road. Take this jeep trail across the meadow. It will begin climbing through a beautiful

The buff-colored volcanic tuff, or hardened ash, forms beautiful cliff bands throughout the Jemez Mountains.

grove of aspens. You will stay on this road for a quarter of a mile before bearing right when the trail forks. This road will keep climbing for another half a mile to FS 266. Go right on FS 266, which will climb for a short distance before heading down Borrego Canyon. You will then have a fun 5-plus-mile cruise down Borrego Canyon to your car at Paliza Campground.

There is a good option here for making this a longer, more adventurous ride. At the point at where you reach FS 266 you can go left instead of right, and head down Guacamalla Canyon. At 2.7 miles FS 139 comes in and joins FS 266 from the left. FS 266 continues on in a southeasterly direction, but you want to bear right onto what is now FS 139. FS 139 will take you south, down Hondo Canyon. Continue on FS 139 for another 3 miles before reaching FS 137. Go right on FS 137, doubling back up West Fork heading north. You will then climb up to meet FS 266 just above Paliza Campground where you began. This route adds about 6 miles to your ride and takes you through some gorgeous country. On part of this route you will be on the Jemez Indian Reservation; please be respectful.

RIDE 51 *CERRO PELADO LOOKOUT*

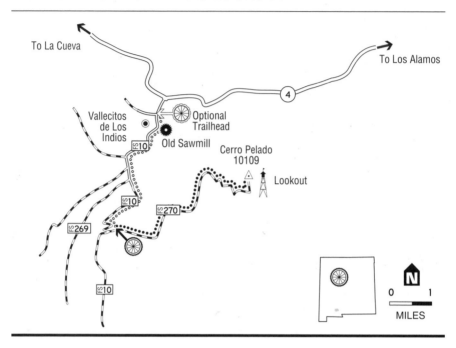

RIDE 51 *CERRO PELADO LOOKOUT*

The ride up to the lookout atop Cerro Pelado Peak will take you to an elevation of 10,109 feet above sea level and is 14 miles up-and-back. While only intermediate riding skills are necessary to negotiate these dirt roads, the extended climb at high altitude will make this ride strenuous for most. There are several very steep and rocky sections that will require some technical skill to get through. Allow three to four hours to complete this ride, more if you want to spend some time taking in the view from the top.

This is a really pretty ride up through mixed conifers and across grassy slopes. There are fantastic views to the north into Valle Grande, and to the south into the maze of canyons and ridges that once drained the snow-capped peaks of a 14,000-foot volcano. Farther to the south you can see the Sandias and in the distant northeast, the Sangre de Cristo Peaks.

General location: Cerro Pelado Peak is within the Santa Fe National Forest, just south of Vallecitos de Los Indios.

The road up to Cerra Pelado Lookout provides incredible views in all directions.

Elevation change: At the beginning of the ride, where Forest Service Road 270 leaves FS 10 and begins climbing, the elevation is approximately 8,000′ above sea level. From there it is a push up to the lookout at 10,109′. Total elevation gain is 2,100 feet.

Season: Because of the high altitudes you will probably have to wait until late spring before this route is dry and clear of snow.

Services: Groceries, gas, and accommodations are available in Jemez Springs and at La Cueva. Bike services are available in Albuquerque, Santa Fe, or Los Alamos.

Hazards: Don't get caught up here in one of those pop-and-crackle thunderstorms that rip through this part of the country summer through fall. You'll have a good view of the weather from here, and if it looks black and threatening, beat a hasty retreat. Notice the scars on some of the bigger trees up here . . . they're not the work of porcupines.

Rescue index: You won't see a lot of vehicle traffic on this road. To find help in an emergency head back to Vallecitos de Los Indios.

Land status: Santa Fe National Forest, Jemez Ranger District.

Maps: The Santa Fe National Forest map shows the route up to the peak with adequate detail. You can also use the USGS 7.5-minute quad for Redondo Peak.

Finding the trail: Drive 40 miles north of Albuquerque to San Ysidro. From the intersection of NM 44 and NM 4, drive north for approximately 27 miles on NM 4 to the intersection at the small settlement of La Cueva. From here, bear right on NM 4 heading east. Continue in this direction for approximately 8 miles to the town of Vallecitos de Los Indios. Drive through town and head south on FS 10 for 5.5 miles to the beginning of FS 270 (Cerro Pelado Road) on the left-hand side of the road. Park here off the road.

Sources of additional information: Santa Fe National Forest, Jemez Ranger District; address and phone are listed in the introduction to this section.

Notes on the trail: Once you are on FS 270 it's all uphill. You will encounter a fork about a mile into the ride on the right; keep left here. This is a straight up-and-back affair with no possibility of getting lost.

If you're hard-core you may want to start this ride from Vallecitos de Los Indios. This will add 11 miles to your total distance.

RIDE 52 *SAN ANTONIO CANYON*

The loop that takes you through San Antonion Canyon is 17 miles long and takes you over hard-packed sand and dirt roads that are rutted and rocky in sections. Intermediate riders in good physical condition will find this ride moderately difficult to easy. Allow four hours' riding time, more to enjoy the natural wonders of this place.

The scenery here is beautiful, very alpine, and quite open, more so than the rides to the south and east. The broad, grassy meadow below you is Valle San Antonio, with a clear sparkling trout stream of the same name winding through it. While riding the ridge, you'll have good views over to San Antonio and Redondo peaks.

This is a good place to spot wildlife, so keep your eyes and ears open. Take a

RIDE 52 *SAN ANTONIO CANYON*

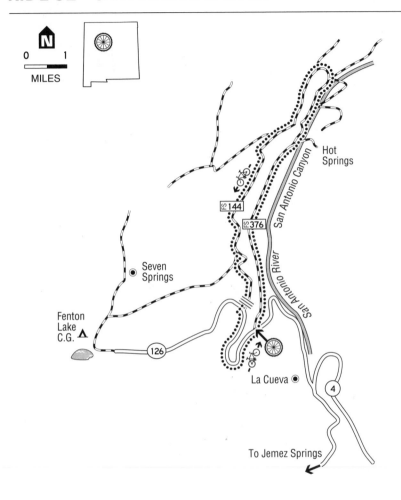

dip in the creek for a refresher in the summer or stop in at the San Antonio Hot Springs in the cooler months for some relaxation. This hot spring stays at a fairly constant temperature of 101 degrees Fahrenheit and is located approximately 2 miles to the south of the intersection of Forest Service Road 144 and 376, or 6 miles up from the beginning of FS 376. The hot springs are situated 250 feet above San Antonio Creek on the east wall of San Diego Canyon. They are on private property, so you will need to get permission to use them.

An abandoned cabin is nestled in peaceful surroundings in San Antonio Canyon.

General location: San Antonio Canyon is within Santa Fe National Forest, just northwest of the settlement of La Cueva, at the intersection of NM 4 and 126.

Elevation change: The ride up San Antonio Canyon starts at an elevation of 8,450' above sea level. This is rolling terrain with several short climbs, none gaining over 500'. The highest point reached is 8,600'. Total elevation gain is under 1,000'.

Season: This is a midspring through late fall ride. The aspens along this route make it a great fall ride.

Services: Groceries, gas, and accommodations are available in Jemez Springs and at La Cueva. Bike services are available in Albuquerque, Santa Fe, or Los Alamos.

Hazards: Vehicle traffic is light on these roads because they are so rough. Be prepared for several water crossings. Don't get overcooked in the hot springs—it will make it hard to stay on your bike on the way down.

Rescue index: The ranger station at La Cueva is the nearest and best option for finding help.

Land status: Santa Fe National Forest, Jemez Ranger District.

Maps: The Santa Fe National Forest map is really all you need for finding this route and for getting an idea of surrounding country. You can also use the USGS 7.5-minute quad for Seven Springs.

Finding the trail: From the intersection of NM 4 and NM 126 reached at La Cueva, you need to go left, up NM 126. From the junction at La Cueva it is just about 4 miles to where FS 376 takes off across a cattle guard on the right-hand side of the road. This is the beginning of your ride. Park here.

Sources of additional information: Santa Fe National Forest, Jemez Ranger District; address and phone are listed in the introduction to this section.

Notes on the trail: Begin this ride by climbing up a gentle hill on FS 376 for about a mile. You will descend into San Antonio Canyon, rolling along for 4 more miles. At mile 5 you will encounter a fork in the road. Keep going straight ahead up San Antonio Canyon. (The right fork takes you up to San Antonio Hot Springs.) In another 2 miles you will encounter a 3-pronged fork in the road; go left up a road that will climb steeply for less than a mile to where it meets FS 144. Go left onto FS 144 and ride this rolling road downhill for almost 7 miles to where it ends at the pavement of NM 126. Go left, downhill to where you left your car at the beginning of FS 376.

For variety, you can ride this loop in the opposite direction. There are many, many possibilities for creating other routes with all the roads in this area. A Forest Service map or topographical maps should be used if you plan to create your own routes.

RIDE 53 *SEVEN SPRINGS LOOP*

This ride is a fun 16-mile loop that gently climbs up one canyon, traverses a ridge line for several miles, and then drops down another canyon. Because of the 1,200-foot gain in elevation, beginning and intermediate riders in good physical condition will find this ride moderate to strenuous. This route follows hard-packed sandy dirt roads that are in good condition for the most part but can become rutted and washed out in sections. Allow three hours to complete this ride.

You will find wonderful, high-alpine scenery on this loop. Heading up the ridge on Forest Service Road 144 you'll have excellent views to San Antonio and Redondo peaks and down into San Antonio Canyon below. This loop allows you to do some easy cruising at a high altitude. Down Oat Canyon on the Rio Cebolla is the State Fish Hatchery, where you can take a tour of the ponds. It's interesting to see what goes into keeping fish on the end of everybody's line. Farther along on your return trip you will pass by the community of Seven Springs.

RIDE 53 *SEVEN SPRINGS LOOP*

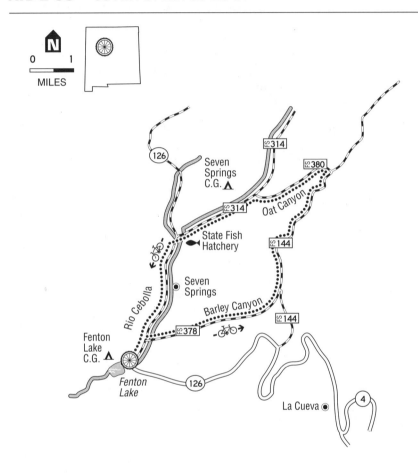

General location: This loop ride is located in the Santa Fe National Forest, just northwest of La Cueva at the intersection of NM 4 and 126.

Elevation change: Where this ride begins at the intersection of FS 378 and FS 126 the elevation is approximately 7,600' above sea level. At the top of Oat Canyon, the highest point on this ride, it's almost 8,800'. Total elevation gain is approximately 1,200'.

Season: Because elevations are not really high and the road surfaces are good, this route should be free of snow and rideable early to midspring through late fall.

Alpine forests of mixed pine, spruce, fir, and aspen can be found in the higher reaches of the Jemez Mountains.

Services: Groceries, gas, and accommodations are available in Jemez Springs and at La Cueva. Bike services are available in Albuquerque, Santa Fe, or Los Alamos.

Hazards: There is a lot of water on this ride—be prepared for several stream crossings. During spring runoff, the amount of water in streams and road ruts is increased.

You will encounter light to moderate four-wheel-drive vehicle traffic up here during certain times of year. Holler to let them know you are there if you need to get by. A bright piece of clothing will help alert both motorists and hunters to your presence.

Rescue index: Along this route you are not too far from help. Your best bet in an emergency is to go to the ranger station back in La Cueva, at the intersection of NM 4 and NM 126. You may also find help at the small summer community of Seven Springs.

Land status: Santa Fe National Forest, Jemez Ranger District.

Maps: The Santa Fe National Forest map shows this route with adequate detail. You can also use the USGS 7.5-minute quad for Seven Springs.

Finding the trail: From La Cueva, at the intersection of NM 4 and NM 126, go left up NM 126, heading west until you reach the campground at Fenton Lake. Park here.

Sources of additional information: Santa Fe National Forest, Jemez Ranger District; address and phone are listed in the introduction to this section.

Notes on the trail: From the Fenton Lake Campground, begin by riding north on FS 378. In approximately 2 miles you will come to a fork where FS 378 bears right, heading east over a bridge that crosses the Rio Cebolla. Take the right fork, cross the river, and continue on FS 378. Climb up Barley Canyon for approximately 3 miles to where the road intersects FS 144 atop a ridge. Go left onto FS 144. Here, you will be rolling along a ridge for another 3 miles to where you will see FS 380, a double-track jeep trail heading up a hill on your left. Go left onto FS 380, which will take you down Oat Canyon for 2 miles. At the bottom of Oat Canyon go through a gate and across a meadow. You will again cross the Rio Cebolla, coming to the intersection with FS 314. Go left onto FS 314, following the Rio Cebolla past the Seven Springs Campground. In another mile you will come to the State Fish Hatchery. Just after the Fish Hatchery cross the Rio Cebolla again and intersect FS 126. Take FS 126 to Fenton Lake where you left your car.

Once again there are many, many options for creating variations on this route or creating your own route entirely.

RIDE 54 *COCHITI CANYON*

This ride goes up Cochiti Canyon, from the Cañada Ranger Station all the way to the private property at the summer community of Tent Rocks and back down, a distance of approximately 15 miles round-trip. The road up the canyon is hard-packed sand and gravel dirt for the most part with sections that are filled with river-worn cobbles. Intermediate and beginning riders will find this route moderately difficult. Allow at least three hours to complete this ride.

Cochiti Canyon is one of the prettiest canyons I found in the Jemez. Beautifully sculpted volcanic tuff and sandstones form the canyon walls here. Pinyon and juniper quickly give way to ponderosas that grow straight and tall from the canyon bottom. You'll probably want to stop in at Dixon's Apple Orchard at the mouth of Cochiti Canyon for some fresh cider or a bushel of crisp apples to take home after your ride.

General location: Cochiti Canyon is located in the Santa Fe National Forest, about 10 miles northwest of Cochiti Pueblo and 15 miles southwest of Los Alamos.
Elevation change: Cañada Ranger Station is at about 6,100'. Tent Rock Ranch is at an elevation of 7,400'. Elevation gain is approximately 1,300'.
Season: You will be able to ride here early in the spring and late into the fall. If this route remains dry and free of snow it is great riding through the winter as well.
Services: All services are available in Los Alamos or Santa Fe.
Hazards: Expect to get your feet wet if you are riding through this canyon in the spring.
Rescue index: Help is close by on this ride. Head down to the Cañada Ranger Station at the mouth of the canyon, or, if you are near the top of this canyon, seek help at Tent Rock Ranch.
Land status: Santa Fe National Forest, Jemez Ranger District.
Maps: The Santa Fe National Forest map is good for finding this route and identifying others in this area. You can also use the USGS 7.5-minute topos for Bland and Cañada.
Finding the trail: From Santa Fe head south on Interstate 25 (also NM 85) 18 miles to the exit for Cochiti Pueblo. This is NM 16, which will take you past Cochiti Lake and past the turnoff for Cochiti Pueblo. Just past the turnoff to Cochiti Pueblo the road will turn into dirt, becoming Forest Service Road 268. In about 4.5 miles, bear right onto FS 89. FS 89 will take you to the Cañada Ranger Station at the mouth of Cochiti Canyon. Park here.

Sources of additional information: Santa Fe National Forest, Jemez Ranger District; address and phone are listed in the introduction to this section.

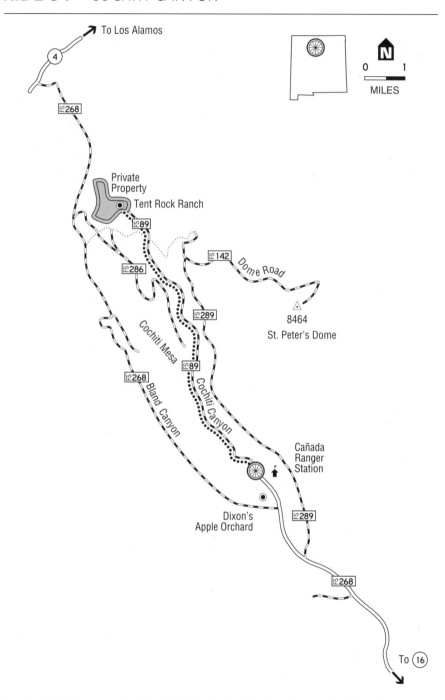

To Los Alamos

4

FS 268

Private
Property
Tent Rock Ranch

FS 89

FS 142

Dome Road

FS 286

FS 289

Cochiti Mesa

8464
St. Peter's Dome

FS 89

Cochiti Canyon

FS 268

Bland Canyon

Cañada
Ranger
Station

Dixon's
Apple Orchard

FS 289

FS 268

To 16

0   1
MILES

N

Cliffs of volcanic tuff in Cochiti Canyon.

Notes on the trail: From the Cañada Ranger Station ride up Cochiti Canyon on FS 89. You are in a canyon bottom here that does not allow you to become lost. You will reach the private property of Tent Rock Ranch at approximately 7.5 miles. Turn around and head back the way you came.

There are many options for creating your own routes in this area. Stop in and ask the ranger about making a loop over to Bland Canyon via the Carl Shipman Trail (FS Trail 113). This trail is steep and hairy with many switchbacks. Or ask about taking the Carl Shipman Trail east to where it hooks up with the Dome Road. These options require technical riding skill, physical stamina, and the spirit of adventure. This is a great area well worth exploring.

RIDE 55 *GUAJE MOUNTAIN CIRCUIT*

The ride around Guaje Mountain, on the eastern slope of the Jemez Mountains, is a 14-mile loop. Intermediate and advanced riders will find that several of the very steep, loose sections will make this ride moderately difficult to strenuous.

RIDE 55 *GUAJE MOUNTAIN CIRCUIT*

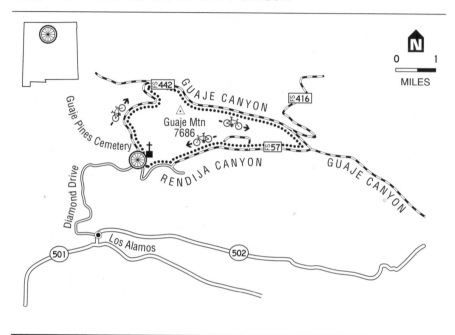

Besides sections of pavement and hard-packed dirt roads, you can expect to encounter a couple of rocky descents. Allow three hours to complete this ride.

This is some rough country, characterized by steeply eroded canyons with large boulders and formations of volcanic tuff. Ponderosa forests thrive at these elevations and in this sandy soil—you'll see them everywhere. This is a fun ride right out of Los Alamos.

General location: This loop is located within the Santa Fe National Forest, just to the north of Los Alamos.

Elevation change: Where you leave your car, just behind Guaje Pines Cemetery, the elevation is approximately 7,100' above sea level. From there you will climb, steeply at times, over several ridges to a high point of 7,759'. You will then drop down, in a short distance, to the bottom of Guaje Canyon at an elevation of 7,172'. Once in Guaje Canyon you will gradually descend, reaching your lowest elevation at the intersection of Forest Service Road 442 and FS 57, at 6,300'. From here you will begin a gradual climb up Rendija Canyon. An elevation of 7,100' is reached before dropping back into the foothills of Los Alamos. Elevation gain is approximately 1,460'.

Season: Spring, summer, and fall are best for this ride. If roads are dry and free

Ponderosa pines thrive in the sandy soils of Los Alamos.

of snow during the winter, and you've got some warm tights and gloves, go for it.

Services: All needs and services can be found in Los Alamos.

Hazards: Parts of this ride are steep and loose, so use caution. Guaje Canyon gets a moderate amount of vehicle use, so keep your eyes and ears open.

Rescue index: Help is close by in Los Alamos.

Land status: Santa Fe National Forest, Jemez Ranger District.

Maps: The Santa Fe National Forest map is fine for finding this route and others nearby. You can also use the USGS 7.5-minute quads for Guaje Mountain and Puye.

Finding the trail: In downtown Los Alamos find Diamond Drive, which bisects the west side of town in a north/south direction. Take Diamond Drive north and continue as the road bends around and heads east for just over 2 miles until you reach the Guaje Pines Cemetery Road. Go left here and follow the road around behind the cemetery to where the pavement ends and the dirt road begins. Park here.

Sources of additional information: Santa Fe National Forest, Jemez Ranger District; address and phone are listed in the introduction to this section.

Notes on the trail: Several roads take off in different directions from behind the cemetery. Take the road to your right, the one that heads downhill for a short distance before it begins to climb. The climb is steep at first, then the road levels, then climbs again to a second ridge before dropping into Guaje Canyon. Turn right onto Forest Service Road 442 when you reach the canyon bottom and head downhill for just under 5 miles until you reach the junction of FS 442 and FS 57. Turn right onto FS 57 and ride up Rendija Canyon. This is a mellow climb for the most part. Just past the Sportsman's Club shooting range the gravel road will become pavement. Continue to follow this road through the Baranca Drive intersection, where FS 57 becomes San Idelfonso Road. Where this road intersects Diamond Drive, turn right. Take Diamond Drive back to Guaje Pines Cemetery Road where you will turn right again to head back to your car.

There are several options for doing some exploring in this area. You may want to continue past the turnoff taking you back to Los Alamos and explore a little bit farther down Guaje Canyon. This road ends about 7 miles east of Los Alamos at NM 502.

Another option is possible beginning halfway in this ride. Continue on FS 442 and take FS 416 heading north, about a mile past the junction of FS 442 and FS 57. This road rolls steeply up and down, taking you into some extremely rugged country. All of the Forest Service roads that take you out of Los Alamos heading north, west, or east eventually dead-end at either the boundary of the Baca Grant to the west, or at the boundary with the Santa Clara Indian Reservation to the north and east. If you are interested in further exploring options for routes in this area, supplementary maps are a must. The Santa Fe National Forest map shows this area in good detail.

RIDE 56 *PAJARITO MOUNTAIN LOOP*

The ride up to Pajarito Mountain and the Pajarito Ski Area will be strenuous for intermediate and advanced riders who are in excellent physical condition. On this 15-mile loop ride you will gain 2,500 feet on dirt roads that are very steep, rocky, and loose in sections. Other parts of the trail cover roads that are hard-packed dirt and pavement. Allow three to four hours to complete this loop.

You will be riding west toward the ridges of the Sierra de Los Valles here, the mountains that form the eastern boundary of the Valle Grande. Views to the east into the Valle Grande and south toward Los Alamos and Bandelier National Monument are fabulous. The Sandia and Sangre de Cristo mountains are also visible from here.

General location: Parajito Mountain and Ski Area are located just west of the town of Los Alamos within the Santa Fe National Forest.
Elevation change: At the beginning of Pipeline Road the elevation is approxi-

RIDE 56 · *PAJARITO MOUNTAIN LOOP*

mately 7,300′ above sea level. From here you will head up the mountain, reaching a high point on this ride of 9,800′. You will then drop a few hundred feet to where you'll pick up Forest Service Trail 282. This trail will follow a ridge line, reaching a high of 9,600′ before dropping down to 9,200′ where it joins the Camp May Trail Road at the base of the Parajito Ski Area. You will then ride down this road back to Los Alamos at an elevation of 7,100′. Total elevation gain is 2,500′.

Season: Because of the high elevations reached along this route it is not clear of snow before mid- to late spring. Snow will return to these elevations sometime in November.

Services: All services are available in Los Alamos.

Hazards: This ride is at high elevations and may be too much for someone unaccustomed to exertion at altitude or in less than peak physical condition. Certain stretches of this ride are steep and loose, requiring a good amount of technical skill. Make sure that helmet has a snug fit.

Also, don't get caught up here in one of those raging summer thunder-and-lightning storms—they can really put a damper on your outing.

Rescue index: Your only real option for finding help in an emergency is to flag down a jeep or go back to Los Alamos.

The Pajarito Mountain Loop Trail traverses the eastern slope of the Jemez Mountains.

Land status: Santa Fe National Forest, Jemez Ranger District.

Maps: The Santa Fe National Forest map is okay for finding this trail. You can also use the USGS 7.5-minute quads for Guaje Mountain and Valle Toledo.

Finding the trail: From downtown Los Alamos find Diamond Drive. This road bisects the west side of town in a north/south direction. Take Diamond Drive north approximately 1 mile from the intersection with East Jemez Road, to North Road. Go left on North Road and, about a third of a mile later, be looking for the dirt road on the left at the point where the road makes a sharp turn to the right. Park at the beginning of this dirt road. This is Pipeline Road.

Sources of additional information: Santa Fe National Forest, Jemez Ranger District; address and phone are listed in the introduction to this section.

Notes on the trail: Begin climbing up Pipeline Road and continue to climb for approximately 7 miles until FS Trail 282 (really an old road) cuts across. (If you reach signs posting the private property boundary of the Baca Grant, you have gone too far.) Go left onto FS Trail 282, heading south up the ridge. Go through two gates before reaching Camp May at the boundary with the Pajarito Ski Area just below and to the north of Pajarito Mountain. The cut slopes of the Pajarito Ski Area lie just beyond. At Camp May, head downhill on the main road, FS 1. Ride FS 1 all the way down, a little over 5 miles, to where it eventually comes out on West Road in Los Alamos. Go left onto West Road and follow it out to Diamond Drive. Go left onto Diamond Drive and then left once more onto North Road, back to the beginning of Pipeline Road where you left your car.

There are a few options for descents once you reach the higher altitudes in this loop. Two of these options look like they might offer some really excellent single-track riding. Possibilities for route options include riding FS Trail 280. This trail leaves from FS Trail 282 on the the southern side of Pajarito Mountain, about another mile beyond Camp May, and joins FS 1 at the Los Alamos Reservoir. Or, from the parking area, go 7 miles up Pipeline Road to FS Trail 282 north, on the right-hand side of the road. On the maps it looks like this trail crosses over to the beginning of the Guaje Canyon drainage and follows it all the way, about 6.5 miles, to FS 442 (see Ride 55, Guaje Mountain Circuit). Have a look at some topographical maps and chat with the ranger before heading out this way.

Socorro Area Rides

The town of Socorro, in the lowlands of the Rio Grande River Valley at 4,167 feet above sea level, is considered to be one of the oldest towns in New Mexico. Socorro (population 9,000) and Magdalena (population 1,000), just 30 miles to the west, share a rich history that reaches back hundreds of years and across many cultures. Just 75 miles south of Albuquerque, this area offers some excellent riding opportunities as well as the chance to experience a place where the Old West and the new, high-tech West have come together.

Apache, Navajo, Gila, Piro Pueblo, and Comanche all hunted in this area, but the Piro Pueblo Indians were the most permanent inhabitants of the region. On June 4, 1598, Don Juan de Onate christened the adobe town of the Piro Indians he found here "Nuestra Senora del Socorro," or, "Our Lady of Help," because of the corn and provisions the Indians provided his weary expedition. Thirty years later two Franciscan priests began the construction of the Mission de San Miguel at Socorro and set to work at the task of converting the Piro Indians to Catholicism. The Piro were sedentary farmers, peace-loving people who easily accepted the new ways of worship and agriculture brought to them by the fair-skinned fathers. During the Pueblo Revolt of 1680 all 600 of the Piro abandoned their pueblo and joined the stream of refugees fleeing the violence to the north. They, along with many other Indian converts, left with the Spanish to seek safety behind the fortress walls at El Paso. There, the Piro people melted into the thousands of Indians and immigrants from all over Mexico and the west, never to return to their ancestral home.

The burned and looted remnants of the Piro pueblo and San Miguel mission remained undisturbed for over 100 years until 1816 when a land grant from the Spanish Crown ceded the land to 21 families. These families rebuilt the mission and began to farm the fertile lowland river soils. The Apache Indians who continued to range and hunt through this area did not make life easy for these Spanish settlers. With the iron horse, however, there came more settlers, soldiers, and guns, forcing the Apache to retreat farther into the mountains and south, into Mexico.

Silver was discovered in the mountains behind Magdalena in 1863, but was not mined until the 1880s. Later, enormous deposits of lead and silver were discovered, and when the boom hit, the town of Kelly sprang up around it. Most of the ore produced from the Magdalena mining district came from the mines at Kelly, three miles south of the town of Magdalena in a canyon of the Magdalena Mountains. Between 1880 and 1902, the Magdalena district was the richest ore-producing region in the country, yielding $7 to $9 million worth of lead-silver ore in that 12-year period. Kelly was once a thriving community of some 3,000 people, complete with a school, grocery, bank, and church. A few walls and cement foundations, the old bullet-ridden bank safe, and scattered and broken dishes are all that is left of Kelly today. Among the ruins, however, stands the beautifully restored, tiny white church that once served the town. The ruins of the mine works at Kelly are extensive and quite interesting. There is also good mineral-hunting in the mine's tailings. The old structures and mine dumps sit on private property today, off-limits to the public.

Until the railroad branched from Socorro and headed south through Texas, Magdalena was the "end of the line" for the infamous cattle drives that brought beef to market. It was to Magdalena that ranchers drove their longhorns, thousands of them, prodding them along for weeks and sometimes months across the grasslands of the southern plains, to the stockyards at Magdalena. Here, cattle, as well as timber, minerals, and flour, were loaded onto boxcars and sent to the East and West coasts. Socorro was a major shipping center in the late nineteenth century, sending natural resources produced in the West away to meet the demands of a rapidly growing country. Socorro long held the reputation as one of the West's roughest frontier towns, where hard-bitten miners, cattlemen, and anyone looking to make a buck eventually passed through.

Concealed beneath lava flows and the remnants of volcanos that form the mountains to the west of Socorro are the Rio Grand Rift and many other faults. The rich ore deposits of the region were created by intrusions of molten rock along these faults into limestone bedrock. The perfect chemical environment for the formation of minerals carried by metal-bearing fluids was thus created. These super-rich deposits of ore made Socorro the mining capital of the West for several decades. In 1889 the main smelter in Socorro was producing 300 bars of silver a day from ore that was shipped from Arizona, Colorado, and Mexico. The New Mexico School of Mines, established here in 1882, is known today as the New Mexico Institute of Mining and Technology. The New Mexico Bureau of Mines and Mineral Resources is also headquartered here. Excellent rock and mineral displays, as well as historical background on the area, can be found at the Mineral Museum in the Workman Center on the campus of the Institute.

The land surrounding Socorro is open desert grasslands, with riparian woodlands along the Rio Grande. Clump grasses, chamiso, yuccas, agave, cholla, and prickly pear cactus dominate the landscape around town. Cottonwoods reach down with long roots to tap the water found in drainages, springs, and along the river; their leafy heads signal the presence of water in this arid land. Up to about 7,000 feet, the lower slopes of the mountains around Socorro are wooded by pinyon and juniper; these give way to ponderosa pine in the Transition zone, then to aspens and mixed conifers in the higher elevations of the Magdalena Mountains. You may spot antelope grazing along the foothills of these mountains or a coyote darting through the brush. In the higher reaches, you might get lucky and spot a cougar, black bear, or maybe even a bobcat. The cottonwoods and willows that thrive along the river here draw a wide variety of mammals and birds, including white-tailed deer, red and gray fox, eagles, cranes, songbirds, and an incredible assortment of waterfowl.

BOSQUE DEL APACHE NATIONAL WILDLIFE REFUGE

The Bosque del Apache National Wildlife Refuge, 18 miles south of Socorro, was created in 1936 to protect the valuable Rio Grande River habitat. The river woodland habitat of the Rio Grande has been greatly changed by human occupation over the centuries, and the portions of it that survive intact today are mainly found in refuges and preserves. All kinds of creatures and migrating birds make their home here. A special resident of the refuge is the sandhill crane. Thousands of them come here to winter from November through March. Even more treasured is the very rare and endangered whooping crane. If you are lucky you may spot the snowy white, red-capped whooping crane; their numbers are now so diminished that wildlife officials have developed a scheme to save them, taking eggs from their nests and slipping them into the nests of their cousins, the sandhill cranes. Born into the care of sandhill cranes, whoopers then follow their adopted parents' migratory patterns to this refuge, instead of heading for the Gulf of Mexico to winter, where their remaining relatives are vulnerable to oil spills and hurricanes, disasters that could wipe them out entirely. Water canals course throughout the preserve and fields are seeded to help the cranes and other wildlife survive. The unique natural beauty and abundant wildlife of this refuge led me to include a ride here which, while it is not technical or even mountainous, is extremely rewarding. The refuge is open from half an hour before sunrise to half an hour after sunset. The Visitor Center has many informative displays, videos, and books and is open Monday through Friday 7:30 A.M. to 4:00 P.M. daily.

Here is a list of places to contact to help you plan your trip to Socorro and the surrounding area:

Socorro County Chamber of Commerce
103 Francisco de Avodo Street
P.O. Box 743
Socorro, New Mexico 87801
(505) 835-0424

Cibola National Forest
Supervisor's Office
2113 Osuna Road NE, Suite A
Albuquerque, New Mexico 87113-1001
(505) 761-4650

Cibola National Forest
Magdalena Ranger District
Box 45
Magdalena, New Mexico 87825
(505) 854-2281

Desert Cycles
105 Plaza
Socorro, New Mexico 87801
(505) 835-4085

RIDE 57 *GHOST TOWN OF KELLY*

This ride is a short junket up to what remains of the formerly bustling little town of Kelly. The six miles to Kelly and back is a fascinating tour of the past that riders of all abilities will enjoy. In just under three miles you will gain 845 feet on a dirt road surface that is routinely graded. Starting from the ranger station in Magdalena this route will take about an hour round-trip, not including time spent poking about the ruins at Kelly.

The little white church that has been restored in recent years, the cement and stone walls of the former bank, complete with safe, and the head frame to the main mine shaft are all that remain of the once thriving town of Kelly. The setting of this old church and the tower frame of the old mine building are quite pictur-esque; bring your camera along. The ruins of mine buildings and their contents, scattered all through the hills behind the mine, are fun to explore. The tailings dumps from the mine can yield some fine mineral specimens, including pyrite, azurite, turquoise, and Smithsonite, a rare zinc carbonite found in this area. The dumps and main mine building are on private property, so get permission to hunt around here; inquire through the Forest Service office in Magdalena.

General location: The ruins of the town of Kelly are 3 miles south of Magdalena in the Magdalena District of the Cibola National Forest.
Elevation change: Where this ride begins in the town of Magdalena the eleva-tion is approximately 6,600' above sea level. From here you will ride up to the ghost town of Kelly at an elevation of 7,445'. Elevation gain is 845'.
Season: This route will remain dry and free of snow and mud during much of the year.
Services: Accommodations, food, and gas are available in Magdalena. Bike ser-vices are available in Socorro.
Hazards: Always be extremely careful when walking and exploring around old mines. Open mine shafts are often unmarked and are very dangerous. Poisonous gases can build up in these old shafts and quickly overcome the unsuspect-ing. Abandoned mine shafts and building structures should never be entered or climbed on as most are in various stages of decay and could easily collapse.
Rescue index: You are not far from help on this ride. In case of an emergency seek aid just 3 miles back down the road at the ranger station in Magdalena.
Land status: Cibola National Forest, Magdalena Ranger District.

RIDE 57   *GHOST TOWN OF KELLY*

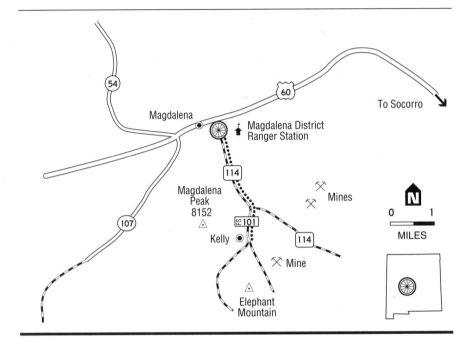

Maps: The Cibola National Forest map for the Magdalena Ranger District does not show a lot of detail for this short ride. Use the USGS 7.5-minute quad for Magdalena.

Finding the trail: In the town of Magdalena you will need to find the intersection of US 60 and County Road 114, the only paved intersection in town. On the southeast corner you will find the Magdalena Ranger District Station; stop in and say hi and see what interesting information they might have to offer. Park here.

Sources of additional information: Cibola National Forest, Magdalena Ranger District; address and phone are listed in the introduction to this section.

Notes on the trail: From the ranger station you will go left on CR 114, riding uphill and south out of town. At 2.5 miles from the intersection at the ranger station where you began this ride, you will encounter a fork in the road. CR 114 takes off to the left, on the graded road; Forest Service Road 101 begins on the right. Go right onto FS 101 and continue for half a mile to the small, white church and just beyond to what was once Kelly. Give yourself some time to poke around up here and then head back to town.

This is just a quickie but there are quite a few roads in this area, many of them

A little white church among the rabbit brush and cholla cactus is all that remains of the once thriving town of Kelly.

quite steep, that offer good opportunities for exploring. A Forest Service map or supplementary topo maps are recommended for exploring this wild and empty country criss-crossed by old mining roads.

One good option for exploring is to bear left at the fork of CR 114 and FS 101 and continue for approximately 1.5 miles to where it ends in a maze of old mining roads in Chihuahua and Mistletoe gullies.

RIDE 58 *HOP CANYON*

The ride up Hop Canyon is a 14-mile up-and-back affair that intermediate riders in good physical condition will find moderately difficult to strenuous. This route follows unmaintained dirt roads that are washed out and loose in sections. Other portions of this ride are very steep and may need to be portaged. Allow two to three hours' riding time.

RIDE 58 *HOP CANYON*

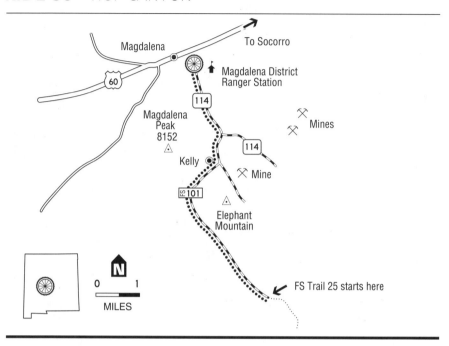

Pinyon and juniper dominate in these ashy gray volcanic foothills. Clumps of chamiso, rabbit brush, and the clownish cholla cactus fill in between. This is some really lovely, empty country. Don't miss the little white church and the rest of the ruins that were once the town of Kelly.

General location: Hop Canyon is located just 3 miles south of Magdalena in the Cibola National Forest.

Elevation change: From Magdalena, at an elevation 6,600′ above sea level, you will ride to the end of the road in Hop Canyon, where the elevation is approximately 8,000′. Elevation gain is 1,400′.

Season: Spring through fall will be the best time for riding in this area. You may find this route dry and free of snow in winter as well.

Services: Accommodations, food, and gas are available in Magdalena. Bike services are available in Socorro.

Hazards: Stay off and well away from any mine openings and old structures in this area; they are unstable and unsafe to be around. If you want to spend time exploring the mine dumps or buildings at Kelly, you will have to secure permission as they are on private property. Inquire at the ranger station before you go.

Ruins of the mine works at Kelly.

Parts of this ride are very steep and require exceptional strength and skill. Don't be discouraged; you can walk your bike around tough spots.

Rescue index: In an emergency, seek help at the ranger station in Magdalena.

Land status: Cibola National Forest, Magdalena Ranger District.

Maps: The Cibola National Forest map for the Magdalena Ranger District is fine for finding this route and others in the area. You can also use the USGS 7.5-minute quad for Magdalena.

Finding the trail: In the town of Magdalena find the intersection of US 60 and County Road 114, the only paved intersection in town. Find the Magdalena Ranger District Station on the southeast corner of this intersection. Park here.

Sources of additional information: Cibola National Forest, Magdalena Ranger District; address and phone are listed in the introduction to this section.

Notes on the trail: Begin by riding left out of the ranger station and heading south on CR 114. You will come to a fork in the road 2.5 miles from town; go right onto Forest Service Road 101 and continue up and around Elephant

Mountain, riding as far as the road will take you. Eventually FS 101 deteriorates and ends where FS Trail 25 begins. This part is a very steep, rugged single-track trail that heads up to South Baldy Peak and is better suited for hiking. Head on back, now.

RIDE 59 *SOUTH BALDY PEAK*

The ride up to South Baldy Peak is an 18-mile up-and-back ride that offers many route options for the adventurous. Riders who are at an intermediate or advanced skill level and who are in excellent physical condition will find this ride strenuous. Over nine miles you will gain 3,750 feet! The way up to the peak follows dirt roads that are sometimes graded. Some sections of this road will be washboarded; others will be rutted and loose. Allow at least five hours to complete this ride.

Gorgeous ponderosa pine forests give way to mixed conifers and aspen as desert scenery melds into wonderful alpine scenery. The stupendous views on the way up and near the top of South Baldy Peak stretch in all directions. The Rio Grande Valley sprawls to the east and you'll be looking across the plains of San Augustin to the west. Although this ride is arduous, it is definitely worth the push.

General location: South Baldy Peak is located due south of Magdalena and west of Socorro inside the Cibola National Forest.
Elevation change: At Water Canyon Campground where this ride begins the elevation is approximately 6,800′ above sea level. You will reach an elevation high near the top of South Baldy Peak of 10,551′. Elevation gain is more than 3,750′.
Season: Mid- to late spring through fall is the best time to do this ride. South Baldy Peak, at an elevation of 10,783′ above sea level, receives substantial amounts of snow in the winter months, so early spring riding will be extremely muddy and wet.
Services: Accommodations, food, and gas are available in Magdalena. Bike services are available in Socorro.
Hazards: Be informed about dominant weather patterns before you head up this way. Summer thunderstorms can pop up in an hour around here and they pack a lot of electricity. Get away from exposed ridges and peaks should it start looking dark and threatening. Also, temperatures can drop in a hurry. Be prepared and play it safe.

This is a tremendous amount of elevation gain for a single day's ride, so be sure you are in excellent physical condition before you attempt it. Also, be sure to bring plenty of fluids and good, high-energy snacks—you're going to need them.

RIDE 59 *SOUTH BALDY PEAK*

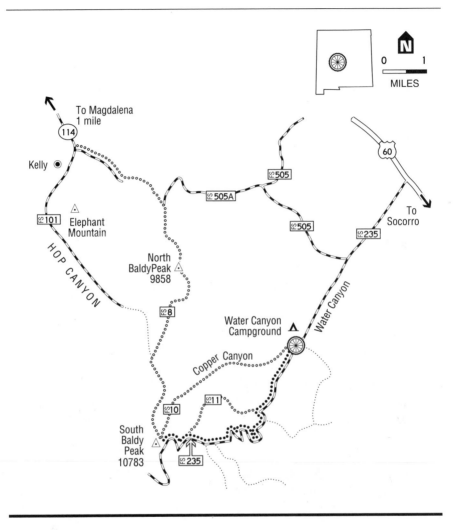

Rescue index: Good planning and preparation is the best way to avoid an emergency. You are not close to help here. You will need to backtrack off the mountain, get to your car, and head to either Magdalena or Socorro to find help.

Land status: Cibola National Forest, Magdalena Ranger District.

Maps: The Cibola National Forest map for the Magdalena Ranger District is fine for finding this route and possible route options. You can also use the USGS 7.5-minute quad for Magdalena and South Baldy Peak.

Water Canyon Campground remains in the sunlight while South Baldy Peak is swallowed by clouds.

Finding the trail: From Socorro drive west on US 60 for approximately 15 miles to Forest Service Road 235. FS 235 takes off at a right angle toward the mountains from the left-hand side of the road. Drive approximately 4.5 miles to Water Canyon Campground. Park here.

Sources of additional information: Cibola National Forest, Magdalena Ranger District; address and phone are listed in the introduction to this section.

Notes on the trail: Ride up FS 235, climbing for the next 9 miles until you reach the peak. The road continues past the summit of South Baldy Peak for another 1.5 miles to a lower summit to the southwest.

There are many excellent options for riding single-track descents off the top of South Baldy Peak. Most of these will require a drop-off, pick-up, or shuttle, as well as a good amount of technical skill and adventurousness. Supplementary maps are a must if you are interested in trailblazing off this mountain.

The best option is to take FS Trail 10, which leaves from the north side of South Baldy Peak. This trail will take you down an excellent single-track that follows Copper Canyon. Eventually this trail hooks up with FS 406, which will take you right into the Water Canyon Campground.

Another good option is to take FS Trail 11, which leaves from the left-hand side of FS 235 (as you are riding down) just over a mile below South Baldy Peak. This single-track makes about a 3-mile loop, hooking back into FS 235 2.5 miles above Water Canyon Campground.

FS Trail 8 leaves from the north side of South Baldy Peak and takes you down and across to North Baldy Peak (elevation 9,858') and then down the north side of this peak on FS 505A to CR 114 and into Magdalena. It is about 12 miles from the summit of South Baldy Peak down to the town of Magdalena.

RIDE 60 *BOSQUE DEL APACHE NATIONAL WILDLIFE REFUGE*

This ride is a 15-mile loop on well-maintained dirt roads inside the refuge. Riders of all abilities will enjoy cruising along this almost flat route that takes you through the beautiful river woodlands habitat of the Rio Grande River Valley. You can plan on taking at least two hours to complete this route around the refuge, with numerous stops for viewing bird and animal life.

This lowland river bottom is plowed and seeded specifically for the cranes and other wildlife protected here and so in many places takes on the appearance of a farmer's fields. Each field is separated by areas of willow and underbrush and usually bordered by tall, leafy cottonwoods that turn a fantastic gold in the fall months when the birdwatching is best. The sheer numbers of birds you will see at the refuge during peak season is astounding. At one time the refuge hosts as many as 10,000 cranes, 16,000 ducks, and 40,000 snow geese. Egrets, eagles,

RIDE 60 *BOSQUE DEL APACHE NATIONAL WILDLIFE REFUGE*

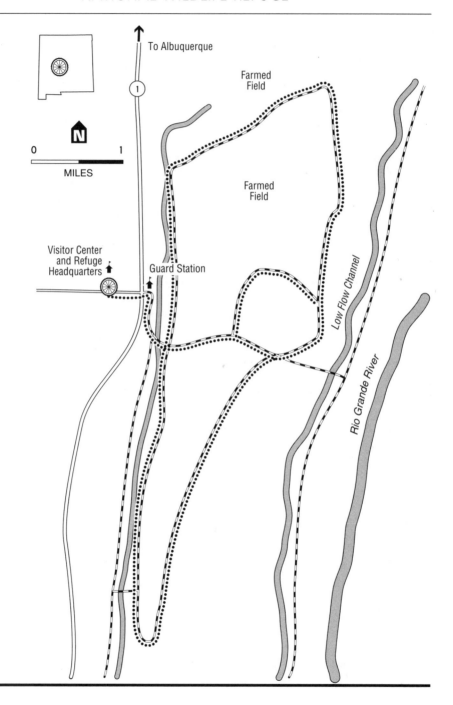

To Albuquerque

1

N

0 — 1
MILES

Farmed Field

Farmed Field

Visitor Center and Refuge Headquarters

Guard Station

Low Flow Channel

Rio Grande River

pheasants, and a variety of song birds pass through here as well. You may see a healthy stag bound across the road, or a red fox dashing into the brush. Riding in the company of so many wild creatures is an experience you won't want to miss.

General location: The Bosque del Apache National Wildlife Refuge is located approximately 18 miles south of Socorro and 5 miles east of Interstate 25.

Elevation change: Elevation at the refuge, right on the Rio Grande River, is 4,500'. There is little or no elevation change in the distance you will be riding.

Season: The refuge is open year-round. Wildlife is most active and most abundant in the spring and fall. These roads are rideable almost anytime, though they may be muddy after rain or snow showers.

Services: All services are available in Socorro.

Hazards: This loop is traveled by most people visiting the refuge. They will be in cars looking at the wildlife, not the road, so keep an eye out for them.

Riding slowly and keeping voices down helps keep disturbance to wildlife at a minimum.

Rescue index: If you need help, ride out to the refuge entrance, where you'll find a gatekeeper, or ride back to the Visitor Center.

Land status: U.S. Fish and Wildlife Service National Refuge, Department of the Interior.

Maps: Maps that show the various routes through the refuge can be obtained at the Visitor Center or at the entrance to the refuge.

Finding the trail: From Socorro head 18 miles south on Interstate 25 to the town of San Antonio and US 380. Get off at this exit heading east and follow the signs for the Bosque del Apache National Wildlife Refuge.

Sources of additional information: Bosque del Apache NWR, P.O. Box 1246, Socorro, New Mexico, 87801, (505) 835-1828.

Notes on the trail: Check in at the Visitor Center for a map of the refuge and an update on which refuge roads are open.

Alamogordo Area Rides

The town of Alamogordo (Spanish for "big cottonwood"), rests against the foot of the Sacramento Mountains in south-central New Mexico at an elevation of 4,335 feet above sea level. The town's economy has long been rooted in ranching and farming, supplemented in more recent times, like other New Mexican communities, by the space and nuclear age industries. Alamogordo enjoys mild seasons and the benefits of both desert and mountain climates. Summers can get hot in the Tularosa Basin, but you can always escape into the Sacramento Mountains just minutes away. With peaks that rise to 9,000 feet and above in this range, there are cooler temperatures and lots of gorgeous mountain scenery to enjoy while hiking and biking in the summer. There is plenty of snow during the winter months as well, enough to support two alpine ski resorts and keep nordic skiers, who ski the old logging roads, rail beds, and trails up here, happy.

The small town of Cloudcroft, located just 20 miles east of Alamogordo, was established by the Southwestern Railroad in the late 1880s. In order to push the tracks through the open deserts of southern New Mexico, the railroad had to get timber for ties from the forested mountains. The company built elaborate bridges to span steep canyons and blasted a level surface into the mountainside to bring down the timber of these higher elevations. Several of these beautifully constructed bridges still stand in the canyons of the Sacramento Mountains and can be seen from the road that takes you up to Cloudcroft from Alamogordo. The railroad eventually built a lodge at the present-day site of Cloudcroft as a vacation spot for its executive employees. Today Cloudcroft serves as the area's recreational hub and destination vacation spot for tourists from all over the Southwest. Cloudcroft is a charming little resort town that supports a healthy population of artisans and craftspeople as well as a small but avid population of outdoorspeople.

There is extensive evidence in the Alamogordo area of habitation by prehistoric Indians that lived in this region as long as 10,000 years ago. Caves in the foothills of the Sacramento Mountains have yielded artifacts that trace the advances of ancient people through many stages of development, including the building of pit houses, primitive walled structures, and the more sophisticated multi-roomed stone pueblos. When settlers first arrived at the site that was to become Alamogordo, they found two abandoned pueblo structures. What remains of these structures now lies buried beneath the pavement of Alamogordo's streets. About the time the pueblo builders began to disappear, Apache Indians began to move through this area, hunting and gathering. While the Apache ranged widely across the Southwestern states and Mexico, one particular band, the Mescalaro Apache, settled in the Sacramento Mountains and called them home. The Mescalaro Apaches' fierce determination to remain on the land they claimed as their homeland eventually rewarded them with a reservation that stretches across the spine of the Sacramento Mountains and reaches from Cloud-croft to the town of Ruidoso in the north.

Alamogordo sits at the edge of a broad depression known as the Tularosa Basin. This basin, or valley, was created by rift faults associated with the rifting Rio Grande Valley. The mountains of the Sacramento, San Andreas, Oscura and Organ ranges have then risen as fault blocks to enclose this valley. Sediments eroding from the rocks of the San Andreas Mountains to the west deposit in the dry lake beds of Lake Lucero and Lake Otero in the bottom of the Tularosa Basin. Because this valley is so low it has no outlet and no drainage for the sediments brought down with rainwater and snowmelt that collects in these low-lying depressions. When the water evaporates, gypsum crystals begin to grow in the lake beds. These crystals are then broken down by the desert weather into tiny white sand grains that are picked up and blown into dunes. The beautiful snow-white sand of these gypsum dunes covers some 300 square miles and is the centerpiece of White Sands National Monument. Any trip to this part of the country would be incomplete without a visit to this fantastic natural wonder.

The distance between Alamogordo and Cloudcroft encompasses five life zones, with views to a sixth. The Lower Sonoran desert country around town supports agave, yucca, creosote, mesquite, ocotillo, and many varieties of cactus. The Upper Sonoran life zone is accented by the rounded shapes of pinyon and juniper trees and, toward its upper limits, by ponderosa pines. The Transition zone is dominated almost exclusively by ponderosa, but eventually gives way to the firs, spruce, and pine of the higher, wetter reaches of the Canadian zone. Picturesque Sierra Blanca (12,003 feet) to the north falls well inside the Hudsonian and even into the Alpine zone. All the critters found in other parts of New Mexico at these elevations can be found here. In some of the higher, emptier places in the Sacramento Mountains you may be lucky enough to spot a black bear, cougar, or bobcat.

This is high, mountainous country where the weather can change rapidly. Even a midsummer storm can drop temperatures substantially in a short period of time. Rain, hail, and lightning usually accompany these storms, which occur most frequently during the monsoon season, mid- to late summer through September. Cloud buildups occur on a daily basis during this time of year, letting loose with loud claps of thunder and rain by early afternoon. It is a good idea to plan your ride for early in the day if thunderstorms are in the forecast. Stay off high and exposed areas such as ridges and peaks when lightning is present. Check in with a forest ranger in the area where you will be riding and/or camping for weather forecasts and hunting season schedules and areas. Here are a few numbers and addresses you will need to plan your trip to this area:

Alamogordo Chamber of Commerce
1310 White Sands Boulevard
Alamogordo, New Mexico 88310
(505) 437-6120

Lincoln National Forest
Supervisor's Office
Federal Building
11th and New York
Alamogordo, New Mexico 88310
(505) 437-6030

Lincoln National Forest
Cloudcroft Ranger District
P.O. Box 288
Cloudcroft, New Mexico 88317
(505) 682-2551

Outdoor Adventures
1516 Tenth Street
Alamogordo, New Mexico 88310
(505) 434-1920

RIDE 61 *PUMPHOUSE CANYON*

This is a quick, seven-mile loop that is just outside Cloudcroft and can be ridden from town. Intermediate and beginning riders will find this loop only moderately difficult. Although you reach an elevation of 9,000 feet, the route is short enough to require only a moderate fitness level. This route includes hard-packed dirt roads, rough, four-wheel-drive jeep roads, a section of single-track, and a section of paved road. Allow one to two hours to complete this ride.

This ride is perfect for a shorter outing and serves as a good introduction to the beautiful, rolling, wooded mountains of the Sacramento Range. While cruising through the forests and canyons of these mountains it is easy to forget that the arid, barren expanse of the desert is less than an hour away!

General location: This loop ride is less than a mile outside Cloudcroft, to the southeast, in the Lincoln National Forest.
Elevation change: At the beginning of Pumphouse Canyon where this ride starts, the elevation is 8,250′ above sea level. On this loop route you will reach a high elevation, where the trail hits NM 24, of 9,000′. Total elevation gain, 750′.
Season: Due to the elevations reached on this ride it will not be dry and free of snow until midspring. The snow usually returns to these mountains sometime in November.
Services: All services are available in Alamogordo. Basic services are available in Cloudcroft.
Hazards: Quickly changing weather accompanied by a fast drop in temperature

RIDE 61 *PUMPHOUSE CANYON*

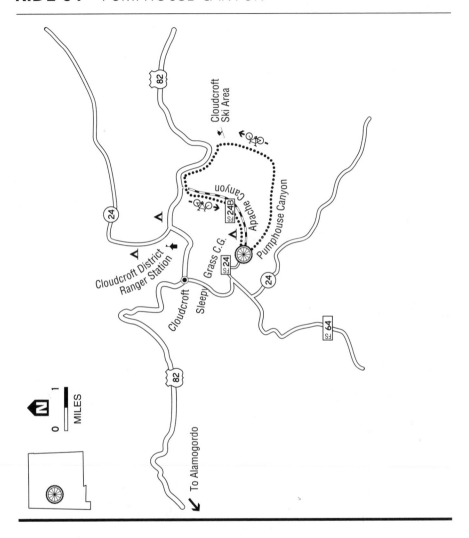

is common in these desert mountains. Be aware of local forecasts, especially in the summer months. Also, check with a forest ranger for hunting season schedules in this very popular hunting area.

Rescue index: You are never far from help on this ride. The Cloudcroft District Ranger Station is just a couple of miles away back in the town of Cloudcroft.

Land status: Lincoln National Forest, Cloudcroft Ranger District.

Maps: The Lincoln National Forest map does not show the trail through Pumphouse Canyon, but it is good for finding most trails in this area. Use the USGS 15-minute quad for Cloudcroft.

Finding the trail: This loop can be ridden right from the town of Cloudcroft or from Sleepy Grass Campground. To reach Sleepy Grass Campground, head south out of Cloudcroft on NM 24. Drive for approximately 1.3 miles to Forest Service Road 24, go left on FS 24, driving about a third of a mile to the campground. Park here.

Sources of additional information: Lincoln National Forest, Cloudcroft Ranger District; address and phone are listed in the introduction to this section.

Notes on the trail: From Sleepy Grass Campground ride back out toward NM 24. Ride about 200 yards back the way you came in, looking for a trail leaving on the left side of the road. This is the trail that will take you up Pumphouse Canyon. You will climb gradually up this trail for approximately 2.5 miles to where it comes out at the Cloudcroft Ski Area. Ride out to US 82 and go left, riding for approximately 1.5 miles to FS 24B, which leaves on the left-hand side of the road and heads down Apache Canyon. This road eventually ends up at Sleepy Grass Campground, where you began this ride.

You may also want to try riding this loop in the other direction.

RIDE 62 *SILVER SPRINGS LOOP*

This is another great loop route that can be ridden right from the town of Cloudcroft. This loop is 12 miles long, covering 6.5 miles of pavement and 5.5 miles of hard-packed dirt road through Silver Springs and La Luz canyons. An excellent one-mile spur that takes you up to Wofford Lookout can be added to this ride as an option. Beginning and intermediate riders in good condition will find this ride easy to moderate. Allow at least two hours to complete this ride.

This route provides a good tour of the rolling mountains and winding canyons around Cloudcroft. Beautiful alpine forests of mixed conifers and aspen glades that turn a brilliant yellow in fall cloak these desert mountains. Breathe deep and enjoy the sweet smells of the pines as their needles warm in the sun. Check out the views from Wofford Lookout.

General location: The Silver Springs Canyon Loop takes you through two canyons just north of Cloudcroft in the Lincoln National Forest.
Elevation change: Where this ride begins in the town of Cloudcroft the elevation is approximately 8,640' above sea level. From there you will ride down to the beginning of Forest Service Road 162 at 7,787'. A high point is reached along this route of 8,750'. Total elevation gain is 963'.

RIDE 62   *SILVER SPRINGS LOOP*

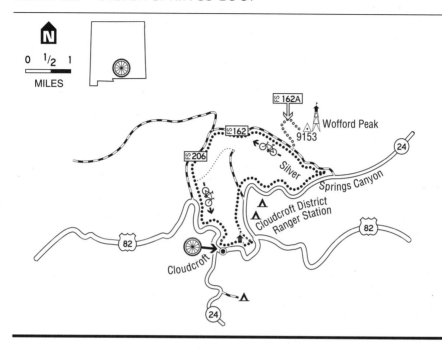

Season: Provided that the route is dry and free of snow, you can ride here mid- to late spring through late fall.

Services: Basic needs can be met in Cloudcroft. All services are available in Alamogordo.

Hazards: Vehicle traffic and hunters are your biggest hazards on this ride. Wear a bright piece of clothing to help alert motorists and hunters to your presence.

Rescue index: You are never far from help on this loop route because it takes you along busy sections of roadway and through the town of Cloudcroft. The district ranger station in Cloudcroft is a good place to seek help.

Land status: Lincoln National Forest, Cloudcroft Ranger District.

Maps: The Lincoln National Forest map is fine for finding this route. You can also use the USGS 15-minute quad for Cloudcroft.

Finding the trail: This loop can be ridden right from town. Drive to the ranger station, stop in and say hi, and see what the weather looks like and where the hunters are going to be before you go. Park here or somewhere in town.

Sources of additional information: Lincoln National Forest, Cloudcroft Ranger District; address and phone are listed in the introduction to this section.

You'll find an alpine environment and enjoy cool days riding high in the peaks of the Sacramento Mountains.

Notes on the trail: From Cloudcroft ride east and north out of town on NM 24, also listed as NM 244 on some maps. From the ranger station it is approximately 4.5 miles to where dirt road FS 162 takes off on the left-hand side of the road; turn here and head up Silver Springs Canyon. You will come to FS 162A leaving to your right in 1.5 miles. This is the spur road that will take you up to Wofford Lookout. Go up, have a look, come back and continue on FS 162A. Another 2.3 miles beyond the turnoff to Wofford Lookout you will come to a fork in the road.

Bear left onto FS 206, which will take you downhill to US 82. You will then turn left and ride back up US 82 to the town of Cloudcroft to where you left your car.

RIDE 63 *LA LUZ CANYON*

The route that takes you down La Luz Canyon is a 15-mile loop that will be moderate to strenuous for beginning and intermediate riders in good to excellent physical condition. This ride includes five miles of pavement, but consists mostly of hard-packed dirt roads in good condition, with sections that are washboarded and periodically washed out due to heavy rain or runoff. Allow three hours to complete this loop.

This ride is a great tour of some of the Sacramento Mountains' prettiest country. At the highest point in this ride you will be cruising through conifer forests common to an alpine environment. These deep piney forests intermittently reveal grassy gullies and meadows crossed by streams and laced with wildflowers.

General location: La Luz Canyon is located northeast of Alamogordo and north of US 82 between the towns of High Rolls and Cloudcroft in the Lincoln National Forest.

Elevation change: The town of High Rolls, where this ride begins, is 6,691' above sea level. You will then ride up to where Forest Service Road 206 leaves the pavement at an elevation of 8,000'. At the intersection of FS 206 and FS 162 you will reach an elevation of 8,750'. From here you will follow La Luz Canyon downhill back to High Rolls. Elevation gain is approximately 2,060'.

Season: This route should be dry and free of snow by midspring, and rideable until snow returns again sometime in November.

Services: All services are available in Alamogordo. Basic services are available in Cloudcroft.

Hazards: Be aware of weather forecasts and hunting season schedules for this area; getting caught in a lightning storm or a hail of hunters' bullets can really put a damper on your ride. Be wary of vehicle traffic while riding US 82.

Rescue index: You can flag down help on US 82. Or, go back to High Rolls or to the Cloudcroft district ranger station.

Land status: Lincoln National Forest, Cloudcroft Ranger District.

Maps: The Lincoln National Forest map is fine for finding this route and others nearby. You can also use the USGS 15-minute quad for Alamogordo.

Finding the trail: From Alamogordo head north on US 54/70 to US 82 heading east. Go east on US 82 for 9 miles to the small town of High Rolls. Once you reach town, take the third left, directly across from the Mountain Park Road (FS 339). This left turn is the beginning of FS 162, where you'll be coming out at the end of your ride. Park here.

RIDE 63 *LA LUZ CANYON*

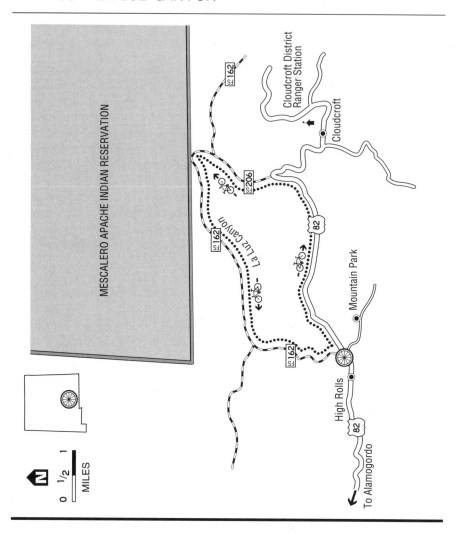

Sources of additional information: Lincoln National Forest, Cloudcroft Ranger District; address and phone are listed in the introduction to this section.

Notes on the trail: Begin riding by heading back out onto US 82 and taking a left. Ride approximately 5 miles on the pavement to where FS 206 leaves on the left-hand side of the road. FS 206 leaves off the elbow of the first major switchback of US 82 as it winds toward Cloudcroft. From here FS 206 follows the old railroad grade as it climbs. Ride FS 206 just over 2 miles to the intersection with FS 162, where you will go left. Six miles from this intersection you will encounter a fork in the road; go left again, continuing on FS 162, down to High Rolls and back to where you left your car.

You may want to continue up US 82 to Silver Springs to the beginning of FS 162 and start from there. A shuttle or drop-off would be a good option here as it would cut out miles of riding on busy US 82. This option adds quite a bit more climbing and almost 12 more miles of distance to this ride.

RIDE 64 *RIM TRAIL*

The portion of the Rim Trail that is featured on this ride makes a total round-trip approximately 19 miles long. This is a great single-track trail on hard-packed alpine soils, covering mostly rolling terrain on an old railroad bed. Roots, rocks, and water bars in the trail will require intermediate skill and the elevation of this ride will require a good amount of physical fitness and stamina. A quick spur on a paved road will take you up to Alamo Peak, the highest point along the ride. Allow four hours to complete this route.

The Rim Trail traverses the spine of the Sacramento Mountains, winding through miles of gorgeous spruce and pine forests. Views from this ridge are fantastic. To the west bright dunes of white sand can be seen in the Tularosa Basin. Behind the dunes are the San Andreas Mountains. The Rim Trail is a good opportunity to ride some moderately difficult, really fun single-track. This ride is worth trying out even if you only have a couple of hours: it is easy to lengthen or shorten it by using the many access points along the way.

General location: The Rim Trail begins 3 miles south of Cloudcroft and is within the Lincoln National Forest. Cloudcroft is about 20 miles east of Alamogordo.
Elevation change: At the point where the Rim Trail begins, at Slide Campground, your elevation is 8,839′ above sea level. The trail gently rolls along the old railroad grade, making only modest gains and losses in elevation as it traverses a ridge line. A high point of 9,500′ is reached at Alamo Peak. Total elevation gain is 661′.
Season: Because of elevation this trail is rideable mid- to late spring through fall. Fall foliage is gorgeous up here.
Services: Basic services are available in Cloudcroft. Bike needs can be taken care of in Alamogordo.
Hazards: Your biggest concerns up here are quickly changing weather and exposure in the event of an electrical storm.

This trail receives a fair amount of traffic from other trail users, including,

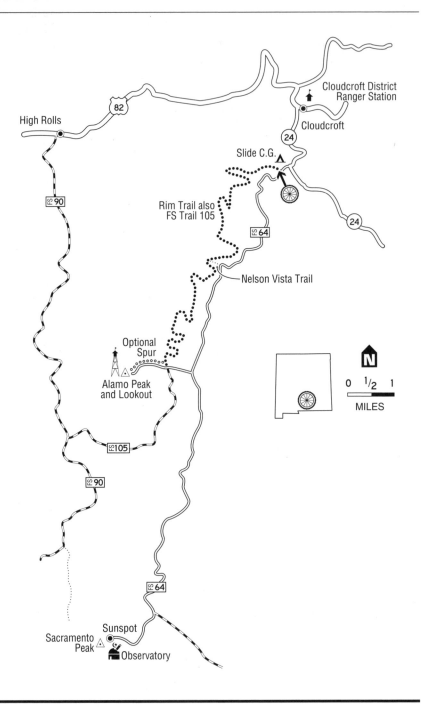

High Rolls

82

Cloudcroft District
Ranger Station

Cloudcroft

24

Slide C.G.

FS 90

Rim Trail also
FS Trail 105

FS 64

24

Nelson Vista Trail

Optional
Spur

Alamo Peak
and Lookout

N

0   1/2   1

MILES

FS 105

FS 90

FS 64

Sunspot

Sacramento
Peak

Observatory

A little trail-side maintenance before riders take off on the Rim Trail.

along certain sections, off-road motorcycle riders. Remember, all hikers, equestrians, and motorcycles have the right of way. Pull over, be courteous, and say hello.

Rescue index: The Rim Trail parallels the paved road out to the Sacramento Peak Solar Observatory and the small settlement of Sunspot. The paved road is never more than a mile to the east and there are many spur trails that will take you there. Your best bet for getting help in an emergency is back in the town of Cloudcroft, at the district ranger station.

Land status: Lincoln National Forest, Cloudcroft Ranger District.

Maps: The Lincoln National Forest map shows the Rim Trail, but not with a lot of detail. Use the USGS 15-minute quads for Cloudcroft and Alamogordo.

Finding the trail: From Alamogordo head north on US 54/70 to US 82 heading east. Head east on US 82 for approximately 15 miles to the town of Cloudcroft. Paved Forest Service Road 64 leaves from the right-hand side of the road just as you enter town. Continue on to the far end of town first and check in with the Cloudcroft Forest Ranger. Once on FS 64 proceed approximately 2 miles to the Slide Campground Area. Park here.

Sources of additional information: Lincoln National Forest, Cloudcroft Ranger District; address and phone are listed in the introduction to this section.

Notes on the trail: Find the trailhead for FS Trail 105, or the Rim Trail, at the Slide Campground Area. This trail is well marked and well worn—there is little or no possibility of getting lost. Approximately 4.5 miles from the trailhead you will encounter the Nelson Vista Trail joining from the left. Eight miles from where you began you will cross the dirt road FS 63. In another half mile you reach the Alamo Peak Road. Go right and ride for another mile up to the lookout. Go back the way you came or take the paved FS 64 back to Slide Campground.

Silver City Area Rides

The town of Silver City (population, 11,000) is a place rich in the history of the Southwest. Silver City lies at the southern edge of the 3.3-million-acre Gila National Forest and is the jump-off point to some of the emptiest and most beautiful wilderness New Mexico has to offer. At an elevation of 5,900 feet above sea level, Silver City and the surrounding mountains enjoy four mild seasons. Temperatures during the summer frequently reach 100 degrees, while winter brings enough snow to nearby mountains to keep cross-country skiers happy. The Victorian-style buildings and sidewalks of downtown Silver City, the old mines that dot the hillsides behind town, and the stories of Billy the Kid's younger days here all help to maintain a Wild-West feeling that the townspeople love to share with their visitors. Today's inhabitants of Silver City are a mix of fiercely independent cattlemen and miners and more liberally minded, environmentally concerned newcomers seeking a simple life far from the city. Many of this latter group found themselves here by way of Western New Mexico University. Often these two groups are at odds, fighting over issues related to the land they love. Once you've spent several days riding around this country, its not hard to understand why passions run high among Silver City's inhabitants.

While the Anasazi were developing into a highly complex society, building the beautiful stone kivas and pueblos that are found scattered all over the northern parts of Arizona and New Mexico, the Mimbres Indians, a branch of the Mogollon culture, were flourishing in this region. Living mainly along the banks of the Gila and Mimbres rivers, these devoutly religious people farmed squash and beans and developed their pottery-making skills. Today the Mimbres are credited with creating some of the finest and most beautiful pottery ever produced by ancient peoples.

Distinguished by black-on-white, sometimes red-on-white, geometric designs with animal shapes incorporated into them, many well-preserved pieces of Mimbres pottery serve as a fascinating record of the imaginative lives of these people. Their pots undoubtedly had an important place in their lives: they left behind hundreds of them at grave sites, most with a small hole in the bottom, ceremoniously broken out to release the spirit of the pot so it might accompany its owner to the next world. Like the Anasazi, the Mimbres disappeared sometime near A.D. 1300, leaving few clues as to the cause for their departure. Growth rings in the trees of this area indicate a severe drought had lasted several years around this time. There is a good possibility that these people migrated north in search of a wetter climate and were assimilated into the Pueblo culture developing there. Soon after the departure of the Mimbres, those who would become the Apache people moved into this region, hunting and gathering. Several different bands of Apache called the mountains of southern Arizona and New Mexico home until

215

the end of the eighteenth century, when a flood of European settlers, prompted mostly by mineral riches discovered in the region, demanded their final defeat and removal.

The history of the Anglo and this land revolves around the riches found here and the struggle to mine them from the earth. Deposits of copper were first mined in the hills surrounding Silver City by the Spanish more than 300 years ago. Shortly after the Civil War gold was discovered and the old Spanish mines were reopened; by 1870 silver was discovered here as well. What began as a stream later became a flood of rough and ready men looking to "get rich quick." Substantial amounts of gold, copper, and silver were taken out of mines like the Legal Tender Mine, right behind the Silver City courthouse, the Cleveland Mine, and the Santa Rita del Cobre Mine. The Santa Rita del Cobre Mine eventually became an open pit mine when ore was exhausted in the shaft mine. This open pit mine, now called the Santa Rita/Chino Mine, kept widening until it swallowed the town of Santa Rita. The pit, now over a mile and a half wide and 1,000 feet deep, still produces some copper, but today mining in the area as a whole is very limited.

Throughout the nineteenth century many of these mining operations were repeatedly attacked by the Apache and sometimes had to be abandoned. Still, a hardship-resistant brand of adventurer, driven by the dream of riches, persisted, producing the likes of Henry McCarty, otherwise known as "Billy the Kid." McCarty's career began at the age of 12, so the story goes, when he murdered his first man in Arizona. His first arrest was not until the age of 15: he was thrown in the Silver City jail, only to escape by shinning up the building's chimney. McCarty went on to commit as many as 21 murders and countless robberies on a path that led him from Silver City to New York City and then back to Fort Sumner, where he was shot by the Lincoln County sheriff, Pat Garrett.

The mountain ranges that surround Silver City and extend far to the north include the Burro, the Mogollon, the Tularosas, the Diablo, the San Mateo, the Black, the Mimbres, and the Pinos Altos mountains. Virtually all of these ranges are contained within the Gila National Forest. This mass of mountain ranges, bisected by 170 miles of the Continental Divide, actually belongs to the Basin and Range province that extends across the southern half of Arizona and New Mexico. Although this rugged tangle of ridges, peaks, and valleys does not fit the standard monolithic range type of most Basin and Range mountain ranges, each identified group of peaks was thrust up as an individual fault block. Many of these fault blocks, or mountain ranges, are volcanic in nature, and they are often referred to as the volcanic highlands of southwestern New Mexico. Lava once flowed over and around these fault blocks, which were then uplifted, broken, and eroded into what is called the Gila Conglomerate. Lava chunks, ash, and other volcanic materials were deposited in layers that welded together, forming such features as the caverns and canyons of Cliff Dweller Canyon in the Gila National Monument. The ore bodies that occur in the mountains surrounding Silver City were created by intruded fault slices of Precambrian granite and Paleozoic limestones. Mineral enrichment occurred along these contact zones, leaving behind substantial deposits of silver, lead, copper, zinc, and gold.

From the low-lying desert surrounding Silver City to the snow-capped peaks of the Gila Wilderness, six out of seven life zones can be found. Cactus such as prickly pear and cholla associated with Lower Sonoran life zone stud the grassy plains leading up to the foothills of these mountains, which are covered with healthy stands of pinyon and juniper. Large, beautiful clump grasses and agave are also found in these foothills, and occasionally mistletoe hangs from the branches of an oak or other deciduous tree where it flourishes as a parasite. Ponderosa pine, limber pine, and Engleman spruce are some of the conifers that cloak the higher elevation of the Canadian life zone. These are also the trees that are sacrificed to produce the millions of board feet of commercial timber that come out of the Gila National Forest each year.

Nearly 400 miles of streams and a handful of small lakes sustain healthy populations of trout as well as bass, bluegill, and catfish in the Gila National Forest. Beaver also make the waterways of these mountains their home. The most numerous large mammal found in the Gila is the Rocky Mountain mule deer, followed by the smaller Sonoran white-tailed deer. Pronghorn antelope can be seen grazing on the grassy flatlands that surround these mountains. Both elk and bighorn sheep have been reintroduced to the mountains of the Gila after having been hunted out in the past. Several different herds of elk in the Gila have now grown over 1,000 strong and continue to maintain healthy numbers. The occasional cougar or bobcat can be spotted from time to time in this country, while black bear stay mostly to themselves in the higher timbered regions. A substantial number of migrating birds heading south into Mexico and Central America visit the canyons of these mountains in the spring and fall, including tanagers, orioles, warblers, phoebes, cardinals, hummingbirds, and a host of waterfowl. Anyone with an interest in birding will be thrilled with the number and variety of birds that come to the Gila. The Gila National Forest contains several wilderness areas that are off-limits to mountain bikes, including the Gila, Aldo Leopold, and the Blue Range Primitive Area, which extends into Arizona.

Some interesting stops in and around Silver City will give you insight into the history of the area and enrich your riding experience here. The Silver City Museum has many mining and household items dating from the mid- to late 1800s, a collection of Mimbres artifacts, and a great assortment of old photos from the area's heyday. The Western New Mexico University Museum has the largest collection of Mimbres pottery in the world, some pieces dating to the eighth century. If you've never seen an open pit mine, the Santa Rita/Chino Mine, over a mile and a half across and 1,000 feet deep, is something to see. The Hearst Museum in Pinos Altos displays the work of local artists and tools from the old mining days. The Gila Cliff Dwellings National Monument features a series of twelfth- and thirteenth-century stone dwellings tucked into the overhangs and caves of the beautiful Cliff Dweller Canyon. This monument is a little over 90 miles from Silver City and takes about two hours to drive to.

There is a lot to see and do in this wild and empty corner of New Mexico. Those who have the time and energy, and are interested in doing a little exploring, will be well rewarded for their efforts. Here are a few places to contact to help you start planning a trip to the Silver City area:

Silver City Chamber of Commerce
1103 North Hudson
Silver City, New Mexico 88061
(505) 538-3785

Gila National Forest
Supervisor's Office
2610 North Silver Street
Silver City, New Mexico 88061
(505) 388-8301

Gila National Forest
Mimbres Ranger District
Box 79
Mimbres, New Mexico 88049
(505) 536-2250

Gila National Forest
Silver City Ranger District
2915 NM 180 East
Silver City, New Mexico 88061
(505) 538-2771

Gila Hike and Bike
103 East College Street
Silver City, New Mexico 88061
(505) 388-3222

RIDE 65 *CLEVELAND MINE*

This ride is an easy cruise up to the old Cleveland Mine site. Total distance from town up to the mine and back is just under ten miles. Half of this ride is on pavement and the other half is on an unmaintained dirt road. Riders of all abilities who are in good physical condition will take two to three hours to complete this tour.

This ride serves as a good introduction to the town of Silver City, giving a feel for the history, surrounding country, and some of the issues facing its modern-day inhabitants. The Cleveland Mine is federal property and is listed as a Super-fund

RIDE 65 *CLEVELAND MINE*

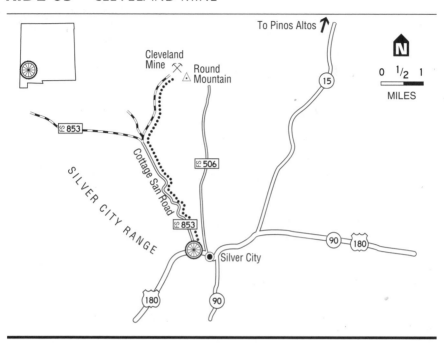

clean-up site. The mine came to life around the turn of the century, producing modest amounts of gold and silver. The acrid smell of the air and burnt orange color of the rocks and water seeping from these old mining works is caused by arsenic and other heavy metals seeping from the ground to the surface. The heavy metals and arsenic carried by the water running away from this mine site are toxic, and threaten the town's groundwater supply. *Do not handle the rocks or drink the water around this old mine site.*

General location: The old Cleveland Mine site is 5 miles north of the town of Silver City.

Elevation change: Where this ride begins in the town of Silver City the elevation is 5,938′ above sea level. You will reach a high point on this ride at the mine at an elevation of 6,550′. Total elevation gain is just over 800′.

Season: This route will be rideable almost year-round. It may get muddy up near the mine if the ground is super-saturated, and you don't want that corrosive stuff stuck to your bike, so wait till things dry out.

Services: All services are available in Silver City.

Hazards: Don't handle those sticky orange rocks and definitely don't drink any

Ruins of the Cleveland Mine just outside Silver City.

of the water you see running out of these tailings. Be careful of car traffic on your way up.

Rescue index: You're not far from town on this ride. Get out to the pavement, flag down help, or get back to town to find help.

Land status: The ground you will cover on this ride is the property of the town of Silver City. The mine site is owned by the federal government and managed by the Bureau of Land Management.

Maps: The Gila National Forest map is a little large and unwieldy for finding this little ride, but it does show the route up to the mine and is good for looking at other trails and landmarks in the region. You can also get the USGS 7.5-minute quad for Silver City.

Finding the trail: Right in town, park your car off US 180 heading west near Alabama Street.

Sources of additional information: Gila National Forest, Silver City Ranger District; address and phone are listed in the introduction to this section.

Notes on the trail: Ride north on Alabama Street from where it leaves US 180 on the right-hand side of the road. (This is less than half a mile west of the intersection of US 180 and NM Highway 90.) Follow this paved road as it becomes the Cottage San Road and then the Bear Mountain Road (Forest Service Road 853). Continue for just over 3 miles to where the pavement ends. At this point you will find dirt roads taking off in 3 different directions. To the left, FS 853 continues up toward Bear Mountain; the route straight ahead takes you to some private homes; and the right turn takes you up to the mine. Go right and continue up this dirt road until you come to the old mine site. Head on back the way you came.

RIDE 66 *SILVER CITY LOOP*

This 12-mile loop can be ridden right from town and will take beginning and intermediate riders in good physical condition about two hours to complete. A little less than a third of this ride is on the pavement; the rest is on dirt roads that are in good condition.

On this ride you will head up and out of Silver City to the northwest of town, and return to town via a Forest Service road that parallels the peaks of the Silver City Mountain Range along its eastern flank. The views out across town are good from up here. The Continental Divide follows the ridge of the Silver City Mountains before heading south to the Burro Mountains.

General location: This loop route begins in Silver City and heads northwest into the Gila National Forest.

Elevation change: In Silver City where this ride begins the elevation is 5,938' above sea level. From here you will climb gently to reach a high elevation of 6,648' on this loop. Total elevation gain is 710'.

Season: Because this route is a little lower in elevation it will stay rideable late into the fall or even early winter and be ready to ride again by early spring.

Services: All services are available in Silver City. The guys at Gila Hike and Bike are very knowledgeable about this country and have got some good wrenches working for them. Go see them for any and all biking needs.

Hazards: Watch out for cars as you ride out of town on the paved road.

Rescue index: You are never far from help on this ride. The town of Silver City is close by and within view part of the time.

Land status: The ground you will cover on this ride is under the jurisdiction of the town of Silver City, the Bureau of Land Management, and the Gila National Forest.

Maps: The Gila National Forest map is good for finding this ride, the other

RIDE 66   *SILVER CITY LOOP*

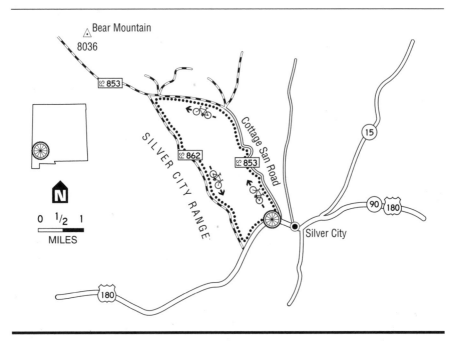

rides in this section, and other possible routes in the 3.3-million-acre national forest. You can also use the USGS 7.5-minute quad for Silver City.

Finding the trail: Start this ride in Silver City from Alabama Street, at the intersection with US 180, half a mile west of NM 90.

Sources of additional information: Gila National Forest, Silver City Ranger District; address and phone are listed in the introduction to this section.

Notes on the trail: In Silver City ride north on Alabama Street from where it leaves US 180 on the right-hand side of the road. (This is less than half a mile west of the intersection of US 180 and NM 90). Follow this paved road as it becomes the Cottage San Road and eventually turns into the Bear Mountain Road (Forest Service Road 853). Continue for just over 3 miles to where the pavement ends. At this point dirt roads take off in 3 different directions. To the left, FS 853 continues up toward Bear Mountain; going straight ahead takes you to some private homes; and the right-hand road takes you up to the Cleveland Mine. Take the dirt road that is farthest to your left, the Bear Mountain Road (FS 853). Just under 2 miles from where the pavement ended you will come to a fork. Stay left, continuing on FS 853 heading toward Bear Mountain. At the next intersection go left onto FS 862. FS 862 now heads in a southeasterly direction along the

The agave, used in the past by the region's native inhabitants for needles, thread, and many other things, is found throughout New Mexico.

eastern slope of the Silver City Range for approximately 5 miles until it drops down and intersects US 180 just to the west of town. Ride back into town on the pavement for just over a mile to the intersection of US 180 and Alabama Street where you began.

RIDE 67 *CONTINENTAL DIVIDE*

This fabulous loop route encompasses paved and dirt roads as well as single-track in just under 20 miles. The single-track portion of this ride traverses the Continental Divide for almost six miles between Bear Mountain and Little Walnut Canyon north of Silver City. The single-track is rocky and loose in sections and requires at least intermediate technical riding skill and a good, strong pair of legs. A big pair of lungs will come in handy on this ride as well. This ride will take about four hours to complete.

This route is a favorite among local riders and it's not hard to see why. Proximity to town, variety of trail conditions and terrain, and incredible high-desert scenery all combine to make this a five-star ride. You'll ride up and out of

RIDE 67 *CONTINENTAL DIVIDE*

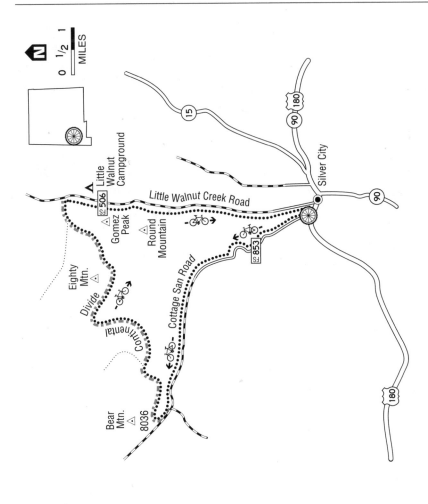

town through the rolling pinyon-and-juniper–covered foothills of the Pinos Altos Range. The views from the higher ridges along the Divide are great, revealing a maze of more blue ridges and valleys to the north and east.

General location: This loop route is located north of Silver City and falls mostly within the boundaries of the Gila National Forest.

Elevation change: From where you begin this ride, in the town of Silver City,

Riding the Continental Divide in the Pinos Altos Mountains just north of Silver City.

the elevation is 5,938' above sea level. From there you will climb to where the Continental Divide Trail leaves Bear Mountain Road at an elevation of approximately 7,000'. The highest point on this ride is 7,800', reached in the next 1.5 miles on the slope of Bear Mountain. You will then descend to a saddle at 6,600' and then climb to Eighty Mountain, at an elevation of 7,467'. Total elevation gained on this ride is approximately 2,730'.

Season: Because of the high altitudes reached along this route, this ride is best ridden spring through fall.

Services: All services are available in Silver City.

Hazards: Be aware of hikers and equestrians using this trail. Smile and give them the right-of-way. Also, be aware of vehicle traffic on the paved roads going out and coming back from this ride. Parts of this single-track are rocky and wild, so use caution and don't forget to wear your brain bucket!

Rescue index: Silver City isn't too far away on this ride; head back there for help.

Land status: This route covers the property of the town of Silver City, Bureau of Land Management (BLM) land, and Gila National Forest land in the Silver City Ranger District.

Maps: The Gila National Forest map is fine for finding this route. You can also use the USGS 7.5-minute quad for Silver City.

Finding the trail: This ride starts right in town; you can leave your car somewhere between Little Walnut Creek Road and Alabama Street off US 180.

Sources of additional information: Gila National Forest, Silver City Ranger District; address and phone are listed in the introduction to this section.

Notes on the trail: Ride north on Alabama Street from where it leaves US 180 on the right-hand side of the road. Follow this paved road as it becomes the Cottage San Road or Bear Mountain Road. Continue for just over 3 miles to where the pavement ends. At this point you will find dirt roads taking off in 3 different directions. Take the road to the left, which continues up toward Bear Mountain and becomes Forest Service Road 853. Continue on the dirt FS 853 heading in a west-northwest direction for approximately another 3 miles to where you will find a sign marking the beginning of the Continental Divide Trail on the right-hand side of the road. Go right onto this trail and be prepared to climb somewhat steeply for three-quarters of a mile to the top of Bear Mountain. From the top of Bear Mountain you will drop down to the east and begin riding the trail along a rolling ridgeline. Continue riding this single-track for the next 5 miles to where it begins to turn into a double-track and then a dirt road as you intersect FS 506. Go right onto FS 506 and head downhill; go right again when you come to a "T" intersection. You are still on FS 506 and will continue your descent, going past Little Walnut Campground. It is another 1.5 miles on this dirt road that becomes paved Little Walnut Creek Road, which takes you back to Silver City.

RIDE 68 *SIGNAL PEAK*

This ride is a fairly grueling push on a good riding surface up to one of the highest peaks in the immediate Silver City area. This up-and-back adventure climbs to the peak on a dirt road that gets steep and loose in spots. Intermediate and advanced riders in excellent physical condition will take two hours to complete this 14-mile round-trip.

You will climb out of Cherry Creek Canyon up into the realm of the straight, tall, red-barked ponderosa pine. Over seven miles you will gain 1,700 feet to arrive at Signal Peak summit and lookout. Once you reach the peak you'll want

RIDE 68 *SIGNAL PEAK*

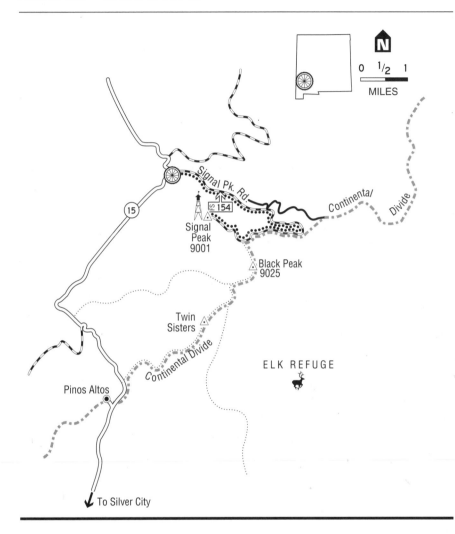

to take a break and have a good look around before heading back down. Check those hubs and brakes, cinch on that helmet, and away you go!

General location: Signal Peak is located approximately 15 miles north of Silver City inside the Gila National Forest.

Elevation change: Where this ride begins at the start of Forest Service Road 154 the elevation is 7,293' above sea level. From there you will climb to 9,001' at the summit of Signal Peak. Total elevation gain is 1,700'.

Season: This is a spring, summer, and fall adventure. Plan your ride for the early morning or early evening hours during the summer months to avoid the really hot hours of the day.

Services: All services are available in Silver City.

Hazards: Don't hang out up here if you see dark, rumbling clouds approaching; you're very exposed. Also, check your speed and use caution on this descent— it's steep and you can find yourself traveling at mach speeds before you know it.

Rescue index: In an emergency get down to NM 15 and head to Pinos Altos, where you'll find help and a phone.

Land status: Gila National Forest, Silver City Ranger District.

Maps: The Gila National Forest map shows this route, but not with a lot of detail. Use the USGS 7.5-minute quad for Twin Sisters.

Finding the trail: From Silver City head north out of town on NM 15 to the town of Pinos Altos. Continue past Pinos Altos for another 7.5 miles to where FS 154 leaves on the right-hand side of the road. Pull off and park at the beginning of FS 154.

Sources of additional information: Gila National Forest, Silver City Ranger District; address and phone are listed in the introduction to this section.

Notes on the trail: Begin riding by heading up FS 154 (Signal Peak Road). Approximately 2 miles from where you started you will encounter a fork. Bear right, heading uphill, continuing on FS 154 to Signal Peak. Another 2 miles beyond that fork the road will bend around and head west while still climbing. For the next 1.7 miles, climbing toward Signal Peak, you will be traversing the Continental Divide as you go. It is another mile to the summit of Signal Peak past where the Continental Divide Trail takes off to the left and heads toward Black Peak. Head back down the way you came.

RIDE 69 *PINOS ALTOS LOOP*

This 19-mile loop includes paved road, dirt road, and some great single-track. Intermediate and advanced riders in good physical condition will love this ride that will take three to four hours to complete.

The Pinos Altos loop starts from the town of Pinos Altos and takes you up NM 15, up the Signal Peak Road, then branches off taking you up and over Black Peak, down over the Twin Sisters Peaks, and back into town on a single-track trail. Black Peak is the highest peak in the Pinos Altos Range, at 9,025 feet above sea level. This is a really fun ride through pine forests and across peaks that also offers several great options.

RIDE 69 *PINOS ALTOS LOOP*

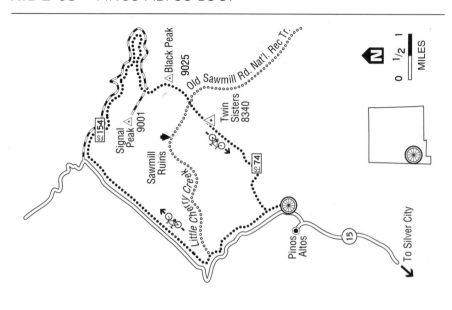

General location: This loop route is located in the Gila National Forest immediately to the north of the community of Pinos Altos, which is 7 miles to the north of Silver City.

Elevation change: At the point where this ride begins in the town of Pinos Altos the elevation is 7,840′ above sea level. From there you will ride to a high elevation, atop Black Peak, of 9,025′. Total elevation gain is 1,185′.

Season: This route reaches elevations that will keep things snow-covered and muddy until at least midspring.

Services: All your services are available in Silver City. Basic services are available in Pinos Altos.

Hazards: You are pretty exposed once you reach these higher peaks, so be aware of those towering cumulus clouds should they turn black and start to rumble. Be careful of car traffic on NM 15 on your way up here.

Rescue index: In an emergency seek help in Pinos Altos.

Land status: Gila National Forest, Silver City Ranger District.

Maps: The Gila National Forest map is good for finding this ride and route options. You can also use USGS 7.5-minute quads for Twin Sisters and Fort Bayard.

Riding the Pinos Altos Loop.

Finding the trail: From Silver City drive north on NM 15 from where it forks left off of NM 90 and US 180 in town. Drive 7 miles to the little town of Pinos Altos. Park here.

Sources of additional information: Gila National Forest, Silver City Ranger District; address and phone are listed in the introduction to this section.

Notes on the trail: Begin riding by heading up the pavement on NM 15. Continue for approximately 7 miles to where Forest Service Road 154 (Signal Peak Road) leaves on the right-hand side. Go right onto the dirt Signal Peak Road. About 2.5 miles after leaving the pavement you will come to a fork; bear right and continue on FS 154. Ride up FS 154, climbing for 5.5 miles to where the trail to Black Peak, FS Trail 74, leaves on the left-hand side of the road. (The summit of Signal Peak is 1 mile beyond where the trail to Black Peak leaves FS 154. You may want to ride up FS 154 to Signal Peak as a quick spur option.)

Once you leave FS 154 to go to Black Peak, you will be riding single-track. Climb up to Black Peak and then get ready for a really fun, fast, rolling descent down over Twin Sisters Peaks (8,340'), down over Cross Mountain, and into Pinos Altos. At the saddle between Black Peak and Twin Sisters Peaks you will come to an intersection. The trail that branches off to the right heads north and east, down Little Cherry Creek drainage. Bear left and continue on toward Twin Sisters to the south. Just before you reach the Twin Sisters there will be another trail forking off to the left; this is the old Sawmill Road. Stay right to get to the top of the Twin Sisters. From there the trail will take you straight into Pinos Altos.

A great option: Take that right-hand turn off the saddle between Black Peak and Twin Sisters Peak onto the trail that takes you down Little Cherry Creek. This trail will take you to the ruins of an old sawmill before dropping down and becoming FS 855. FS 855 intersects NM 15 3.5 miles above Pinos Altos. Go left to head back to your car.

You can also explore the old Sawmill Road, part of a system of roads and trails designated as National Recreation Trails just outside of Silver City. You can pick up the old Sawmill Road where it heads south from just north of Twin Sisters Peaks. From the intersection with FS Trail 74, Sawmill Road heads south for over 8 miles, coming out at Fort Bayard, just north of the town of Central, 7 miles east of Silver City. Ride back the way you came to return to Pinos Altos.

RIDE 70 *FORT BAYARD HISTORICAL TRAILS*

Fort Bayard is an important historical site in the Silver City area, and the trails around it make for some excellent mountain biking. The old Sawmill Road is a National Recreation Trail, a double- and single-track trail that starts at Fort

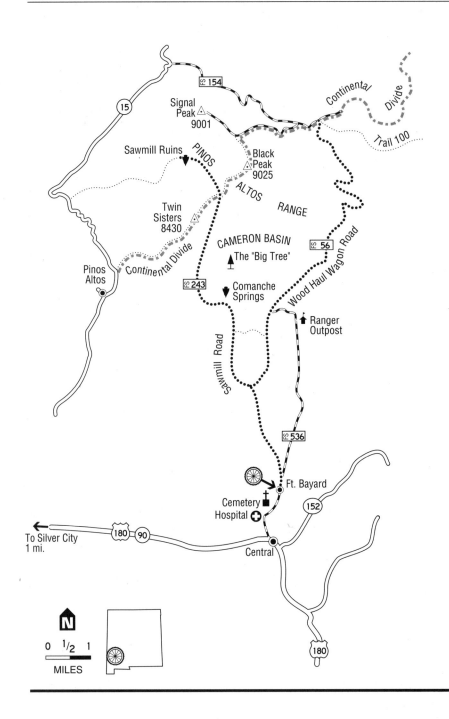

Bayard and winds its way north through the foothills of the Pinos Altos range, for almost 10 miles to the ruins of the old sawmill just below Signal Peak. The Fort Bayard Wood Haul Wagon Road branches off the Sawmill Road and heads north and east, reaching all the way to the intersection of Forest Service Road 855 and FS Trail 100, a distance of 9 miles from where it forks and 12 miles from the fort. No specific route is given here; the idea is to get out and do some exploring, ride to some of the historical landmarks scattered through these hills, create your own routes, and ride for as long as you like. All of the trails in this area are only moderately difficult and well suited to riders of all abilities.

Fort Bayard was erected in 1866 during a time when the United States Army was getting ready to secure the Southwest for settlement and deal with the problem of hostile Apache Indians. The Ninth and Tenth Cavalry, the famous Buffalo Soldier divisions, were black soldiers who had distinguished themselves as strong and fearless fighters in the Civil War. Believing that they were especially well suited to the task, the Army sent the Buffalo soldiers to this country to fight the Apache. Many of them died and were buried here, in the Fort Bayard National Cemetery. In this cemetery you will find veterans of not only the Civil War, but World War I, World War II, the Korean War, and the Vietnam War. Fort Bayard was run as a military outpost until the turn of the century, when it was turned into a hospital for war veterans suffering from consumption.

The land directly behind Fort Bayard is managed by the Gila National Forest and the Division of Wildlife Resources as a National Elk Refuge. As you are riding along, keep voices down and eyes peeled to see these regal beasts grazing and sunning at their leisure. Ride these trails to "The Big Tree," the old sawmill, or the ruins at Comanche Springs. Make your own routes, ride for three hours or three days, and enjoy!

General location: Fort Bayard is located 9 miles east of Silver City and 1 mile north of the town of Central.

Elevation change: Fort Bayard is 6,067' above sea level. From there, the old Sawmill Road gains in elevation only very gradually as you head north until you approach 8,000' at the saddle of Twin Sisters and Black Peak on your way to the sawmill. The Wood Haul Wagon Road rolls along, gaining and losing only modest amounts of elevation until it approaches the Continental Divide, where this road meets Forest Service Trail 100, at elevations close to 8,000'. It is possible to gain 2,000' riding in this area.

Season: This is a great place to ride year-round as long as the ground is not covered with snow or soaked by rain.

Services: All services are available in Silver City; basic services can be found in Central.

Hazards: You'll encounter few hazards riding in this area—no hunters or off-road vehicles. You may want to equip yourself with topographical maps if you're going exploring.

Rescue index: Help is not far away on this ride. Head back to the hospital at Fort Bayard or to the ranger's outpost at the end of FS 536.

Land status: Gila National Forest, Silver City Ranger District.

Maps: The Gila National Forest map is quite good for finding the trails in this area. You can also use USGS 7.5-minute quads for Fort Bayard, Twin Sisters, and Allie Canyon.

Finding the trail: From Silver City head east on US 180, also NM 90, 9 miles to the town of Central. Go north from Central 1 mile to Fort Bayard. Park here.

Sources of additional information: Gila National Forest, Silver City Ranger District; address and phone are listed in the introduction to this section.

Notes on the trail: Find the beginning of the Sawmill Road National Recreation Trail where it leaves to the north off the road to the cemetery. Follow this trail north approximately 2.5 miles to where the Wood Haul Wagon Road forks to the right. Continue on the Sawmill Road or try the Wagon Road; it's your choice.

You can start either ride by heading up FS 536. This dirt road leaves from Fort Bayard, just to the east of the Sawmill Road, and takes you up past a ranger outpost to join the Wood Haul Wagon Road approximately 5 miles from the start. Supplementary maps are worthwhile here.

RIDE 71 *TRAIL 100*

Forest Service Trail 100 runs east to west for approximately nine miles from the Mimbres District Ranger Station all the way west to where it joins the Signal Peak Road. This is an up-and-back affair giving you a round-trip of 18 miles. This trail has portions of fabulous single-track riding and will take intermediate and advanced riders in good physical condition about four hours riding time to make it to the Continental Divide, at the Signal Peak Road, and back.

From the Mimbres Ranger Station you will ride all the way up Allie Canyon. The trail begins in pinyon and juniper and climbs up to ponderosa forests near the Divide. This is a great ride that features many water crossings.

General location: FS Trail 100 is located north and east of Silver City in the Gila National Forest. The trailhead is almost 40 miles from Silver City by car.

Elevation change: At the Mimbres District Ranger Station where this ride begins the elevation is 6,247' above sea level. From there you will climb up Allie Canyon to the Continental Divide, at 8,068'. Total elevation gain is 1,821'.

Season: This is a spring, summer, and fall ride. Expect to find a good amount of runoff coming down this drainage in the spring.

Services: All services are available in Silver City. Basic conveniences such as gas

RIDE 71 *TRAIL 100*

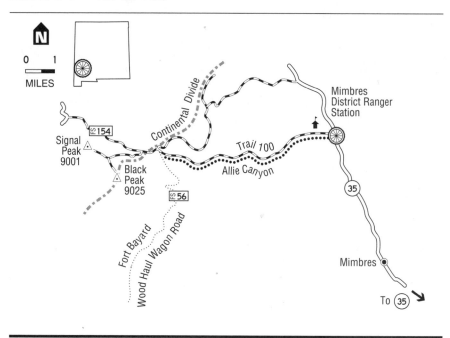

and water can be found along the way to the trailhead in the small towns of Bayard, Hanover, Turnerville, and San Lorenzo.

Hazards: Check in at the ranger station for an update on times and locations for deer hunts. Outside of hunting season there are few hazards.

Rescue index: In an emergency head down to the district ranger station located at the trailhead.

Land status: Gila National Forest, Mimbres District.

Maps: The Gila National Forest map is fine for finding this route and getting to the trailhead. You can also use the USGS 7.5-minute quad for Allie Canyon.

Finding the trail: From Silver City head east on US 180, also NM 90, for 9 miles to the small town of Central. In Central get on NM 152 heading east. Stay on NM 152 for another 17 miles to the intersection with NM 35 at the small town of San Lorenzo. Head north on NM 35 almost 12 miles to the Mimbres District Ranger Station. Park here.

Sources of additional information: Gila National Forest, Silver City Ranger District and Mimbres Ranger District; address and phone are listed in the introduction to this section.

A rider splashes through a puddle on his way down Allie Canyon on Trail 100.

Notes on the trail: After you've gone in and had a chat with the ranger to learn about ride conditions and options, find the trailhead for FS Trail 100 where it leaves just to the south of the ranger station at the mouth of Allie Canyon. Ride up FS Trail 100 as it follows this drainage for the next 9 miles. The trail remains clear, although it gets quite rocky in spots, and because it stays in the canyon bottom it is hard to get lost. When you reach the Signal Peak Road at the Continental Divide turn around and head back the way you came.

If you were lucky enough to get someone to drop you off, you can ride the Signal Peak Road out to NM 15, go left, and follow NM 15 down to the towns of Pinos Altos and Silver City.

Afterword

LAND-USE CONTROVERSY

A few years ago I wrote a long piece on this issue for *Sierra* magazine that entailed calling literally dozens of government land managers, game wardens, mountain bikers, and local officials to get a feeling for how riders were being welcomed on the trails. All that I've seen personally since, and heard from my authors, indicates there hasn't been much change. We're still considered the new kid on the block. We have less of a right to the trails than horses and hikers, and we're excluded from many areas, including:

    a) wilderness areas
    b) national parks (except on roads, and those paths specifically marked "bike path")
    c) national monuments (except on roads open to the public)
    d) most state parks and monuments (except on roads, and those paths specifically marked "bike path")
    e) an increasing number of urban and county parks, especially in California (except on roads, and those areas specifically marked "bike path")

Frankly, I have little difficulty with these exclusions and would, in fact, restrict our presence from some trails I've ridden (one time) due to the environmental damage and chance of blind-siding the many walkers and hikers I met up with along the way. But these are my personal views: The author of this volume and mountain bikers as a group may hold different opinions.

You can do your part in keeping us from being excluded from even more trails by riding responsibly. Many local and national off-road bicycle organizations have been formed with exactly this in mind, and one of the largest—the National Off-Road Bicycle Association (NORBA)—offers the following code of behavior for mountain bikers:

1. I will yield the right-of-way to other non-motorized recreationists. I realize that people judge all cyclists by my actions.
2. I will slow down and use caution when approaching or overtaking another cyclist and will make my presence known well in advance.
3. I will maintain control of my speed at all times and will approach turns in anticipation of someone around the bend.
4. I will stay on designated trails to avoid trampling native vegetation

and minimize potential erosion to trails by not using muddy trails or short-cutting switchbacks.

5. I will not disturb wildlife or livestock.
6. I will not litter. I will pack out what I pack in, and pack out more than my share whenever possible.
7. I will respect public and private property, including trail use signs, no trespassing signs, and I will leave gates as I have found them.
8. I will always be self-sufficient and my destination and travel speed will be determined by my ability, my equipment, the terrain, the present and potential weather conditions.
9. I will not travel solo when bikepacking in remote areas. I will leave word of my destination, and when I plan to return.
10. I will observe the practice of minimum impact bicycling by "taking only pictures and memories and leaving only waffle prints."
11. I will always wear a helmet whenever I ride.

Now, I have a problem with some of these—number nine, for instance. The most enjoyable mountain biking I've ever done has been solo. And as for leaving word of destination and time of return, I've enjoyed living in such a way as to say, "I'm off to pedal Colorado. See you in the fall." Of course it's senseless to take needless risks, and I plan a ride and pack my gear with this in mind. But for me number nine smacks too much of the "never-out-of-touch" mentality. And getting away from civilization, deep into the wilds is, for many people, what mountain biking's all about.

All in all, however, NORBA's is a good list, and surely we mountain bikers would be liked more, and excluded less, if we followed the suggestions. But let me offer a "code of ethics" I much prefer, one given to cyclists by Utah's Wasatch-Cache National Forest office.

Study a Forest Map Before You Ride
Currently, bicycles are permitted on roads and developed trails within the Wasatch-Cache National Forest except in designated Wilderness. If your route crosses private land, it is your responsibility to obtain right of way permission from the landowner.

Keep Groups Small
Riding in large groups degrades the outdoor experience for others, can disturb wildlife, and usually leads to greater resource damage.

Avoid Riding on Wet Trails
Bicycle tires leave ruts in wet trails. These ruts concentrate runoff and accelerate erosion. Postponing a ride when the trails are wet will preserve the trails for future use.

Stay on Roads and Trails
Riding cross-country destroys vegetation and damages the soil.

Always Yield to Others
Trails are shared by hikers, horses, and bicycles. Move off the trail to allow horses to pass and stop to allow hikers adequate room to share the trail. Simply yelling "Bicycle!" is not acceptable.

Control Your Speed
Excessive speed endangers yourself and other forest users.

Avoid Wheel Lock-up and Spin-out
Steep terrain is especially vulnerable to trail wear. Locking brakes on steep descents or when stopping needlessly damages trails. If a slope is steep enough to require locking wheels and skidding, dismount and walk your bicycle. Likewise, if an ascent is so steep your rear wheel slips and spins, dismount and walk your bicycle.

Protect Waterbars and Switchbacks
Waterbars, the rock and log drains built to direct water off trails, protect trails from erosion. When you encounter a waterbar, ride directly over the top or dismount and walk your bicycle. Riding around the ends of water-bars destroys them and speeds erosion. Skidding around switchback corners shortens trail life. Slow down for switchback corners and keep your wheels rolling.

If You Abuse It, You Lose It
Mountain bikers are relative newcomers to the forest and must prove themselves responsible trail users. By following the guidelines above, and by participating in trail maintenance service projects, bicyclists can help avoid closures which would prevent them from using trails.

I've never seen a better trail-etiquette list for mountain bikers. So have fun. Be careful. And don't screw up things for the next rider.

Dennis Coello
Series Editor

Glossary

This short list of terms does not contain all the words used by mountain bike enthusiasts when discussing their sport. But it should serve as an introduction to the lingo you'll hear on the trails.

ATB
all-terrain bike; this, like "fat-tire bike," is another name for a mountain bike

ATV
all-terrain vehicle; this usually refers to the loud, fume-spewing three- or four-wheeled motorized vehicles you will not enjoy meeting on the trail—except, of course, if you crash and have to hitch a ride out on one

bladed
refers to a dirt road that has been smoothed out by the use of a wide blade on earth-moving equipment; "blading" gets rid of the teeth-chattering, much-cursed washboards found on so many dirt roads after heavy vehicle use

blaze
a mark on a tree made by chipping away a piece of the bark, usually done to designate a trail; such trails are some-times described as "blazed"

BLM
Bureau of Land Management, an agency of the federal government

buffed
used to describe a very smooth trail

catching air
taking a jump in such a way that both wheels of the bike are off the ground at the same time

clean
while this may describe what you and your bike *won't* be after following many trails, the term is most often used as a verb to denote the action of pedaling a tough section of trail successfully

deadfall
a tangled mass of fallen trees or branches

diversion ditch
a usually narrow, shallow ditch dug across or around a trail; funneling the water in this manner keeps it from destroying the trail

double-track
the dual tracks made by a jeep or other vehicle, with grass or weeds or rocks between; mountain bikers can ride in either of the tracks, but you will of course find that which-ever one you choose, and no matter how many times you

change back and forth, the other track will appear to offer smoother travel

dugway   a steep, unpaved, switchbacked descent

feathering   using a light touch on the brake lever, hitting it lightly many times rather than very hard or locking the brake

four-wheel-drive   this refers to any vehicle with drive-wheel capability on all four wheels (a jeep, for instance, has four-wheel drive as compared with a two-wheel-drive passenger car), or to a rough road or trail that requires four-wheel-drive capability (or a *one*-wheel-drive mountain bike!) to negotiate it

game trail   the usually narrow trail made by deer, elk, or other game

gated   everyone knows what a gate is, and how many variations exist upon this theme; well, if a trail is described as "gated" it simply has a gate across it; don't forget that the rule is if you find a gate closed, close it behind you; if you find one open, leave it that way

Giardia   shorthand for *Giardia lamblia,* and known as the "backpacker's bane" until we mountain bikers expropriated it; this is a waterborne parasite that begins its life cycle when swallowed, and one to four weeks later has its host (you) bloated, vomiting, shivering with chills, and living in the bathroom; the disease can be avoided by treating (purifying) the water you acquire along the trail (see "Hitting the Trail" in the Introduction)

gnarly   a term thankfully used less and less these days, it refers to tough trails

hammer   to ride very hard

hardpack   used to describe a trail in which the dirt surface is packed down hard; such trails make for good and fast riding, and very painful landings; bikers most often use "hardpack" as both a noun and adjective, and "hardpacked" as an adjective only (the grammar lesson will help you when diagramming sentences in camp)

jeep road,   a rough road or trail passable only with four-wheel-drive
jeep trail   capability (or a horse or mountain bike)

kamikaze   while this once referred primarily to those Japanese fliers who quaffed a glass of saki, then flew off as human bombs in suicide missions against U.S. naval vessels, it has more recently been applied to the idiot mountain bikers who, far less honorably, scream down hiking trails, endangering the physical and mental safety of the walking, biking, and equestrian traffic they meet; deck guns were necessary to stop the Japanese kamikaze pilots, but a bike pump or walking staff in the spokes is sufficient for the current-day kamikazes who threaten to get us all kicked off the trails

multi-purpose   a BLM designation of land which is open to many uses; mountain biking is allowed

out-and-back   a ride where you will return on the same trail on which you pedaled out; while this might sound far more boring than a loop route, many trails look very different when pedaled in the opposite direction

portage   to carry your bike on your person

quads   bikers use this term to refer both to the extensor muscle in the front of the thigh (which is separated into four parts) and to USGS maps; the expression "Nice quads!" refers always to the former, however, except in those instances when the speaker is an engineer

runoff   rainwater or snowmelt

signed   a "signed" trail has signs in place of blazes

single-track   a single, narrow track through grass or brush or over rocky terrain, often created by deer, elk, or backpackers; single-track riding is some of the best fun around

slickrock   the rock-hard, compacted sandstone that is *great* to ride and even prettier to look at; you'll appreciate it even more if you think of it as a petrified sand dune or seabed, and if the rider before you hasn't left tire marks (from unnecessary skidding) or granola bar wrappers behind

snowmelt   runoff produced by melting snow

snowpack   unmelted snow accumulated over weeks or months of winter—or over years in high-mountain terrain

spur   a road or trail that intersects the main trail you're following

technical   terrain that is difficult to ride due not to its grade (steepness) but to its obstacles—rocks, logs, ledges, loose soil . . .

topo   short for topographical map, the kind that shows both linear distance *and* elevation gain and loss; "topo" is pronounced with both vowels long *trashed*   a trail that has been destroyed (same term used no matter what has destroyed it . . . cattle, horses, or even mountain bikers riding when the ground was too wet)

two-wheel-drive this refers to any vehicle with drive-wheel capability on only two wheels (a passenger car, for instance, has two-wheel-drive); a two-wheel-drive road is a road or trail easily traveled by an ordinary car

water bar   An earth, rock, or wooden structure that funnels water off trails to reduce erosion

washboarded   a road that is surfaced with many ridges spaced closely together, like the ripples on a washboard; these make for very rough riding, and even worse driving in a car or jeep

wilderness area land that is officially set aside by the federal government to remain *natural*—pure, pristine, and untrammeled by any vehicle, including mountain bikes; though mountain bikes had not been born in 1964 (when the United States Congress passed the Wilderness Act, establishing the National Wilderness Preservation system), they are considered a "form of mechanical transport" and are thereby excluded; in short, stay out

wind chill   a reference to the wind's cooling effect upon exposed flesh; for example, if the temperature is 10 degrees Fahrenheit and the wind is blowing at 20 miles per hour, the wind-chill (that is, the actual temperature to which your skin reacts) is *minus* 32 degrees; if you are riding in wet conditions things are even worse, for the wind-chill would then be *minus 74 degrees!*

windfall   anything (trees, limbs, brush, fellow bikers) blown down by the wind

SARAH BENNETT grew up in Salt Lake City, biking and skiing in the Rockies and hiking southern Utah's desert canyonlands. She took her BA degree in English literature at the University of Colorado, and combined her love for the West and the written word into an occupation of writing sports, outdoor, and environmental articles for a wide variety of publications. An avid sportswoman, Sarah competes in national and international telemark skiing contests. She worked as a cook on a sailboat in the Caribbean for a year, and for twice as long mountain biked the mountains and deserts of Arizona and New Mexico for her two books in this series. "I've toured the Roman ruins in southern France," says Sarah, "as well as those in Greece and Italy. They're fascinating . . . a real thrill. But there's *nothing* more exquisite than pedaling or hiking up to the ancient Indian dwellings in our own Southwest." Not surprisingly, her favorite author is Wallace Stegner.

DENNIS COELLO'S AMERICA BY MOUNTAIN BIKE SERIES

Happy Trails

Hop on your mountain bike and let our guidebooks take you on America's classic trails and rides. These "where-to" books are published jointly by Falcon Press and Menasha Ridge Press and written by local biking experts. Twenty regional books will blanket the country when the series is complete.

Choose from an assortment of rides—easy rambles to all-day treks. Guides contain helpful trail and route descriptions, mountain bike shop listings; and interesting facts on area history. Each trail is described in terms of difficulty, scenery, condition, length, and elevation change. The guides also explain trail hazards, nearby services and ranger stations, how much water to bring, and what kind of gear to pack.

So before you hit the trail, grab one of our guidebooks to help make your outdoor adventures safe and memorable.